Igor Stravinsky

THE MAN AND HIS MUSIC

BY

ALEXANDRE TANSMAN

Translated by

THERESE *and* CHARLES
BLEEFIELD

G. P. PUTNAM'S SONS
New York

Copyright, 1949, by G. P. Putnam's Sons

All rights reserved. This book, or parts thereof, must not be reproduced in any form without permission.

MANUFACTURED IN THE UNITED STATES OF AMERICA

The excerpts from the *Symphony in Three Movements* are reprinted with the permission of the Associated Music Publishers, New York, and are copyright, 1946, by the Associated Music Publishers, Inc. The excerpts from the *Danses Concertantes* are reprinted with the permission of the Associated Music Publishers, New York, and are copyright, 1944, by the Associated Music Publishers, Inc. The excerpts from *Le Sacre du printemps* are reprinted with the permission of the Associated Music Publishers, New York, and are copyright, 1945, by the Associated Music Publishers, Inc. The excerpts from the *Sonata for Two Pianos* are reprinted with the permission of the Associated Music Publishers and Chappell & Co., Inc., New York, and are copyright, 1943, by Chappell & Co., Inc. The excerpts from *Petrouchka* are reprinted with the permission of Boosey & Hawkes, Inc., New York, and are copyright, 1947, by Boosey & Hawkes, Inc.

Igor Stravinsky

Translators' Note

A DEFINITIVE and up-to-date critique on Igor Stravinsky in English certainly needs no justification. Apart from the composer's own *Poétique Musicale* (1947), and the *Chroniques de ma Vie* (1935), there have been remarkably few works of any real consequence since André Schaeffner's *Stravinsky* (1931). Schaeffner's work has as yet to be translated. The scarcity of such studies is very surprising, considering the impact of Stravinsky's work and personality on contemporary music.

No amount of analysis can reduce the content and the meaning of a work of art to words. But Mr. Tansman is highly successful in helping the reader to come closer to Stravinsky's music itself. He presents it in the light of the composer's own intentions and as he sees it. He writes with conviction and awareness of the fact that he is differing with a number of critics and musicologists.

But it is not only as a study of a very significant composer that this book is important. Stravinsky has been in close contact, through the ballet, with the entire contemporary movement in art; Mr. Tansman's analysis of Stravinsky's creative temperament, substantiated by his own experience and thinking as a composer, is highly rewarding to anyone with an interest in the philosophy and the psychology of art.

We have attempted, in this translation, to render the author's thought with clarity and exactitude. It has not been an easy task to convey in another language the boldness of Mr. Tansman's metaphors and the subtleties of his style, necessitated by the complexities of his thought as he analyzes Stravinsky's music. But the experience has been a most rewarding one, and we are grateful for the privilege of presenting Mr. Tansman's work to the English reader.

THERESE AND CHARLES BLEEFIELD

Los Angeles, California
June 10, 1949

Contents

Introduction ix

PART I

1. General Outlook 3
2. Stravinsky and the Phenomenon of Music 9
3. Discipline and Attitude 39
4. Creative Typology and Craftsmanship 69

PART II

5. Life and Works, 1882–1920 143
6. Life and Works, 1920–48 207

Conclusion 275
Chronological List of Works 279
Index 287

Introduction

NO ARTIST will have provoked so many commentaries, discussions, and polemics, in short, will have stimulated so much critical writing during his lifetime as Igor Stravinsky. Indeed, innumerable essays concerning him—biographical, æsthetic, and analytical—have already been published in every language, and each of his new works serves as a point of departure for discussion and for the revision of former theories. The fact that I have been asked to write a new book on Stravinsky proves that the subject has lost nothing of its current value, and that the question has not as yet been clarified in such a way as to give a sharp and lucid picture of the artistic discipline and the musical and spiritual significance of his work.

How is it that the music critics have seized upon a musician so extremely lettered and yet so unliterary? The slogan, so convenient in its vagueness, "this man will never cease to astonish us," is not only superficial, but, in my opinion, of little value and completely outside the pale of the Stravinsky phenomenon. For, as anyone knows who is intimate with the composer as a man and an artist, nothing is more foreign to his nature than to astonish, to strive for the unheard of, and to disturb by deliberately premeditated novelty.

Trained in self-discipline, Stravinsky, a lucid artist as sensitive as he is perceptive, is a man most removed from seeking after effect for its own sake. This axiom applies, in his case, on the æsthetic as well as the technical plane, particularly in his spiritual attitude with regard to the goal and the elements of the musical art. This seeker sets no other goal for himself than to succeed in applying his doctrine, the rigidity and clarity of which preclude not only unforeseen elements of an extraneous nature, but also every factor that might be foreseen by any cerebral or experimental process apart from the genesis of the creative act itself.

Is there a Stravinsky case? That would depend, above all, upon the meaning one gives to the notion of a "case." If one considers every original personality, every creator of genius as a case, then obviously Stravinsky is one. But a somewhat equivocal and ambiguous element often colors the conventional meaning of the term. A confused meaning is given to it, implying a certain lack of balance between appearance and intrinsic reality, and favoring the mistaking of the latter for the former, in brief, making the reality open to discussion, if not altogether doubtful. That is how Case X is opposed to Case Y. In my opinion, this attitude is æsthetically unjustifiable when applied to a personality of Stravinsky's caliber. An obvious disproportion makes it pretentious and even somewhat ridiculous.

It seems hardly necessary to state that the Stravinsky phenomenon, by the scope of the composer's work and his sheer presence, precludes comparison with any other contemporary case. It is possible and desirable that among the composers of the next generation, similar or different

Introduction

personalities may reveal themselves, but one cannot compare a promise, however significant, to a fulfillment of such definite and crystallized accomplishment. The object of such a comparison would be made ridiculous, as a young shoot compared to a tree that has already borne much fruit.

Stravinsky is no obstacle to the development of future geniuses. He in nowise prevents them from appearing. On the contrary, he paves the way for them by his achievement, both positive and negative. We would have to wait for a body of works as well balanced as his to assume the same importance before we could place it on the same level. For the moment, the most striking personalities of this generation are intensely aware of the beneficent example that his discipline offers them, as well as of the contributions of his musical technique, while among the youngest of them, we have as yet to discover a personality approaching that of Stravinsky in scope. We ought to understand, once and for all, that the creative movement in music is not a tournament or a contest, and that no question of competition or comparison can have any intrinsic value here.

Everything true is useful to art and to its development. The opposition of tendencies should manifest itself on the music staves, and not in the pages of newspapers and magazines. This opposition should have an earnest æsthetic basis, and should not depend upon the narrowness of cliques or upon personal taste.

To admire a work it is not necessary to belong to the same school, since it is the completed work that is the object of our admiration, and not the school that it represents. Admiration, moreover, is not synonymous with love. It is even possible to hate subjectively that which we objectively admire. But neither love nor hatred should blind us to the merit of a work. I shall return to the question once again when I discuss certain phenomena pertaining to Stravinsky's path, but for the time being let us return to the Stravinsky case.

It is, above all, the immense diversity of its manifestations that has contributed to the creation of a case around Stravinsky's work. The diversity of the problems that each particular work poses is sometimes misinterpreted as a lack of unity, or as the absence of a directive line in his evolution. The principle aim of our work is to oppose such interpretations and to affirm that the variety of the problems that manifest themselves in Stravinsky's work in no way excludes from it the admirable unity of the whole and the logical connection of the parts. It is to show that one work, aimed at answering certain problems or at fulfilling another function, is not placed in a direction opposed to that of the preceding work, and that it in no way excludes the authenticity of the past or a future renewal. Each one of these manifestations remains subordinated to the hold of the same unifying personality.

The forcefulness and significance of a work by Stravinsky carry with them, above all, a factor that is of the present, but the surprise that they provoke, even the possible sensation, never has a quality of passing actuality. It does not act like a heavy stone that, when thrown into a calm sea, creates a formidable but momentary backwash. Once the shock of it has worn off, a work of Stravinsky continues to move along on its own momentum; it integrates itself within that movement as a contribution surviving its original effect; it remains to participate in a renewal of the tides, a determining factor whose contribution it is impossible to ignore. It is supported by the internal law of the creator and does not depend upon immediate effect. It is this quality that differentiates a work *of the present* from a *modern* work. The former corresponds to the potential aspirations of a spiritual present, while the latter caters to the external, collective demands of a passing actuality and loses its meaning as soon as these exigencies show themselves to be overreached. On the general plane, the spiritual aspirations of a present art always remain the aspirations of Art, pure and simple, fulfilled by present means.

Has too much, then, been written about Stravinsky? No, because the theme seems inexhaustible, each new work contributing far more than a new subject for discussion— a new spiritual wealth, a new aspect of a complete work that manifests a different projection of a general problem, in short, a new object of study. The knowledge and the understanding of the composer's creative process and the aims that he sets for himself are often lacking, and commentators have all too often tried to make his work fit their personal conception of it, discovering that which lends itself to bias, and eliminating, for lack of insight or good faith, the elements that are an essential part of his true creative nature.

Theories, tempting but unsubstantiated because of their complexity, have been elaborated to categorize his work and to force it into predetermined conceptions that are often artificial and self-contradictory, ignoring the unerring success with which he has forged the particular links and imposed æsthetic and technical logic upon them— theories about his "Pygmalionesque" nature, about his genres which vary, depending upon their particular period, and obscure the logic of his development; theories about the sudden shifts and zigzags of his evolution, his character as a creative craftsman, the cosmopolitanism of his art, since he is supposed to have "turned his back" on his Russian background, his so-called indifference to the musical material he employs, his conception of the "typical work," the so-called intellectuality of the creative process excluding the factor of sensitivity. These various theories deal with Stravinsky's artistic typology as well as the technical means of expression he employs in his work, although, in a nature like his, these elements interpenetrate and should be perceived together and in perspective.

If then it seems opportune to me to add to the considerable number of commentaries on the work and the æsthetic of Igor Stravinsky, it is without the slightest intention of creating a new outlook on his case, but rather to place his works, at least partially, in the spiritual frame that seems to me to be his own, and to refute certain points of view about his work that are very clever indeed, but also quite arbitrary in their hasty generalization.

Having had the occasion, as a result of personal circumstances, to live close to Stravinsky for several years and to discuss problems of every kind with him many times, I do not think that I am betraying his thought and his friendship by writing this book, in which I shall attempt to destroy certain myths and conventional judgments rather than to seek to replace them by another "mystery" of a subjective nature. For nothing is as far removed from Stravinsky's human and artistic nature than the elaboration of gratuitous theories.

His musical theory has been defined once and for all. It postulates music as an absolute, autonomous art, and tradition as the internal law of its evolution. It is secondary, and even unimportant, to agree with every consequence of this discipline, which is a true artistic and spiritual attitude, and not the pedantic result of an intellectual system. We are concerned with making an analytical judgment on the problems of Igor Stravinsky, and not, as is often the case, on those of his commentators. In its

Introduction

solution of artistic and technical problems, Stravinsky's entire work bears the mark of genius so apparent, manifests an integrity and an honesty so irreproachable, an artistic conviction and a logic in its evolution so pronounced, that the objectivity of the analysis naturally confuses itself with personal admiration.

All of Stravinsky's work shows a constant effort toward the perfecting of his craft, toward the fulfillment of an artistic ideal placed at the summit of his spiritual conception, an ideal which, in his effort as a human creator, he comes ever closer to achieving, probably without ever wishing to reach it completely, for an ideal, once achieved, leaves a void with the very ceasing of the human struggle against the rebellious organic element.

As we shall see later on, the struggle, whether it involves the solving of an artistic problem or a material restraint, is the vital element indispensable to the creative nature of the composer. To explain its function we must first integrate Stravinsky's creative process in the ensemble of the principles that govern art as a spiritual manifestation.

PART I

CHAPTER I

General Outlook

EVERY work of art necessarily implies a "convention," taken in its etymological Latin meaning—"*conventum*," that is to say, a pact, a rule of the game, a tacit agreement between the active and passive elements of the creative process, between the creator of the work of art and the perceiving agent. In most of the highly developed arts, this convention rests upon a centuries-old tradition that provides it with the possibility of a logical and continuous renewal. It seems to me that it would also be useful to establish some sort of convention or rule of the game between the reader and myself in order to avoid any misunderstanding arising from the debatable interpretation of a term or a concept. For the meaning of certain terms is not the same for everyone. Without maintaining that my definitions are the closest approximation of the exact idea, I shall define my terms with the sole purpose of clarifying my exposition.

Contrary to recognized procedure, I shall first discuss Stravinsky's artistic discipline before I go on with the details of his work. It seems to me that analytical detail in so important a work is more readily understood once the spiritual and æsthetic aspect of the artist has been established.

Synthesis, then, will precede analysis. My book will not include a detailed technical analysis of Stravinsky's method of writing, for each one of his works might well justify an individual essay. An approximate analysis could give only an extremely incomplete and superficial idea of Stravinsky's innovations in the realm of musical expression.

I am well aware that a work of musicology looks more professional, more scholarly, when it is crammed full of musical quotations, captioned with complicated and repellent terms. I should rather not place too much stress upon a fact that experience has often made clear to me: that these overtechnical analyses, when examined at close range, often prove to be quite open to discussion and sometimes even incorrect. They rely often upon the hope, sometimes justified, that only a few readers will go and seriously check whether a chord really is a third inversion of a thirteenth, with altered third and seventh, omitted fifth and anticipated ninth, etc., which, after all, can result in a very different essential chord. The reader would rather take the author's word for it, and I wonder whether he isn't right in doing so. I consider that deductions drawn from a sampling, made either deliberately or at random, are of very debatable importance.

To us, the most interesting thing is a general harmonic or melodic principle, acting as a guiding force upon a style as a whole, and not a theme or a chord that loses all determining significance once it has been removed from its particular context. With Stravinsky, all the means of expression are so interdependent, so intimately bound up with his creative thought, that a chord or a timbre takes its real significance only from its relation to the other component elements—the melody, the rhythmic framework, the general or specific goal sought in that work, the position of a chord in relation to what precedes and follows—in short, everything that constitutes the spring that nourishes him and whereby he emanates radiance.

Since I am not trying to write an encyclopedia of all the innovations and peculiarities of the technical language belonging to Stravinsky, I should rather limit myself to a few examples, whose details may enlighten us concerning the principles by which he composes, than skim through quotations too numerous or too dissimilar to prove anything when isolated from the musical context.

To some, this book may seem to be too much of a eulogy. But although as an artist I feel in no way committed to follow Igor Stravinsky blindly, except in his spiritual discipline, which seems to me to be of a purely abstract and impersonal nature, I should be lacking precisely that objectivity and impartiality in criticism by making this analysis of his works in any other fashion.

Like every work of man, that of Stravinsky probably and necessarily comprises weaknesses, but these seem to me very slight and can in no way invalidate the universal scope of his contribution to our art. The man is too great not to take criticism, and he could easily forgo a panegyric. My attitude, then, is dictated only by a thorough, reasoned study, both intellectual and emotional, of an artist of genius whose friendship has in no way influenced me, but who has helped me to consider certain phenomena from the angle most suited to them.

I have tried, therefore, to see Stravinsky's work in relation to what *he* intended, and not to what *I* would do in his place or what I should like him to have done. This, in my opinion, is the only true criterion of objectivity. Any criticism based upon the personality of the critic instead of that of the subject under discussion is subjective. A truly objective critic must ask himself two essential questions: has the artist accomplished what he set out to accomplish; and was the goal he set for himself worth the trouble?

I have limited myself, then, to studying Stravinsky's musical works, and to considering, in the first place, what he did and what he did not intend to achieve in each one of his creative undertakings. Therefore, I will have to motivate my conclusion, which may seem eulogistic, solely by the value of Stravinsky's work taken as a whole. Furthermore, I believe that one should not undertake to study an artist of such stature for any reason but to show what is universal and immortal in his work. I leave it to others to discover its apparent weaknesses, which are due more to the paths that these critics expected him to follow than to any real defects. The artist in Stravinsky is as perfect as human nature makes it possible to be, if one evaluates him in accordance with the goals that he proposed to himself and not with the desires of critics.

I shall return now to the question of convention and tradition, which, as we shall see, is of great importance in understanding and penetrating more deeply into Stravinsky's artistic discipline. We have observed that a convention, by which we mean here a pact, a rule setting limits to arbitrariness, is not a factor that makes for conventionality in a work of art in the sense usually given to that term, and moreover, that on the contrary, it is an element indispensable to the co-ordination of the active and perceptive moments that the work implies. A convention that develops in a logical order, holding onto what is essential while gradually casting off what belongs to contingent, "modern" actuality, becomes a tradition in the course of time. The tradition, then, is no hard-set academicism, no catalogue of clichés and unchanging processes. On the contrary, it is the fountainhead of logically ordered and determined survival, and of a healthy germination.

There often is confusion, too, between the definition of musical language and that of style. We shall define the *language*, then, as the means of expression peculiar to one artist, while *style* implies a notion of abstract universality, and should, therefore, be considered as a way of using language. The language of an author can be personal or eclectic, while his style can be pure or baroque. That is why we often confuse academicism with the use of a traditional style, which to me seems to be an error. This distinction is of extreme importance when applied to Stravinsky's language and style. Academicism does not consist in the use of a style already established, such as, for example, that of the great classical masters; it manifests itself, just as often, among vanguard groups. Academicism is a scholastic and static attitude toward tradition and current convention; it is routine, what the English call "commonplace" and the French, *"pompier."* *

When, in the course of my work, I use the idea of classicism and romanticism in the art of music, I do not feel myself bound to consider them as phenomena of an exclusively chronological order: the classic period, the romantic period. The classicism of a musician is not determined by the use of a certain style, associated with the manner of writing of a given period, but only by the use that he makes of it, by the attitude of the creating ego with regard to his work in the abstract, by the extent to which it intervenes and consciously participates in the elaboration of that work. In the course of this essay, classicism and romanticism will be treated chiefly as psychological factors

* *Pompier*—French expression for bourgeois conventionalism, from the "fireman" helmets worn by Roman heroes in nineteenth-century neoclassical paintings (translators' note).

participating in the genesis and in the creative process of the artist, and not as historically determined dates and periods.

My main sources of information were, first of all, documents that I consider authentic and about whose interpretation no doubt is possible: the musical works of Stravinsky, the *Chroniques* of his life, his *Poétique Musicale,* the interviews with him, and, last but not least, his personality as a man and an artist as I came to understand it thanks to our relationship and our very numerous conversations, from which the formal atmosphere of an interview was eliminated.

I am well aware of the extent to which several views of Stravinsky's personality, his doctrine, and his work methods have had to be repeated in the course of this work, sometimes in identical words. This is not due to clumsiness on my part, or to a faulty outline. It seemed unavoidable, since we are concerned with seeing how the same phenomenon reflects itself in each particular factor, technical and spiritual; how a single spring distributes its active flow in each one of the directions that the creative personality may take.

Therefore, I deliberately decided to be repetitious rather than run the risk of omitting some facet of my conception of Stravinsky's art that might lead to new misunderstanding. Unfortunately, there is no lack of misunderstanding concerning the composer's work.

CHAPTER II

Stravinsky and the Phenomenon of Music

I

WE SHALL consider Stravinsky's work, monumental in its volume as well as in its intrinsic value, first of all from the point of view of the "rule of the game"—a complex, varied, stimulating game, governed by an honest, genuine rule, established once and for all, like a law inherent in the musical art itself. The rule of the game is characterized by a single common denominator, in its widest but also in its most restricted sense: music, nothing but music, the whole of music.

Though Stravinsky frequently changes his game, it is not because he has come to consider the previous game unsatisfactory in its essence or in its realization. On the contrary, it is because he believes that the more successful a game has been, the more necessary it becomes to invent another one, instead of making an infinity of variations upon the first. To Stravinsky, each work presents a particular problem to be solved, something for the intellect to put in order, an obstacle to overcome, and if there is no obstacle, one must be created for the sake of conquering it. For art, like every purely human contribution to organic existence, requires an element of contrivance, necessitated by man's struggle against difficulty and the constraint of order. Stravinsky is aware of this obstacle and acts with a regard for it, for anarchic license precludes artistic quality.

(We are assuming a priori the presence of a latent gift, whose existence must be taken for granted; in speaking of an artist like Stravinsky, it is impossible to doubt this gift.)

When once the difficulty and the obstacle stand before him with precision and clarity, he encloses them and fixes their limits in order to grasp the problem to its fullest extent and with all its potentialities. This work of organization is in no way strictly intellectual or pedantic, for it constitutes the first contact of human intelligence with the material perceived by grace of his vocation and his latent gift. Once a problem is solved, Stravinsky loses his interest in it as such and begins work on another.

When he changes the game, Stravinsky never changes the rules of the game: whichever manner he adapts to his art, apart from the æsthetic or stylistic character of the individual problem, his artistic attitude before his task as a musician always remains the same. Stravinsky considers egocentric sincerity as an excess of honesty—a dangerous excess, since it suppresses the indispensable element of convention. However, he holds to the notion of honesty as an essential condition of his work and of his relationship to the perceptive element of his art. He does not consider it at all necessary to disclose everything he thinks; but what he does see fit to disclose is always true and genuine beyond question. Stravinsky believes, with Rémy de Gourmont, that sincerity is an explanation, but never an excuse. It is not a question of keeping some secret or other to one's self, but of avoiding the disclosure of truths which, in his opinion, should not be of interest to anyone and which have no relation to music as he understands it.

In his *Poétique Musicale*, as well as in many passages of the *Chroniques* of his life, Stravinsky substantiates theoretically this necessity to enclose and define the problem posed by each particular work. Before understanding a work, it is less important to know what one is going to do than to decide clearly upon what should be avoided.

II

"The creator's function is to sift carefully the elements which are given to him, for human activity must impose limits upon itself. The more art is controlled, limited and worked upon, the freer it is." * And further: "If everything is permitted to me, the worst and the best, if nothing offers me any resistance, effort of any sort is unthinkable, there is nothing upon which I can build, and therefore, all undertakings are in vain."

This conscious restraint, necessary to the creative process, is imposed upon him sometimes by circumstances (material necessity, commissions) independent of his will, but principally by himself, as an intellectual problem to be solved, a fixed goal to be reached. In the first case, he succeeds in making external circumstances his own, and works as though he had imposed them upon himself.

It is extremely significant that a work like *L'Histoire du Soldat* and after it, the whole conception of the chamber orchestra, "individualized" according to the particular demands of each work, owed their origin and their realization, above all, to external circumstances beyond the com-

---

* Igor Stravinsky, *Poétique Musicale* (Cambridge: Harvard University Press, 1942).

poser's personal or artistic choice, these circumstances being of a purely material and even financial nature. Stravinsky, in the *Chroniques de ma Vie* and Ramuz, in his *Souvenirs sur Igor Stravinsky*, tell us how the composer found himself in Switzerland after the Russian Revolution, in difficult financial circumstances, and how the idea occurred to both of them to compose a work that might be transported from place to place and be given on an improvised stage in the course of a tour.

They had to manage with extremely limited means, especially for the musical part of the work. Stravinsky proceeded to limit the data of his problem. He first reduced to a minimum the very number of the musical ensemble which he would be able to use for future performances, and was then confronted with the difficulty of choosing the instruments themselves. But, as we know, for Stravinsky necessity makes the law, and also, satisfaction. The problem was to limit that choice in order to achieve the sonority that fitted his idea, in a manner, at once most simple and precise, and best suited to his musical and lyrical intentions.

Everything was considered, weighed, and analyzed, and Stravinsky finally decided upon an ensemble exactly suited to his needs, by using the two extremes of each instrumental group: violin and contrabass for the strings, clarinet and bassoon for the woodwinds, cornet and trombone for the brasses, and a percussion battery from which the timpani are omitted, but which includes a whole assortment of instruments handled by a single performer. The choice was rather novel at the time (we shall discuss it when we study that particular work), but restrictions of an economic nature made it necessary: its origin was not at all capricious or eccentric; it was the result of a clear choice of limitations.

Stravinsky and the Phenomenon of Music

And now began the joyful struggle against difficulty, against the imposed and circumscribed obstacle. This labor of the intellect, this prodigy of artifice, was to result in a marvelous masterpiece both of content and of technical achievement: *L'Histoire du Soldat.*

For a work like *Apollon-Musagète,* Stravinsky had to face, once more, a double limitation, both æsthetic and external.

First, an instrumental ensemble that had already been decided upon, limiting the orchestra to the strings, then, its use according to the æsthetic idea he conceived for his music in this particular work, music of a "white," monochromatic character. The problem was to create "expressionless" music by means of an instrumental choir that is pre-eminently expressive and vibrant.

After the first rehearsal, Stravinsky decided upon the number of musicians in each group; he thus assured for the polyphonic interplay of the melodies a feeling of spaciousness, which he considered necessary. Then, he changed the proportions of the volume, by an *ad hoc* distribution of the high, low, and middle voices. He used this ensemble with sobriety, austerity, rigidity, and even a coldness of style in order clearly to create a work which, while it reveals an apparent dryness, offers the initiate a depth of infinite tenderness, serenity, and tranquillity.

In other cases, when the difficulty is not external in origin and independent of his choice, Stravinsky imposes the problem and restraint upon himself, whether it be æsthetic or orchestral, harmonic or tonal. In the *Concerto for Piano,* for example, the problem consisted in the opposition of the solo instrument to an orchestra of wind instruments. Another variant revealing the composer's technical preoccupations had already occurred in the *Symphonies for Wind Instruments. Les Noces,* after several trials and hesitations, results in the solution of opposing the four pianos and the percussion to the entire vocal choir. In the *Duo Concertant,* the problem is to combine the violin and the piano, which usually do not get along very well from the point of view of sonority. In the *Ebony Concerto,* Stravinsky's idea is to adapt himself to a professional jazz orchestra, which he had, until then, completely ignored, but which he finally used with incomparable mastery, while retaining his individuality from beginning to end.

One might thus cite every one of Stravinsky's works, since every one contains a restraint imposed from without and that the composer has made his own. This restraint is always welcome, since each particular case offers him the joy of discovery and the incentive to overcome the obstacle in a medium whose very difficulty increases and stimulates his creative faculty.

A curious fact, but one very characteristic of a nature like Stravinsky's, is that this restraint, this struggle against latent material difficulties, finds expression even in the effect that it has upon the sonority of the ensemble as reflected in each performer.

I shall only cite, as the first example which comes to mind, the beginning of the *Rite of Spring.* The opening phrase is given to the bassoon. It is perfectly playable, but its high register makes it difficult to perform, and requires a certain tension, a certain physical effort on the part of the performer. This tension is not accidental: it creates the somewhat forced and strained sonority that engenders what we would not call the "atmosphere," a term foreign to Stravinsky's æsthetic, but the musical and sonorous climate that the composer intuitively or deliberately wished to create at the outset of his work. Another composer might have given that phrase to an instrument that would have played it in its favorite register, such as the

Stravinsky and the Phenomenon of Music

flute in the lower register, or the clarinet in the middle register, but this would have changed the entire musical character, since it would thus have replaced the moment of tense effort and strained breath with a climate of technical security, and therefore, of musical serenity.

We shall return later and at greater length to the discipline that governs Stravinsky's work, from *Petrouchka* to his most recent creations: a discipline that remains the rule of the game common to his entire production, apart from particular problems or the successive periods of his activity.

III

In my opinion, Stravinsky's work should be evaluated exclusively from the purely musical viewpoint in relation to the laws of composition. It should not be evaluated from any positive consideration of a subjective, dialectical, or æsthetic nature. Although this fact is less apparent in the few works that precede *Petrouchka*—except in the *Feu d'Artifice*—it is already embryonic, and the composer's whole production progresses by degrees toward the conception of music as a complete and autonomous art. Considered from that viewpoint, this work, so complex and varied in its richness, becomes clear in its unity and unified in its apparent diversity. It is not a technical process or system that characterizes Stravinsky's creative organization, but a spiritual attitude, whose significance goes far beyond the means of expression, which, by its novelty, would be sufficient in itself to place him at the summit of the musical art.

This above all is what the greatness of Stravinsky's admirable example consists in: to have tried to bring music back to its essential and natural ends, and to set limits upon its spiritual and emotional action, to eradicate the weeds that had invaded it and impoverished it like an abuse of ill-gotten wealth.

The expressive aspect of music, its action upon the senses, had become the pretext for an unbridled, exasperated individualism, which the late romantics had confused with natural creative individuality. The expression, or rather, the externalization of the ego through the medium of music, began little by little to assume, in the perceptive reaction to our art and its creation, the place of the ability to *compose* music, that is to say, to organize concrete material for an abstract end in accordance with precise laws.

In its effort to express too many things and to demonstrate its individuality in all its aspects, this art was in danger of no longer being able to express anything in its own field of action. In claiming that its virtue consisted more in the imaginative correlation between the effect of sound and a state of the soul or a state of material things than in an organized display of the elements peculiar to it, strictly defined and co-ordinated, music was unconsciously abandoning the tradition of an independent art.

The only æsthetic end to which Stravinsky's art pays reverence is that of being a musician, nothing but a musician, and a complete one. So that the principle of limiting and enclosing that the composer adapts to the solution of the problem he poses for himself in each particular work acts also as a generating principle of his whole æsthetic attitude toward the art of music in general.

He does not consider this as a material restriction, but, on the contrary, as an enrichment of the common method and of his own personal activity, as the freedom to move within the boundaries of a circle defined by art itself.

"Liberty, then, consists for me in the possibility of moving within the framework which I assign to myself for each one of my undertakings. I should say, moreover, that my liberty is greater and deeper in proportion as I limit my field of action more strictly and surround myself with more obstacles. What I lose in restraint, I lose in strength; the more restraint one imposes upon one's self, the freer one is from the chains that shackle the mind." *

When thus considered from a dogmatic point of view, Stravinsky's lesson in discipline is an answer to all æsthetic or stylistic tendencies, while detracting nothing from their individuality or originality. It is above all the discipline of an artist, a spiritual attitude of absolute integrity, a renunciation, conscious and motivated, of whatever does not seem indispensable, so that whatever survives becomes necessary.

IV

It is extremely significant that in such a lucid and deliberate pursuit of an "abstract" end, of a work in itself, Stravinsky should lean, in his work, exclusively upon what is real and concrete—which does not in the least mean that his conception is "realistic," but rather the contrary. No one is more suspicious than Stravinsky of approximations, vagueness, and working in the dark. Stravinsky never yields to the vague fancies of uncontrolled imagination: imagination plays only the part of a source that feeds the inventive process with no unexpected increases in the flow. Thus, the composer's lucidity could never be overwhelmed by an exaltation that might exclude organization by human intelligence. In his creative process, Stravinsky applies the inverted maxim: *Sum, ergo cogito.*†

* *Poétique Musicale.*
† I am, therefore I think (translators' note).

The composer considers his work in a quasi-elementary light: for him, to compose is to form, to organize a whole out of the chosen elements that are his material.

Ramuz, describing the "complete man" Stravinsky is, grasps with rare penetration, in his *Souvenirs sur Igor Stravinsky,* this love of his for what is concrete, well grounded, and well defined. "Stravinsky, how, like me, you loved bread when it was good, wine when it was good, the one for the other, the one with the other! Here, your personality starts, and here your art; that is to say, the whole of you." And also, "What I perceive in you is the very taste and meaning of life, the love of everything alive, and the fact that everything alive is for you, as if in advance and potentially, music." *

No musicologist ever defined the humanity and reach of Stravinsky's art with such insight; no one was ever able to explain more simply the composer's repugnance for what is cloudy, improvised, unprecise, for, as Ramuz also says, Stravinsky's nourishment comes from "below," which means from what is concrete, alive, and tangible.

This attachment for what is real, for what comes from "below," manifests itself in Stravinsky not only in the sources or reasons behind his work, but even in the material and practical organization of his activity. And on that plane, too, the concreteness of things resolves itself in a problem of inner, human order and shares in the act of creation, but it never goes beyond its part as a source, and never penetrates the abstract realization.

In his *Chroniques,* for example, Stravinsky humbly confesses that he composes at the piano.

Is it necessary to assert that the most sensitive and imaginative ear in the world—that of Stravinsky—has no need of a piano to "hear" abstractly the real effect of his work?

* C. F. Ramuz, *Souvenirs sur Igor Stravinsky.*

We should concede without too much effort that he ought to know enough *solfège*. The psychological explanation of this habit lies in his preference for a concrete and live source for his work. He likes to lean upon that polyphonic instrument, a tangible entity that produces the sound itself, and opens infinite possibilities to him, even in its limitations, since it is, musically speaking, a "live thing." It certainly is not a matter of improvising, but a sort of shock to stimulate himself.

In Switzerland he bought a cymbalum, an instrument in which he had become interested after hearing the virtuoso, Aladar Racz, performance on it. He studied it at close range, exploited all its possibilities, and used it in a masterly way in *Le Renard*, for purposes that the performers who usually play the instrument had never suspected until then. He lived in Switzerland, and later at Pleyel's, in Paris, surrounded by an amazing family of percussion instruments, as one would live with live creatures. He has a rare gift for observation, and nothing alive, organic, or natural escapes him; everything is considered as potential art, so long as one takes things for sources only, without trying to "transpose" them artificially, using art to transform them into realistic or descriptive products.

Inspiration comes to him, while working, as appetite comes while eating, for to him, inspiration is not an *état d'âme*, coming on in fits, but a latent, permanent faculty, manifesting itself in the course of the actual work and the inventive struggle against the imposed restraint.

The choice of his texts is usually based upon this same concrete level of sound. It was not the poetic significance, pictorial or literary, that charmed Stravinsky in the primitive texts he chose for the *Pleasant Songs* (*Pribaoutki*), the *Berceuses du Chat*, the *Four Russian Songs, Les Noces*, and *Le Renard*. He chose these texts, rather for their "phonetic" sonority, and he himself composed the text of *Les Noces,* arranging the syllables for his musical purposes. Here, music makes no attempt to adapt itself to the prosody of the sentence, but fuses itself with the sound factor, embraces it, makes it but one sound, simultaneously emitted.

It matters little to Stravinsky that these texts should have neither head nor tail from a literary point of view, that they should be absurd and anodyne in their primitiveness, that they should have practically no meaning as regards subject matter, atmosphere, or action. They are a "pretext for music," and this seems to him enough to obtain a perfect and unified synchronization of the dismembered phonetic sound with the complementary musical construction. It is then the sonorous potential, the "concatenation of words and syllables, as well as the cadence which they engender, and which produces upon our sensitivity an effect akin to that of music," [*] that interests Stravinsky in that concrete source, that "pretext for music."

This syllabic conception, eliminating, as we said, any preoccupation with correspondence between the meaning of the word, or the sentence, and the music, ignoring both the expressiveness of the text and its correct prosody, manifests itself with the same conviction in the various songs and in *Les Noces,* the text for which Stravinsky composed himself in an archaic, folklike style. I remember Stravinsky, one evening, analyzing for us the principle of the vocal flow in *Les Noces,* and singing a fragment to us *sotto voce.* We really had the impression that the words were part of the music, that the combination of the syllables was just as important as the striking of the xylophone, and that the text of the choruses was also an instrumental

[*] Igor Stravinsky, *Chroniques de ma Vie* (Denoël & Steele, Paris, 1935).

group indispensable to the organization of the synthetically integrated sonority.

For *Oedipus-Rex*, Stravinsky fixed his choice upon archaic Latin, hard set and hieratic, the sonority of which would adapt itself to the definite character he wished to impart to his music. This is a language as clear and precise as that of the Roman jurists and the pharmacists, one in which nothing is left to interpretation. He bends its prosody at will, forcing it, whenever necessary, in order to make it follow the current of his creative, purely musical thought.

"It is not with respect that one begets children." His own vision of *Oedipus-Rex* is a strictly autonomous one of a sonorous drama, internal and nonillustrative, as a matter of fact, like the rest of Stravinsky's lyrical works.

Stravinsky, then, always leans upon a concrete point of departure, but he never sacrifices it to the abstract, plastic conception of his work. He always remains the artist of "actual reality," but, at the same time, remains as removed as possible from artistic realism. Concrete reality is, for him, a starting point, but never becomes the final goal, for musical realism necessarily bears with it an element of approximation, of derivation, something superimposed, while music always remains, for Stravinsky, an art in itself, whose expressive aspect should be completely eliminated during the active moment of creation.

"I consider music to be, in its very essence, incapable of expressing anything whatever, be it a feeling, a psychological state, a natural phenomenon etc. If, as is nearly always the case, music could express something, it would be but an illusion and not a reality. It is just an additional element which we have lent it by inveterate and tacit convention, which we have imposed upon it as an etiquette, a protocol, in short, an attitude, which, out of habit or unconsciousness, we have come to confuse with its essence. Music is the only sphere in which man realizes the present. . . . The phenomenon of music is given with the sole end of establishing an order among things, including, above all, an order between man and time. To be realized, it requires, necessarily and only, a construction. Once the construction is made and the order achieved, everything is said." *

One might say, inverting the terms of Schelling's definition, that for Stravinsky, music is a moving architecture.†

The element of sensitivity being latent and outside the organizing action, it belongs to intelligence and inventiveness to arrange the available elements and to realize all their potentialities. The only contribution of human ingenuity to the work of art consists in choosing the material element as though by "delegation," ‡ within the limits defined by that art, and to work it out from immanent premises.

This conception of art makes it possible for Stravinsky to exercise his admirable inventive intelligence exactly as though he were applying a pragmatic method, without it ever resulting in formulas or in pedantry. His personality thus manifests itself in the very fact that he does not at all feel committed by his former solution of a problem when he undertakes some new musical work. He is the slave of no derivative technical system, of no intellectual æsthetic, but only of the discipline that he imposed upon himself in

---

* From an interview of Igor Stravinsky by Ingolf Dahl on "Music and the Film," from the *Musical Digest*. Reprinted by permission of the Editor, Alfred Human.

† Schelling said that architecture is frozen music (translators' note).

‡ This is apparently an allusion to Stravinsky's conviction that—as Nadia Boulanger, his close friend and associate, expressed it to me—the function of the creative artist is to express what has been given to him (by the Divinity?) to express (C. B.).

Stravinsky and the Phenomenon of Music

the very conception of his art. This also explains the fact that he retains only what is strictly necessary, thus avoiding any danger of eclecticism or uncontrolled facileness.

It follows, as a result, that this conscious acceptance of a general constraint—in addition to those he imposes upon himself in the realization of each particular work—carries with it no arbitrary factor, but remains of a dogmatic and unifying character: it puts no obstacle in the way of personal expression, but only denies it an egotistical anarchy in the pursuit of the goal to be attained and of the paths leading to it.

When he has once eliminated what he does not want to do, by virtue of the general principle and of the necessities of the particular case, Stravinsky works on solid and fertile ground, appropriate to his purpose, and cleansed of any borrowed elements or parasites that come from other realms of human spirituality.

V

Such restrictions obviously make the task both easier and more difficult, for if on the one hand they leave certain factors open to choice, on the other hand it is always more difficult to do with little than with much. But this circumscription gives a precise meaning, not only to the elements to be inventively treated, but also to the end to be attained, for it makes it possible to determine the goal with complete clarity.

This apparent renunciation could then be summarized in a very simple but very demanding maxim: let us do only what we *can* do, with tools that are truly our own; let us not try to express anything but what we have a need to express, and for that purpose, we must be satisfied with our own tools. If we borrow others, we may, perchance, express something "richer" in volume and complexity, but it overreaches the limits of our art, which loses some of its purity, integrity, and independence thereby.

Of course, this is only an æsthetic theory, as Stravinsky conceives it in relation to his working processes.

But has not Stravinsky abundantly proven, by the works that he has already created, that music, when left to its own ends, without overlapping other spiritual or creative manifestations, could be self-sufficient as an acting force and satisfy itself with its own riches—as is the case, so long as it does not wander out of the path of its traditional evolution—and that it could come out of the experience purer and less pretentious, as a result of owing its spiritual and emotional action only to its own substance, to its own laws and means of expression?

Thus, Stravinsky uses in his art only those means that he considers as the exclusive property of that art. However, that principle once established, he keeps at his disposal all of those purely musical factors, without exception, as the material, whose choice he will determine, and whose treatment he will organize.

In short, he puts himself under the obligation of subordinating his work to the latent, but strictly circumscribed, limits of music as an autonomous art.

VI

One might object to this postulate of pure music with the fact that Stravinsky composed innumerable works with a well-defined subject for the ballet and the theater. I shall treat this problem later, in detail, when I discuss the composer's lyrical conception, but I can assert now, as a general principle, that none of these works owes its artistic

Stravinsky and the Phenomenon of Music 25

value to the dramatic or poetic end toward which it aims, but only to its musical essence and its realization.

Obviously, most listeners place a work like *Petrouchka* on a partially visual and descriptive plane, by evoking the episodic action of the ballet. But this detracts nothing from the autonomous value of *Petrouchka* as a work with a purely musical construction and import, one that is self-sufficient in the development of its own material, apart from any sort of scenic suggestion.

Without going so far as Mr. Boris de Schloezer, who perceives in *Petrouchka* a four-movement sonata, built in accordance with the traditional form of the genre—a view that seems somewhat arbitrary from an architectonic point of view—the work has no *sine qua non* need of being realized choreographically to justify itself musically.

I shall take the liberty of putting forward my own experience here, since I heard *Petrouchka* many times in the concert hall before I saw it in its ballet version. Now my admiration, my complete perceptive reaction to the work, had been acquired by hearing alone, without any suggestion of the visual element.

In Stravinsky's æsthetic intention, the developing of the elements peculiar to music is what determines their worth, and each one of his lyrical works—which excludes any descriptive or illustrative moment as a motor force of the music, since, in any case, it can be nothing more than a pretext—is self-sufficient, and holds together as a concert piece without the need of an episodic program or a literary guide.

"My music expresses nothing of a realistic nature," Stravinsky said in the interview on film music, already quoted. This principle has frequently been affirmed in his *Chroniques* and in his *Poétique Musicale*. This is not a mere word or a sally, but a creed that inspires the composer in his whole art. Of course, the active principle in this attitude was not revealed in all its frankness and clarity in his first work, but established itself as a dogmatic norm in a gradual way. As we shall see, the *Firebird* is still conceived as action music. In *Petrouchka*, we shall find instances externally synchronized with the scenic action. But even at that time, the germ of the future discipline already manifests itself, for the music seeks, in the episodes of which it is made, an architectonic mold that contains them, as much as a correspondence between the sonorous development and the poetic movement of the text.

VII

To place in the general framework of artistic laws this restrictive attitude of Stravinsky, which is his real "rule of the game," I shall take the liberty of making a short digression of an æsthetic nature with regard to the very essence of our art.

These remarks certainly do not try to be original or new, but the uneasiness and confusion now prevalent in our musical movement, and certain quick and ready criticisms, directed at the evolution of Stravinsky's art itself, seem to indicate that sometimes very old and simple things lose nothing by being repeated, be it only to clarify a misunderstanding, oppose bad faith, and, above all, circumscribe a problem made knottier by æsthetic deviation. I think that this general digression will contribute to the over-all understanding of Stravinsky's action, by placing it in the category of a "return" to order, instead of that of musical "revolution."

Although discussions of school, style, and æsthetic tendency have always been helpful phenomena, that is the case only when they remain on their own terrain, without losing sight of the directing idea or compromising the basis for it. When the discussion forgets that its object should be how to reach a goal, the nature of which has been accepted as a law, and loses sight of the goal itself, it seems fitting to remind ourselves of it.

Artistic discussion has nothing to do with petty personal polemics or quarrels among cliques.

The misunderstandings concerning Stravinsky's works and the line of his æsthetic evolution were born, for a very large part, I believe, from the fact that we often expect of music something other than what it is fated to offer us by its very essence.

It is, then, not only a question of *more or less,* but also and above all, a question of *what* and *how.*

Furthermore, the anarchy of deliberately individualistic languages vitiates in its very roots the organic premises of the musical art by usurping the place of a true style.

Now, although music has elements that relate it to other branches of the manifestations of human intelligence, it also possesses elements that differentiate it very strictly and that assign to it a terrain of its own.

In the first category, that of similitude, we shall cite the following very obvious postulates:

A musical work, like all works of art, has a spiritual, nonutilitarian end. This æsthetic end is attained at the time of its disclosure or transmission, not at the time of its material realization. The process of its action comprises, then, two distinct moments; the act of creation or active agent, and the act of perception or passive agent.

The relationship between these two moments should never be distorted. The passive moment should never be given the direction of the active moment, which means that the producing artist should offer what he has to offer. (Of course, I am setting these remarks on an æsthetic level and not on a material or commercial one, for the artist who renounces the integrity of his conviction and adapts the active moment to the demands of the passive cannot be the object of a strictly theoretical discussion.)

A musical work is a manifestation of human individuality, therefore of intelligence. It is the manifestation of a personal thought, not a collective or anonymous one. This thought can be, and in most cases is, a product of the anonymous collective mind whose possibilities it realizes or synthesizes. But the primordial condition of a work of art is the authenticity of its source and of its realization, to which are added the qualities inherent in the personality of the composer—particular talent, aptitude, and professional education, the particular character of the realized substance and expression, which we call personality, originality, and individuality.

The greater or lesser predestination determines what we call gift, talent, or genius; its appreciation always remains subjective and elastic.

The idea of a creator of any work of art whatever involves that of an individual, noninterchangeable talent, which is employed in the service of a technical knowledge of fixed laws, of a craft of a general order to which it brings an individual realization.

The personality of the artist does not make itself manifest only in the originality of his means of expression—which are a temporary factor in a general evolution—but also and chiefly in the general attitude that he adopts with regard to his art and in the ends that he assigns to himself.

From its outset, then, the art of music admits of a synthesis of creative thought (a particular manifestation of a latent state of affairs), and of the technical working out. It

Stravinsky and the Phenomenon of Music 29

also requires imagination and order. The absence of one of these two elements makes a work of art incomplete. Without an imaginative content, it is sterile; without technical and constructive balance, it is misshapen and merely amateurish.

Intelligence, then, manifests itself in a work of art in different guises; starting with a sense of discrimination and self-criticism in the choice of materials to be used, it arrives at the invention of the means best fitted to coordinate these materials, and builds with them a logical construction of a particular kind.

If we assign its place to Stravinsky's case in music, considered as an art with qualities common to all the arts, we find him to be a *complete* artist, as he is a complete man.

While humanizing the artist and bringing him back to his proper and traditional function, Stravinsky restores to him, at the same time, his personal dignity.

The romantic period had created—apart from the notion of the professional as a man devoted, by his predestined vocation and by his intelligence, to the production of works of art of one kind or another—the somewhat ambiguous notion of the artist as a peculiar personality, somewhat on the fringes of the order established by society.

After remaining parallel for a while, these two notions, by an unconscious but effective process of evolution, came, little by little, to dissociate themselves from each other, to the point of becoming opposed as though they were two separate entities. Bad literature concerning art contributed considerably to accentuate this artificial dichotomy by separating the essential factors of artistic creation, and opposing sensitivity to intelligence, or by emphasizing the one at the expense of the other. We thus arrive at an artificial splitting of the artist's personality; instead of the struggle of the artist against the constraint of the chosen material, we have the internal struggle of the artist against himself.

This æsthetic deviation created the type of the so-called "inspired" artist, an ecstatic being, partaking of the Greek pythoness and of the village idiot, creating by shock, in a sort of fit or unconscious trance.

Now, in the best artistic tradition, inspiration is not a temporary psychological state, manifesting itself at times like a morbid symptom, but a definite gift, a natural and permanent faculty.

By returning to his roots, Stravinsky brings the creative artist back to the path he has left and to his rightful place as a *man* who works at musical composition, instead of making him a being separated from the rest of humanity by some mysterious and impenetrable mark.

It is not very probable that Leonardo da Vinci, Rembrandt, or Degas pulled their hair out as they painted, that Shakespeare, Molière, or Valéry wrote, or that Bach, Mozart, or Debussy composed, covering sheets of paper in a burning fever or a state of ecstatic exaltation. Rather, they created, like Igor Stravinsky, lucidly realizing the chosen and limited material, seeking perfection and striving for balance between innate sensitivity and inventive intelligence.

VIII

But the art of music, as everyone knows, also admits of important elements, which are very special and which, by their essence and their emotional and intellectual action, differentiate it from the other arts, and require of it other disciplines and other accomplishments.

The art of music is the only one that involves no re-

Stravinsky and the Phenomenon of Music

creation of something that "exists" outside of itself—I mean thereby a similarity with some determined palpable reality. Any external correspondence imposed upon the art of sound is necessarily artificial and is the result of a compromise, assigning to it a rule of the game applied by complaisance.

The very etymology of the phenomenon of music is sufficiently indicative, and clearly reveals its abstraction from any essential factor of realistic or expressive correspondence. Without discussing the term "music," itself, which owes its name to the universal notion of the Muses, without emphasis upon any sort of concretely realistic manifestation, the fact that in every language this action is related only to "sound" or "play" (*suonare*, to play, *jouer, spielen*, and the same is true of the Slavic languages) clearly indicates that, from its inception, the musical art was thought of as foreign to any derivative, utilitarian consideration.

We know perfectly well that music, like every other art, implies in its very essence the convention of a rule of the game, but it is still necessary that everyone should play his own game.

Now, no factor of idiosyncrasy or real resemblance is perceptible in the morphology of the "art of musical composition," which treats abstract notions, like mathematics, instead of visible phenomena that it is possible to compare: therefore, and because of that unmaterial character, any correspondence of the sounds with a realistic state or phenomenon is the result of an artificial stimulation of the imagination through the introduction of a foreign element and never through the direct action of its organized unfolding in time.

This "a-realism" of musical creation very strictly circumscribes its emotional field of action, but, at the same time, frees it from innumerable shackles.

If, as Stravinsky asserts, and as he applies it in his work, music is powerless to *express* reality, it need not distort that reality to act; it possesses wings with which to fly alone, acting in accordance with its own inherent laws, with no ties to the ground to guide it on its way.

One can describe, paint, or build something real; one cannot "compose a thing out of music." Any music that seeks to illustrate a philosophical or literary thesis admits of an element of æsthetic compromise that may, at times, be of use for some particular purpose, background music for example, but that belongs to another artistic level.

Although it is possible and legitimate to employ music for auxiliary ends, it does not follow that its original purpose is thereby changed.

And Stravinsky never loses sight of the essential, primordial end of this art. In addition to its character as an art organized by human artifice, music also possesses those acoustical and physical characteristics which belong to sound. Its power in that direction can obviously be used in more ways than one, as a suggestive element in the frame of a general action.

But for Stravinsky, one should not confuse the potential elements and qualities of the art of music with its ends and its æsthetic postulates as tradition established them. Music has always been used for utilitarian or auxiliary purposes: to stimulate work or the martial spirit, to express joy, pain, surprise, and anguish, even to illustrate realistic situations, synchronized correspondences, as in the *verismo** opera or the movies. All these uses necessarily resulted in a number of devices, conventions, clichés, and

* *Verismo* (Italian, realism). An Italian operatic school of the late nineteenth century, representing the musical counterpart of the literary "realism" of Zola, Ibsen, and others, and expressed in such operas as Mascagni's *Cavalleria Rusticana* (1890) and Leoncavallo's *Pagliacci* (1892) (translators' note).

Stravinsky and the Phenomenon of Music

formulas that are often mistaken for active qualities and the authentic convention of the musical art. Recently, the virtues of sound, inherent in our art, have also been used scientifically in musicotherapy with what seems to be considerable success. There is no harm in that but rather the contrary. The qualities inherent in literature are also used in publicity, and those of painting in evocations that are foreign to it, which does not prevent real books from being written and authentic pictures from being painted.

But, as we said before, using the potentialities of an art should not reduce that art to those potentialities alone, and above all, should not lead us to ignore its character and *raison d'être* as an absolute art.

The art of music is the only one, with the art of the dance, that unfolds itself through time and motion. This chronic conception of music is essential to the understanding of Stravinsky's work.

A musical work can be perceived only through its dynamic unfolding in time, in its relationship to what is, what precedes it, and what follows. Music is not static, and this quality imposes certain laws upon it, while it frees it from shackles characteristic of arts the perception of which is instantaneous.*

Thus, for Stravinsky, as for the musicians of the pre-Wagnerian schools, the organization of time by human invention belongs to music alone.

IX

The purpose of this digression on general matters was to clarify certain aspects of Stravinsky's æsthetic, and to place them in the framework of the dogmatic postulates governing the normal evolution of our art.

* E.g., the plastic arts (translators' note).

Igor Stravinsky

In spite of all the innovations that Igor Stravinsky has contributed to that art, he objects most strongly to the idea that he is a "revolutionary," and rightly so. Revolution, to him, means the overthrow of a tradition and the rule of anarchy. Stravinsky's action, on the contrary, strives to reestablish a tradition, to bring our art back to the path that it has been threatening to leave, as a result of a misdirection of effort and of a paroxysm of subjectivity. So that if the word did not have a somewhat antiprogressive connotation, one might term Stravinsky's æsthetic influence "reactionary."

Here again, we must make ourselves explicit to avoid any misinterpretation of a statement so contrary to those usually connected with Stravinsky's work.

As we have already observed, music, as a result of the corrupted evolution, first of the neoromantic heritage, then of the impressionist and expressionist schools, was in danger at one time of becoming all things to all men. It had reached a point where it *expressed* not only concrete realities but, in addition, events, personal and psychological situations, philosophical and mystical systems—in a word, everything to which it could contribute by some one of its elements, but all of which are nevertheless very far from its character as an autonomous art.

Now, for Stravinsky, the purpose of art is to stimulate an emotional reaction, not to *express* one, since that belongs to the realm of the author's personal reserve and discretion. Such discretion was on the verge of complete extinction at the profit of a subjective exuberance by means of which the artist sought an outlet for his egocentric personality, rather than to "compose," set in order, or to build a whole out of the concrete elements available outside himself.

Stravinsky tried to bring back the personal contribu-

Stravinsky and the Phenomenon of Music   35

tion to that of constructive intelligence, with the reminder that, apart from an *original* use of materials, there is, first of all, the directing rule and the universal law of tradition, in the discipline as well as in the elements that belong to our art, properly speaking.

"To put it briefly," Stravinsky says in his *Poétique Musicale*, "what is important for the clear ordering of the work, for its crystallization, is that all the Dionysiac elements which set the imagination of the creator in motion and cause the life sap to rise should be properly subjugated and finally subjected to the rule of law before they intoxicate us: for this Apollo demands."

It is obvious that, of the two opposed principles of artistic creation, the Dionysiac and the Apollonian, Stravinsky is more closely akin to the latter. And we shall see that this applies to *Apollon-Musagète* as well as to the sonorous cataclysm of the *Rite of Spring*.

Order is, for Stravinsky, the *sine qua non* condition, and to obtain it, he leans, above all, upon the authentic tradition of our art. This tradition, he believes, eliminates the temporary and defines what is durable and permanent. It is to him a "family possession, an heirloom which one receives on the condition that it will bear fruit before one passes it on to one's posterity."

Liberty, when it is not organized, progresses toward anarchy, and in art, anarchy excludes solidity and durability.

Thus, for Stravinsky, art remains a social superstructure whose means of expression can and must change, although its essential purpose remains independent of the factor of historical period and unchangeable in its principles.

Naturally, in Stravinsky's conception, the opposition between classicism and romanticism is not to be reduced to a notion of chronological order; as is the case with us, it is a matter of artistic attitude. It is thanks to the way in which they ordered their work that a Weber or a Tchaikowsky, both of them romantics in point of historical classification, seem, according to Stravinsky's conception, to have had a "classical discipline." Their themes are romantic, but the use they make of them and the lucid control over organized matter are classical.

For Stravinsky, all "isms," be they classicism, romanticism, or modernism, remain, obviously and with good reason, elastic terms, ambiguous, and overlapping, like the circles that appear when one throws several stones into the water.

For him, the forgetting of tradition in the work of the individual does away with the essential factor of composition—whether it is that of tonality, meter, architectonic form, or instrumentation, or that, finally, of dogmatic discipline, of attitude, and of style.

Stravinsky's "reactionary revolution" was then, it seems to me, an effort to pull music out of a state of continual revolution, to do away with the anarchy that destroys balance and leads to chaos, and to set the house in order, by substituting a universal dogma for subversive and disorderly drives, restoring to that art its constructive essence and its traditional path.

X

There sometimes occur historical situations of such nature that it takes definite genius, extraordinary courage and power of renunciation, and, finally, providential intuition to be obvious and say that a table is a table, and not the sun.

Now, that Stravinsky should be the first and the only

Stravinsky and the Phenomenon of Music 37

one of our time to have understood, asserted, and put to use in his work the fact that a table is indeed a table, and that we will never make a sun out of it, in spite of all our efforts (and above all, that a good table, well built and fit for its purpose, is better than a spurious sun), helps us to understand the phenomenon of a work exemplifying diversified unity and unified variety, and in which, for those who know how to observe, everything seems indispensable and nothing lacking; a work in which the economy of the means used is not a sign of poverty, but a proof of the infallible use of a lucid and discerning intelligence and of a fertile and orderly inventive faculty. Hence this miraculous achievement; the creation of something new at every step, with unchanging means completely devoid of any pretense of being revolutionary.

True originality never was the result of a conscious act of the will. Stravinsky's will does not manifest itself in a desire to be original, for he is original in spite of himself, or without attempting to be. Even if he tried not to be original, he could not help himself, and it is obvious that his discipline *alone,* taken as a theoretical dogma, could not be sufficient to produce such an astonishing body of works, which takes its place even now among the greatest works of all time in the universal treasure of spiritual creation. The phenomenon, then, consists in the adoption of a general rule, made alive by the genius of a man who joins in the rarest fashion the gift of finding infallibly the means of expression necessary to his self-expression and a fertile and profound thought.

XI

Is this discipline the same as artistic objectivity? This depends on the meaning that is given to the word. The fact that Stravinsky submits himself to a general discipline taken as an objective denominator should not make one forget that he remains the only judge in the choice of the problems that he assigns for himself. But if objectivity were defined as an Apollonian conception characteristic of classicism, and subjectivity as the conception characteristic of Dionysian romanticism, Stravinsky would necessarily be put in the category of objective creators.

> "The first painting was the line painted around the shadow of a man projected upon a wall. . . . Experience, the mother of all the arts and sciences, does not cause men to err, but rather imagination, which allows them to sense what experience cannot teach them."
>
> LEONARDO DA VINCI

CHAPTER III

Discipline and Attitude

I

FOR Stravinsky, inventive intelligence, far from drying up a work of art, is on the contrary a fertilizing influence, for it strives to organize dogmatically the dissimilar elements of rebellious matter.

Is Stravinsky indifferent to the thematic material that he makes use of, as some of his critics claim? Is he some diabolical Pygmalion, who, thanks to a mysterious and inexhaustible skill, knows how to create a work of art, a Galatea, from sonorous clay? His Galateas are numerous indeed. . . . One does not become a Pygmalion by wishing to be one, and technical *skill* that would have reached such a degree of mastery and infallibility, without regard to the quality of the materials employed, would be tantamount to genius, and far more obviously so than a certain questionable originality in the "infinite" invention of themes.

In my estimation, no one manifests more lucidity than Stravinsky in the choice of his materials. Who knows better what will fit into his work, who better than he can eliminate what will prove foreign to his art in general, or to his particular problem?

I leave it to professional specialists in the art of splitting hairs to search his work for analogies, borrowings, and thematic reminiscences.

If such a measuring rod were to be applied to all musicians, our art would probably have reached the final stage of its evolution with Orpheus! For every work of art is the result of filiation, a progressive linking, and every thematic element has infinite potentialities. Besides which, we must consider that we know only an infinitesimal portion of the music that has been published, without mentioning that which was composed and remained unpublished, or inaccessible to study and knowledge. The so-called romantic period invented the notion of "thematic copyright." The great classical masters never bothered with it, so that, for example, a large part of Vivaldi's music was worked over by J. S. Bach, and thus became pure Bach, musically speaking.

Certain German musicologists have established with apparent reason that the scherzo of Beethoven's Fifth Symphony is a melodic "ternary variation of the binary finale" of Mozart's Symphony in G-Minor. The rhythm, indeed, is different, as well as the character and the accentuation. But that is precisely why the aforementioned scherzo never ceases for one minute to be pure Beethoven, in spite of the apparent borrowing of the thematic pattern!

Discipline and Attitude

Only a deaf man could fail to realize that a theme from a Russian folksong, or a theme borrowed from Pergolesi, or a Rossinian or Weberian theme, or one borrowed from Tchaikowsky, all become Stravinskyan in Stravinsky's hands, not only because of the stylistic treatment, but *melodically* as well. Stravinsky never adapts himself to a manner: he adapts each manner to his own needs.

The creative invention and the technical building up of his works are so intimately related that for Stravinsky they constitute but one process. The synthetic result alone is important—not the analytical dissection, which can interest only sterile theoreticians and willful detractors.

II

Although Stravinsky is not indifferent to the musical material that he uses, he does remain completely indifferent as to whether or not that material is "officially" on file, classified as having been used before—or whether it is *original* in the romantic sense of the word. He does not borrow freely, however, and I disagree with my old friend Roland-Manuel, who claims (very wittily) that "Stravinsky patronizes a shop in town." Stravinsky considers as his —and everybody else's—every strictly musical potential, every combination of the available notes, whether or not it may have been used before, just so long as it serves some well-defined purpose of his. He is not interested in finding out whether it has been used before, for he knows that in his hands it will give results that can be ascribed to him only.

Stravinsky pays back "with interest" what he seems to have borrowed, consciously or otherwise. Therefore, when they apply to a work of such scope, little investigations into thematic reminiscences seem petty and pedantic.

Those who devote themselves to such work, as groundless as it is sterile, cannot see the forest for the trees. They lose sight completely of the morphology of the musical phenomenon, as it developed throughout the centuries, and before the personality of the artist came to be considered exclusively in relation to the element of *novelty* in his language.

However, novelty is sometimes the result of a real gift and of its thoughtful utilization, whereas sometimes it is merely fabricated out of a desire to be different. As we all know, originality is not achieved by an act of the will, and the method used by inventive intelligence has nothing to do with a cerebral system of language.

III

It would seem superfluous to prove that this or that quotation from Rossini's *Barber of Seville* in the *Jeu de Cartes* or in the recent *Symphony in Three Movements* could easily have been transformed or camouflaged, or even completely avoided and replaced by some other pattern. Musicians far less skillful than Stravinsky perform the trick quite successfully.

If Stravinsky did not find it necessary to do so when he consciously used a pattern familiar to everyone (and he knows the *Barber* to his finger tips), it was because it left him indifferent to realize that these quotations would be criticized as borrowings, or blamed upon a lack of originality. But this does not mean that he was in any way indifferent to the choice of that particular thematic material: on the contrary, the fact that he did choose it after all proves that *that* was what he needed in *that* particular case. His integrity as an artist and his horror of compromise are what kept him from having recourse to a substitution or to some easy trick. As we said before, everything that is potentially music is, in Stravinsky's opinion, absolutely his. If others don't know how to use it, or don't want to use it, so much the worse for them: but that is no reason why one should abstain, so long as the work in its finished form corresponds to the initial intentions, and so long as the *concrete* material becomes a basis for inventive and speculative work, wherein dwells the joy of discovering endless new possibilities.

It is not by making the use of dissonances into a harmonic principle or by indulging in wild and sensational counterpoint that Stravinsky dominates his material. On the contrary, it is because he chooses it deliberately, and uses it with lucidity. This has nothing to do with the self-conscious elaboration of novelty, but remains a creative process. His inventive faculty, guided by his will power, is sure of its means and of the assigned end: he realizes his work with love, and to use the lively and concise word so dear to Stravinsky, with *appetite*.

If we place ourselves on a purely æsthetic level, it is no longer the genesis and the imitative sources of a piece of music that interest us, but its emotional scope and its quality as a finished work of art. If to some the evolution of Stravinsky's art remains enigmatic, if they are baffled by the trend of that evolution, it is because they expected of him not what he had to give them, but what they would have liked him to offer them—either the appearance of a revolution with each new work, or constant repetitions, seasoned with a different sauce each time—instead of a logical and causal evolution of his own particular genius. This logic in the process of self-renewal is often what many commentators of his work have least understood.

It should certainly be easy for the man who contributed so many innovations fraught with endless possibilities for the realm of music to have lived on his own accrued wealth and to have exploited his own stylistic discoveries. He could have gone on working in a classified manner, instead of harnessing himself to a different problem with each one of his works and imposing new restraints upon himself in each case—which is what some call "to turn one's back on one's past."

So many imitators have availed themselves of his discoveries that Stravinsky had neither reason nor desire to repeat himself and to circumscribe his music within one or another to the narrow frames belonging to it.

IV

Here we come to that famous "Russian element" in Stravinsky's work, which so many of his listeners regret his having abandoned. Now this "Russian element" is in reality very different from what it is usually taken to be. Stravinsky is no less Russian now than he was Western at the time when he used the folksongs of his country.

A man does not belong to a country because he uses a given folklore style, but because of his musical affiliation, as it manifests itself in that particular country. Weber did not become Polish because he wrote *Polonaises,* or Beethoven Scotch by writing *Écossaises,* or Russian when he used Russian themes in the quartets dedicated to Razoumovsky; neither did Debussy become Spanish when he wrote *Iberia* and so many other pieces that are Spanish in their inspiration.

Russian art is often confused with its most attractive superficial element, its picturesque, Asiatic aspect, such as became known through the works of the Five. Many insisted upon seeing in *Petrouchka,* the *Rite of Spring,* or *Les Noces* an extension of this primitive element, without realizing that these works are in every way opposed to narrow ethnic or folkloristic conceptions.

Speaking about this Russian category, Stravinsky told me an anecdote that illustrates that habit of confusing everything and remembering only what is considered essential. At a banquet in New York, a very distinguished society woman—the wife of an ambassador—told him, with the intention of paying him a compliment, while showing off at the same time, that her favorite among his works was *Scheherezade*. When Stravinsky tried to correct her politely, telling her that the author was not himself but his master Rimsky-Korsakoff, this woman got herself further involved by protesting, "But, dear master, don't tell me that you didn't write *Prince Igor*, either!"

Russian music, from Glinka and Tchaikowsky on, is as Western as it is Russian in its formation. The Russian musical tradition feeds on the same classical masters as our own. A man like Stravinsky was educated in the same discipline and in the same tradition as any Western composer in Paris, Berlin, Vienna, or Brussels. His musical education, then, was not the fruit of a primitive atmosphere of narrow nationalism: he studied Bach, Mozart, Haydn, Beethoven, and Brahms, like everybody else, and later on, Dukas, Debussy, and Ravel, after Gounod, Chabrier, and Bizet.

His present "Europeanism" is just as much a part of the Russian heritage as his former "Russianism" was founded upon a conception of art that was European, formally and spiritually.

Stravinsky, then, did not betray his Russian tradition, and the absence of ethnic elements in his later works results merely from the phenomenon that we have already observed: he is not given to treating the same problem twice.

Mavra, for example, bears no relation to Russian folk-songs, and uses half-tzigane, half-Italian romances as its material, and yet it is just as much a part of the tradition of Russian music as the *Firebird* or *Les Noces*, for it results from the development of that national art which is not necessarily popular.

However, Stravinsky never created another *Firebird* or *Rite*. He left that for others to do, which obviously baffled many of his admirers. No longer did they find the magic shimmer of the *Firebird*, or the breaking loose of sound and rhythm of the *Rite*. They decided that by becoming "cosmopolitan" Stravinsky had turned away from these great works, which, they thought, should have limited him in his entirety and for the rest of his life.

Stravinsky's example, instead of being related to the classic and Apollonian discipline of his art, has been principally connected with the peculiarities of his language and of his writing, those elements being more immediately accessible to perception. There was a time when everybody seemed to be of Russian origin. Everyone wrote his personal *Rite*. Then everybody became Bachian, Pergolesian, Scarlattian, Rossinian, or Verdian, whereas Igor Stravinsky, who was responsible in spite of himself for these competitions, alone remained infallibly himself, a surprised or aggrieved spectator of a false interpretation of his creative evolution, for which the basis had always been renewal without disavowal.

It is, then, impossible to draw a general conclusion from Stravinsky's work, except by considering it in perspective, and, as we have already observed, by extracting from works varying in their material a common inner denominator, that of a conception of style and the musical phenomenon.

V

Later on, we shall see that Stravinsky's melodic line, whether inspired by Russian folksongs or related to the works of the classical masters, always follows the same personal curve, and that it preserves the same character in its design and inflections. We shall see too that his harmonic writing always moves around the same focus of attraction or radiation; that his rhythmic factor is always organic and, so to say, respiratory; that the polyphonic writing of today is a logical result of that which he anticipated in his first work; that his principle of constructed form is always built upon the same basis of order and traditional discipline; and finally, that his orchestration, while becoming purer, has been, since *Petrouchka,* chiefly based upon musical necessity, instead of being a search for timbres magical and compelling in themselves. But we shall also see that Stravinsky always seeks in music the same essential result, the same solution, and arrives at it thanks to the same attitude and æsthetic method.

The chief characteristic of Stravinsky's work, when considered in perspective, is the surprising diversity of the individual problems and the unity of the general conception. The former often hides the latter, and creates a mistaken impression of contrast and lack of unity. But to do something different is not necessarily to do something opposite, and that maxim applies to Stravinsky more than to anyone else. Here lies, in my opinion, the chief misunderstanding between the composer and one part of his audience, even those who are of good faith. Stravinsky, for the most part, is not *misunderstood,* but *ill understood*—certainly a more serious matter.

When studying the whole of his works, eliminating the classification by periods (so dear to the critic's heart, but of little use here, as I shall explain later on), one is surprised by the æsthetic and technical line going directly from the *Feu d'Artifice* to the *Symphony in Three Movements*—a line that becomes purer and richer as it unfolds itself along its particular path, never deviating from its spiritual direction and end. We find a common denominator in each one of these works, though they may belong to this or that level of Stravinsky's evolution, so that these works, however different, are like the letters of one alphabet. But the letters should not be shuffled around at will or capriciously. Each one has its place within a word that goes into making a sentence. Each letter, in spite of the recent assertions of the "letterist group," takes on meaning only in relation to those that precede and follow it.

As Stravinsky puts it, a nonordered phrase is still noise, while the merest modulation is already art, since it requires invention and human intelligence, artifice and dogmatic law. A measure of music that Stravinsky created in 1947 can be identified among a thousand others, just as is the case with a measure written by Stravinsky in 1911. This should be enough to make it possible to assert that, although an abyss lies between the *Feu d'Artifice* and the *Scènes de Ballet*, each one is still the product of the same genius, which gave it the imprint of its personality: he may have wanted to change the mode of manifestation of that personality, but not that personality itself.

VI

It is rather disappointing to note a total absence of perspective in the appreciation of Stravinsky's evolution. During a recent stay in Italy, I read a little essay of Francesco Malipiero on the subject of Stravinsky, and I was not a little surprised to see him apply to his appreciation of Stravinsky's evolution the subjective criterion of "personal preference," instead of trying to penetrate the structure of the Stravinskyan phenomenon itself. A composer with a personality of his own should evaluate another composer's work with regard to the latter's problems, and not with regard to his own æsthetic or technical preoccupations.

If Mr. Malipiero is sorry to have lost in the Stravinsky of today the "powerful spirit" who gave life to the *Rite* or to *Les Noces,* should one still try to find out whether that is what best suits his nature as a musician, or whether that "powerful spirit" is in itself, and apart from Mr. Malipiero, more precious than the purity of *Apollon-Musagète,* the sensitivity of the *Octet for Wind Instruments,* the discreet grandeur of the last *Symphony,* or the sublimation in the *Symphony of Psalms*—whether it was desirable that Stravinsky should wear himself out to outdo what he had achieved in the *Sacre,* and finally, whether that spirit was not necessarily and progressively to result in that which it did result in?

Now the *Rite* is not diametrically opposed to the *Symphony of Psalms* or to the *Danses Concertantes:* it is just something else, the solution of a different problem, on another level, but always "by the same creative type."

The result of this variety in the problems thus unified by the same method—so characteristic of Stravinsky's art as a whole—is that admirable phenomenon, so rare among men with very strong personalities: his music never is what we call "problem music" (*Problematische Musik*).

It is, of course, legitimate to prefer some works to others, for taste and personal affinities are necessarily involved in our judgment, and may act upon our perception. Some prefer the first two symphonies of Beethoven to the Third, the Fifth, or the Ninth, without taking away from these one iota of their value. Should the evolution of Beethoven's genius have stopped, just because part of his public, and indeed part of the present public, preferred his earlier works?

An artistic genius is always ahead of his public; the latter should make an effort to understand his progress, but never should the creator be expected to go backward, or to mark time.

We should not forget, either, that admiration for some works of art is the result of misunderstanding, so that many music lovers think they like *Petrouchka*, simply because they remember a few catchy folksongs, or the popular French refrain, *"Elle avait une jambe de bois,"* which certainly is more accessible than an inside theme of the *Symphony of Psalms*.

Now the problem of the *Symphony of Psalms* requires different melodic and orchestral material than *Petrouchka,* and the admirers of the latter simply perceive the problems of *Petrouchka* more easily than they perceive those of the *Symphony,* as they are embodied in their respective realizations.

"The Russian manner," and, later on, the "Bach manner" and the "Italian manner" never were exclusive manners in Stravinsky's creative evolution. These favorite sources are always secondary to one and only one thing, the manifestations of which vary in accordance with particular needs: the Igor Stravinsky manner. There is an evolution in the style, never a *change* of style, or of the organizing personality and of his æsthetic discipline.

VII

It is quite unimportant, as a matter of fact, that the inner logic of Stravinsky's evolution, however obvious when considered in perspective, should or should not meet with everyone's approval. For our composer's mission is not to please everyone, but to realize what he has to say to the best of his ability, in a language of his own, to *compose* music, in the strictest and most elementary sense of the term.

The importance of a work is for Stravinsky greater than that of its author, and the success or popularity factor in no way interferes with creation in itself. Stravinsky's art does not aim at popularity among the masses: "The bulk of the people," said he in the interview already quoted, "adds nothing to art, and cannot raise its level. The artist who consciously aims at success with the masses succeeds only in lowering his own level. . . . Music can get no help from an increase in the number of its listeners, but only from an increase in the *quality* of their listening —a quality of the individual's soul." And further on: "Music to me is a power which justifies things, a power which creates organization, harmonizes things. Music was probably there when the Universe was created: *logos.*"

Is such rich variety in the particular manifestations of the composer's evolution reason enough to complain, as the French say, that "the bride is too pretty"? An uninterrupted series of significant and lasting works, without a single failure among them, go into the tracing of a path that renews itself at every step: the *Firebird, Petrouchka,* the *Rite of Spring, Les Noces, Le Renard, L'Histoire du Soldat, The Symphonies for Wind Instruments, Mavra,* the *Wind Octet,* the Concerti *Capriccio, Apollon-Musagète,*

Oedipus-Rex, Le Baiser de la Fée, Persephone, The Symphony of Psalms, Jeu de Cartes, The Dumbarton Oaks Concerto, the two recent Symphonies, *Danses Concertantes, Ode, Scènes de Ballet,* and others that I could quote.

And even if Stravinsky were indeed some sort of chameleon, and took on a different manner with every masterpiece, we would then have fifty composers gifted with genius, instead of only one. Would any one work be less beautiful and less precious as a result? After all, it is music as it is organized in a final work that interests us and nourishes our emotions, and not pointless quarrels concerning its genesis and the relation between one period and another.

However, such an accommodating point of view, which would be justified toward anyone else, is totally inapplicable to Stravinsky, whose line of evolution is as visible as a red thread running through the whole of his works, be it in the maturity of his dogma or the logical progress of his method of writing.

But to perceive that line of development, one must compare Opus 1 with the latest of his works, through everything that took place in between, following each link of the curve in its perspective, and ignoring one's personal bias. Then only does one notice the astonishing unity of the road trodden by an artistic genius conscious of his goal and of the essential limits of his art in each one of its manifestations.

Stravinsky doesn't change—but other people cannot move along. Many admirers of Stravinsky's art are surprised by the very fact that, contrary to expectations, he does not try to surprise them. He is accused of being too cold—but that is because warmth is erroneously considered a necessary concomitant of sensitivity. Now warmth does not necessarily consist in exhibitionistic pathos, and Stravinsky's sensitivity, from which sentimentality is totally excluded, acts exclusively through its purely musical factors, which, if they are less accessible, are far deeper and purer.

Stravinsky's sensitivity needs no help from stimulants of the imagination to express itself; it demands of the listener no reconstitution, no image of a realistic or psychological synchronization. It offers him a pleasure that comes only from the orderly unfolding of the elements that go into the making of his music.

VIII

If such a work of man's art were created by intelligence alone, and resulted in a perceptual and affective impact of such power and universality, the meaning usually given to the term "intelligence" would have to be extended far beyond that which it is usually given.

Bach and most of the great classics also would be nothing but intellectual, since with them, too, the emotional result is obtained exclusively through the interplay of musical factors, and this sensible result of their works is a result of their form alone.

When I compare J. S. Bach and Igor Stravinsky, it certainly is not on the stylistic plane of the so-called "return to Bach," but exclusively on the higher plane of lucid intelligence serving the ends of a sensitivity that compels us through musical means alone, while renouncing any disloyal source of enrichment. It is not because a certain quality of sensitivity is not universally accessible the minute it manifests itself that it does not exist.

Was not Bach himself—whom everyone now claims as his own—considered for more than a century as a "learned musician," cold and cerebral, a builder of abstract methematical structures, seductive when read, but devoid of sensuous appeal? In this case, too, the obstacle to a fair appreciation of his works was not the language he used, but his attitude, his discipline, the source of his creative process. His language was the same as that of his contemporaries, since stylistic universality was the rule at the time. His thematic material was often borrowed in its essential substance from his contemporaries or his predecessors, but his discipline and his work methods were what imposed the unmistakable imprint of genius upon his music.

Like Stravinsky nowadays, Bach in the past conceived of music as the organization of time by human invention, through real and concrete means, while denying himself the use of whatever is realistic and imitative. Not only was he not concerned with knowing whether a theme had already been used by Antonio Vivaldi: he borrowed whole works from him quite naturally to make them his own, with the placidity and serenity of a good craftsman who has found suitable material for his work. At the time, personality was not thought of as including "originality," and we find among the most diverse composers not only common devices, characteristics, and harmonic sequences, but thematic identity as well. No one at the time would have thought of considering Bach's borrowing from the Italians, or from the French clavecinists or the Polish polyphonists, as reflecting in any way upon Bach's personality. It was only later that this false conception of the nature of personality took root, as individual language replaced universal style.

As we have already noticed, Stravinsky is the complete man in the widest sense of the term: "*Homo sum: nihil*

Discipline and Attitude

humanum a me alienum puto." * A man, and complete, above all, in his art. It is, then, through the co-ordination of what is concrete, real, and human that Stravinsky arrives at the abstract and the universal.

It is self-evident that each one of the component elements of this speculative treatment has its intrinsic and autonomous quality, and bears a trade-mark. However, it is through their simultaneous organization that they take on their full significance, the element being nature, and the human contribution art.

Later, we shall analyze the very particular phenomenon that manifests itself in the interdependence of Stravinsky's musical factors, as well as the characteristic features of each one in itself. For the time being we shall take them into account in our over-all appreciation of his discipline.

Each one of Stravinsky's new works, thanks to his own inherent vitality, has immediate and distant repercussions upon the whole of our contemporary musical movement. That is because his work always belongs to the present, without being modern, if modern means "belonging to a passing present tendency."

Through the multiform peculiarities of his art, one can perceive the universality of his dogma and generating direction, from which the most powerfully gifted composers of our time derive a beneficent lesson and which in no way vitiates their own personalities, if they have one to begin with.

Obviously, any unconscious influence from a personality as overbearingly strong as Stravinsky's results only in repetition. It is the universal element in his art that can be followed without danger as a lesson, and not as a

* I am a man, and I consider nothing human foreign to me. Terence (translators' note).

blind imitation of his style of writing, which could result only in sterile conformity.

There is no imitating a perfectly realized work of art: one can only learn from it. The artist should study it, then go his own way, enriched by a lesson in conduct, such as follows upon the habitual study of the great classical masters.

One can therefore accept a line of conduct, an addition to one's education, without sacrificing in any way the expression of one's self.

That is why Stravinsky's example is far less dangerous than that of Wagner, Debussy, or Ravel for those who have an inborn personality and who seek a lesson from him through conscious study, instead of passively submitting to it. It is impossible to follow Debussy without becoming a Debussyist, but one can perfectly well study Stravinsky without becoming Stravinskyan, for such a discipline does not consist exclusively, or even chiefly, in following his school or his style, however winning, but above all in the choice of a "guiding line in the world of musical composition."

IX

It may seem surprising that by giving things their real meaning and trying to restore to the elements composing music their traditional function as tools, Stravinsky should have acted as an innovator, a part that he does not like to claim. And yet, it is in this regard that he is most interesting to us.

We have already tried to understand its significance on the spiritual plane: Stravinsky's dogmatic discipline and attitude, thanks to their universal and organic implications, and the method by which he attains abstract constructiveness through the medium of the concrete.

But as we have already observed, it is also on the level of the very components of the musical art that Stravinsky re-established the traditional order of things, by firmly steering music away from rising anarchy and an exasperated individualism in the means of expression, which necessarily pointed toward a complete disappearance of every factor of universality, since they tended to make impossible any attempt at creating a style.

With regard to its means of expression, our art was becoming a potential Tower of Babel, where everyone spoke a language of his own, and tried to invent one that was novel and deprived of any common denominator with the others.

We shall try later on to analyze the way in which Stravinsky's "revolutionary reaction" has re-established the traditional progress of the means of expression, whether on the level of the melodic, harmonic, or rhythmic conception, or that of constructive form or instrumental organization, after his attempt to give back to the æsthetic conception a spiritual attitude of a dogmatic nature.

On the melodic and harmonic plane, Stravinsky re-established with a brutal and final stroke the concept of tonality. Tonality may not have a natural, organic origin, on a plane with acoustical laws; it constitutes, however, our melodic restraint, and the traditional factor in music as an art organized by human intelligence. It is the creation of human inventiveness, which changes sound and noise into art: to ignore it is to shake the foundations from under the whole structure of the art of music as the evolution of its traditional concept has made it.

Stravinsky restores to the concept of tonality its essential character; he bends it at will, jostles it, uses violence, and struggles joyfully against its hold, but never ignores it as a fact: it remains present in his mind as a framework both firm and flexible, a regulating obstacle of his whole melodic and harmonic structure.

A somewhat noisy controversy was opened lately by some enthusiasts who tried to contrast Stravinsky's work to that of Arnold Schoenberg: the starting point would have been valid, had not this discussion been based upon completely false and artificial, and even naïve, premises: I mean the anti-Stravinskyan campaign of the so-called twelve-tone school (*l'école dodécaphonique*).

No one admires Schoenberg more than I do, and no one is more aware of his invaluable contribution to the music of our time. However, in my opinion, his person and his work would have gained much by staying out of a controversy that is often unpleasant in its methods, and sometimes primitive in its arguments.

But since the controversy exists, and since it is often taken seriously, we shall have to take it into account, and oppose its deductions with objective arguments. I shall ignore the more noisy aspects of this campaign, and try to extract those elements which, from a dogmatic point of view, seem to me to be inconsistent.

As we all know, the Dodecaphonic System is a synthetic label for the twelve-tone system that Schoenberg introduced as a means of musical expression some forty years ago, at first in his works, *Pierrot Lunaire* among them, and then in his theoretical writings.

The claim of "creating a revolution" when one opposes a purely technical system to a method that is first of all dogmatic and spiritual already seems to me to be out of proportion, for an individual factor is thereby opposed to a whole.

Discipline and Attitude

But to present it as a new weapon seems to me to be somewhat disloyal, for Schoenberg had already influenced the preceding generation, which had benefited thereby to the extent that they had retained the possibilities of that new mode of expression, while eliminating whatever scholasticism it could result in when applied as a *sine qua non* system.

Before the First World War, that system was known by the none too precise name of "atonality." Now, etymologically speaking, that term does not exclude the phenomenon of tonality: it merely disregards it as a constructive basis, ignores it as a law; atonality recognizes as its basis the natural, physical laws of sound and its harmonics, rather than the man-created notion of "organized sound."

The more exact name for the system would be "antitonality," or the *necessity* of avoiding any sort of tonal basis in the melodic line and the harmonic fabric.

Now it is my belief that however valuable that system may be as a way of enriching our means of expression (and that is how Arnold Schoenberg often uses it himself, and how his late disciple Alban Berg used it more especially), it goes counter to the evolution of music as a traditional and organized art when established as a universal style; moreover, it leads music to an impasse, to a point where renewal becomes improbable, if not impossible. It necessarily results in a scholastic academicism, in a standardization of the musical language, a thing very different from the universality of a style. For constraint and the surmounting of obstacles, it substitutes occlusion.

In spite of an appearance of order, it results in a practically chaotic organization, by blurring the polyphonic levels, the clarity of which it dispenses with, since they no longer stand out distinctly, each one with its particular tonal relief. Counterpoint loses its clarity for lack of the salient element that defines its contour, harmony is dried up by the loss of tonal polarization and the marvelous possibilities of modulation, form becomes indefinite, for the themes lack in plastic character, and blend into a monotonous similarity, instead of allowing themselves to be constructively perceived.

In my opinion, much as the twelve-tone system can enrich our musical writing with the addition of a new means of expression, it cannot be set up as a style because it lacks every element of universality, and would be an obstacle to the free renewal of the musical language.

At the time of the surprising appearance of *Petrouchka*—the significance of which we shall discuss at length at the proper time—the exasperated chromaticism of most of the European schools, in spite of the presence of great composers (these schools all proceeded, directly or indirectly, from *Tristan*), pointed the way toward this progressive annihilation of the feeling of tonality, and the suppression of a constraint rich in possibilities. We have already noticed how this evolution threatened to result in complete anarchy, for by this invention of a process (which is not the same thing as a method), one was led toward a vanguard academicism, to a codified chaos of musical writing, but not to any sort of a stylistic dogmatism.

It is necessary to insist upon the fact that, in spite of an apparent graphic horizontalism, real polyphony remains imperceptible in a writing that ignores tonality as a basis. In the same way, that system when applied as an absolute rule destroys in the long run the rhythmic life that is the necessary support of the melodic line.

An a priori conception of any kind is the very opposite of a method, as we well know. Therefore, even if one were

Discipline and Attitude

to admit the possibility of opposing a technical conception to an æsthetic attitude, the return to the tonal tradition brilliantly affirmed by Stravinsky would still have been an indispensable salutary measure, however unexpected it may have seemed at the time. For, indeed, the suppression of a constraint affects at times not only the technique, but the very principles of art.

A musical language that, because of its very essence, rejects the tonal basis as a matter of course, allows itself with difficulty to be treated in a purely constructive and abstract manner. It answers better a neoromantic or expressionistic conception of music than an independent and autonomous unfolding of that art in its perceptive action. It is the cause of an exaggerated autonomy of its various elements, such as color, novel timbres, and strange harmonies, thus proving more useful to an imaginative relationship than to the independence of the musical work for and by itself. It aims at effect more than it does at success, because it sacrifices the whole to the perception of a detail.

Now an effect can exist only as a part of a successful whole. It can never replace it. A series of effects will never result in a constructed whole, unless it is intended as applied art.

The technical problem, then, clearly overlaps the æsthetic, and leads us to that of the essential ends of music as a pure art, inasmuch as the atonal language seems to lend itself particularly only to an expressionistic and symbolic conception of that art, instead of obeying its abstract and constructivistic postulates.

I do not deem it necessary to say anything more about this controversy, which is so clearly related to Stravinsky's discipline and work methods. I tried to make clear the extent to which the adoption of a narrow system is contrary to the tradition of the artistic style of music and to the æsthetic postulates of that particular art.

To summarize, the most important thing to us in this development is the fact that, even to be avoided, tonality must be accepted as a fact. The Oriental peoples have varied modes and scales different from our own: their modal scales correspond therefore to their own organization of sound in art, just as our tonalities correspond to a Western organization.

X

It would, indeed, be difficult to make an exhaustive list of the innovations that Stravinsky introduced in the musical art simply by returning to tradition. Whether it is in the design of the melody, in the harmonic invention, in the introduction of a new and more spacious form of polyphony, in the realm of constructive form or that of instrumental conception, the blending of timbres and the writing for instrumental groups, Stravinsky laid new stones, well cemented to the old ones, and bearing the stamp, in their lasting consequences, at once of a definite law and style, and of a striking, undeniable originality.

However, as I already remarked with regard to his æsthetic attitude, we should look upon Stravinsky's work as a complete entity, and consider it in a sort of moving perspective, if we want to grasp the wonderful co-ordination among all its elements and the logical unity of his artistic evolution—and this applies to his technique as well.

It would be interesting to analyze at closer range the cursory criticisms that some level against this work, whose deeper significance they do not fathom, since they sepa-

Discipline and Attitude 63

rate the musical components of Stravinsky's work from his creative thought, thus losing sight of the unity that can be perceived in his work as a whole, although there is no obvious logical connection between one opus and the next.

On the one hand there are those who blamed Stravinsky not so long ago for repeating himself, for using his own recipes and formulas in his writing, and always remaining himself.

Now, some of the above-mentioned "recipes" can in no way be dubbed formulas: most of them have simply become technical discoveries now used by every musician, for they have added directly to the wealth of means of expression that have always been in use. Let us take one example among thousands, and one of a purely instrumental nature. Stravinsky often doubles a legato melodic phrase in staccato by an instrument of the same family—a method born of the traditional arco and pizzicato doubling of the strings. This novelty in the realm of perceptible resonance, with the resulting unification in the tone, has come to be considered a fruitful device and a part of the common property of our contemporary instrumental writing. Everybody uses it, together with numerous other instrumental possibilities that have long been familiar.

There is no valid reason why it should not be used by Stravinsky, who is, so to speak, its inventor. In such a case, he does not repeat a formula: he merely uses a means of expression that has become universal, and answers the need for a particular sonority, just as he might use the mute or any other instrumental effect. It is no more a formula than a sharp or a flat would be: it is just a lucky discovery that has become a part of his instrumental language wherever it fulfills a definite function, and it seems absurd to blame him for retaining it.

Other critics reproach him with the very opposite: according to them, Stravinsky changes from one work to the next, systematically turns away from his past to seek a new vein, and tries to astonish us at every turn with something unexpected.

The fact that at first sight both points of view contain a semblance of truth shows to what extent each side is mistaken in reality. It makes things difficult for many critics, of course, since so many artists live all their lives on the discoveries that they made in a single work, while many others borrow one manner after the other without acquiring a single one that they can finally claim for their own.

As I have already said, and at the risk of repeating myself, the active force of Stravinsky lies in the fact that his personality goes far beyond problems of school or manner, and takes on its full significance in a complex of factors both spiritual and technical. It is because he renounces everything that he does not consider indispensable to the musical art itself that Stravinsky takes possession with appetite, with greed even, of whatever he makes his own.

The *Firebird* and the *Nightingale* still aim partially at an independence of the component elements of the music, as we have already seen—but once he had gotten beyond that problem, Stravinsky was to prefer qualities of solidity and durability to mere glitter.

Here is an artist for whom nothing would be easier than to dip into his own treasures, scattered or amassed, and to take full advantage of them by constantly disguising them—as so many of his imitators are wont to do—but instead, he renounces with apparent humility, but sincere

Discipline and Attitude 65

conviction, everything immediately facile, all direct or camouflaged repetitions (for fidelity to a style is not repetitiousness, but a mark of personality). He had rather harness himself to each new work like a young inventor, his taste made richer by his own experience, but never saturated with it; conscious of his strength, he stumbles upon the welcome obstacle, and enjoys with youthful enthusiasm the obstacle to be overcome in accordance with the law, joining a scientist's pleasure to that of a child, and discovering "the inspiration that comes with work."

What admirable maturity he shows, when he gives us the example of a serene conscience, which only the strength of his conviction, and his inability to surrender the slightest portion of his artistic integrity for the sake of popularity, could make indifferent to praise and blame alike!

These, of course, are manly qualities, as well as the qualities of a "complete man," to use the words of Ramuz: a man whose whole work is built upon the plane of concrete humanity, a plane that always remains lucid and sensitive, scornful of wordiness and redundancy, and mindful to avoid facility and padding.

Stravinsky never recoils before a difficulty: neither does he hide it or get around it; it does not discourage him, but on the contrary, it "inspires" him, and his determination gives him the true joy of "working in tune," which is for him a quasi-physical function, since he realizes himself only in and through music.

XI

Upon reaching the end of this dissertation on Stravinsky's way of reacting, his universal dogmatism, his discipline, and the reach of his æsthetic lesson, we shall summarize this chapter: Stravinsky is opposed above all to the pseudo-expressive, individualistic, and imitative conception of music as meaning "something outside itself" (an idea that developed under the influence of Wagner and the post-Wagnerians). He tried to prove by the example of his work that music should be self-sufficient, that its significance lies in self-realization and in the strict observance of its traditional evolution as an independent art, whose function is to organize the concrete material of sound and to make it an absolute and abstract work of art by organizing its evolution through time.

This discussion on the essential aims of art in general is not entirely new. Such controversies stimulated the eras of Monteverdi, Gluck and Piccini, Richard Wagner and Brahms, not to mention Leonardo da Vinci, Michelangelo, and many others.

But nowadays the contest takes on a far more important and consequential character, for our epoch is seeking a style that has been lost in the abundance and confusion of the languages used. This essentially materialistic era does not lend itself to an abstract, nonutilitarian conception of art: it gives birth to numerous slogans that are tempting but basically contrary to the essential ends of art understood as a phenomenon in itself. Thus the dogmatic doctrine of a man like Stravinsky, animated as it is by his effective creative genius, appears as a sort of a gift from Providence to indicate the normal road, the traditional direction of the musical art.

As we have said before, this example in no wise excludes the rise of other and different personalities, with parallel or even divergent orientations: on the contrary, Stravinsky reinforced their common proclivity toward order by organizing latent gifts and setting them on a purely musical path.

Discipline and Attitude

That word "order," preached by this man, considered as the greatest musical revolutionist of our time, should be emphasized. Order differs sharply from craftsmanship, for order is not a technical, merely constructive quality: it is above all a spiritual, dogmatic, hierarchic quality. Craftsmanship can be taught, order is acquired only by organization, elimination, and renunciation.

Human nature is so made that it is always easier and more pleasant to acquire than to renounce, so that the latter demands a rare quality of humility on the part of the artist, when confronted with work he wishes to mold: an obliteration, not of the personality, but of the individual, an ability to place the desired goal in its complete purity, beyond any desire or possibility to express one's self. In short, it requires a "classical" attitude.

This process is governed in Stravinsky by the laws of a mind both lucid and sensitive. These laws vary in their application with the postulates particular to each work, but they remain for him a universal set of rules of the game, which, by their rigidity, offer him the possibility, even the certainty, of realizing exactly what he sets out to do for himself, without the risk of fanciful improvisation or haphazard success.

Whether or not one likes his work does not affect its intrinsic value: the solidity of his constructive thought goes beyond the momentary aspect of personal affinities and puts his work at the summit of the musical creation of all time.

"An artist who never has any doubts is a mediocrity . . .

"Experience, by separating truth from falsehood, helps us to strive for what is possible, instead of expecting out of ignorance what remains beyond our reach . . .

"False science offers men vanity; true science results in humility . . .

"The greatest rivers flow underground."

LEONARDO DA VINCI

CHAPTER IV

Creative Typology and Craftsmanship

I

COMPOSERS are often judged in this manner: "This one is more of a musician, that one more of an artist." We have already discussed the opposition created between the artist as a producer of art and the artist as a man. We have observed to what an extent this dichotomy seems ambiguous in its vagueness, because it creates a certain unbalance between sensitivity and intelligence, which, in a creator, complement without opposing each other.

Whether the intelligence that builds and orders the work is cold, lucid, and analytical, or whether it is intuitive, synthetic, and warm depends exclusively upon the temperament of the creator-artist, and the history of art presents many examples of these two creative types. If we must relate Stravinsky to some artistic family, we could find numerous examples of his type: the Greeks, Pythagoras or Praxiteles; the Spaniards, Zurbaran, Velasquez, or Goya; the Jew, Spinoza; the Germans or Austrians, Bach, Haydn, and Mozart; the French from Descartes to Valéry; or the Florentine, Leonardo da Vinci.

When we compare the notes on art of Leonardo da Vinci to Igor Stravinsky's *Poétique Musicale* or to certain pages of the *Chroniques de ma Vie*, we are struck by the community of ideas between the Renaissance painter and the contemporary musician.

Both of them take what is concrete, human, and alive for a point of departure, to progress toward the abstract, limiting the difficulty that they choose for themselves. To both of them the profound observation of nature remains an active stimulant, but the work does not strive for realism, or toward an art of imitation and correspondence.

Nature for them is a source, and not a current that carries them away.

The observation of the flight of a bird may be useful to Stravinsky as a starting point to stimulate his "appetite," but he is not the man ever to write a *Flight of the Bumblebee,* or to transpose an impression of industrialism into a musically conceived *Steel Foundry.**

For appetite, with Stravinsky, includes "digestion," and that organic factor, which makes for *creative* music, is of paramount importance: he absorbs realism, but he eliminates it as well; he circumscribes the concrete basis, and never substitutes it for the abstract goal of his work.

We have said that, in our opinion, craftsmanship in

* *The Steel Foundry,* by Soviet composer Alexander Mossolov, b. 1900 (translators' note).

Creative Typology and Craftsmanship 71

Stravinsky is subordinated to his general discipline, as well as to the particular problem that he assigns himself in each work, and moreover, that all the particular elements of that technical realization are interdependent; that each one of these component factors often defines its basic nature, its real significance, in its relation to each one of the others, as well as to the combined whole.

A particular component often originates in another, and acts by direct or indirect repercussion upon the development of that element which gave it birth.

Stravinsky's melodic curve often originates in a dissected chord or a harmonic fragment. His harmony, most often, is the vertical resultant of melodic lines intercrossed and superposed in seemingly independent fashion, though always with a clear relationship between them.

Even his pronounced taste for equivocal tonality, at once major and minor, which is so characteristic of his writing, is manifest in the *Rite of Spring*, where it seems to be of harmonic origin, as well as in the very latest works where it clearly becomes thematic (example 1).

Ex. 1 Symphony in Three Movements, Movement III

Likewise, we often witness the peculiar intervention of the rhythmic organization of a melodic line, which may itself be nothing but the unfolding of a harmonic complex. Since *Petrouchka*, we have become familiar with this way of marking, of scanning, certain parts or portions of a melodic phrase, the result being either a subsidiary thematic pattern—which sometimes takes on a directive importance—or a new rhythm, arising from the doubling of certain elements in a phrase.

The beginning of the first movement of the *Symphony in Three Movements* is an example of surprising effectiveness in the use of that method of simultaneity and interaction of the elements. The tones E, F, and A flat, extracted from the linear pattern, are scanned and accentuated with their respective harmonies by the whole of the string section at the moment when they appear in the phrase exposed by the woodwinds (example 2).

Ex. 2 Symphony in Three Movements, Movement I

This brings in, partially, a short new thematic design that is to be of use in the construction of a moving pedal point of great importance in that movement. But at the same time, this effect of melodic and harmonic origin determines the rhythmic outline of the movement, with its

Creative Typology and Craftsmanship 73

syncopated accents contrasting with the original rhythm of the pattern.

In other cases, this method of extraction by accentuation clearly serves instrumental purposes of partial reinforcement of a volume, resonance effect, etc.

In each one of Stravinsky's works, we can perceive this curious interpenetration of the component musical elements, which, as it seems, feed on the same generating sap, to be then distributed among various sections in order to re-establish their new unity in the final structure.

It is possible, and even probable, that a very large part of this process remains intuitive in origin, and that certain cases of correspondence in the relationship among musical components are due more to the very unity of the work itself than to any deliberate elaboration.

For there certainly is, even in a nature as discerning as that of Stravinsky, a mysterious side inherent in every act of creation; it can be analyzed a posteriori, but its conscious or subconscious source remains unknown. As is the case with Bach or Beethoven, it is sometimes impossible, with Stravinsky, to tell whether his melodic pattern deliberately gave birth to a counterrhythm, or whether that coincidence is the result of unifying intuition.

Let us consider, for example, the "Auguries of Spring" in the *Rite of Spring* (example 3): a unifying chord (the harmonic composition of which is not at all unimportant, contrary to the assertions of some musicologists, since it constitutes a pole for the entire work), F flat, A flat, C flat, and F flat, over G, B flat, D flat, and E flat (a superposition, then, of the tonic of F flat major with the first inversion of the dominant of A flat), gives this episode its rhythmic gait, due to its asymmetrical scansion. This rhythmic harmony gives birth to melodic patterns, all of which correspond by the tones that compose them to

Ex. 3 The Rite of Spring
The Auguries of Spring

some inner tone of these harmonic aggregates, while contrasting by their particular rhythmic movement with the persistence of the unifying hammering rhythm (example 4). Obviously, in spite of the percussive aspect of the

Ex. 4 The Rite of Spring
The Auguries of Spring

strings, these pulsations, with their asymmetrical accents, also serve the purpose of harmonic poles and melodic sources, owing to the detail of their composition.

Numerous examples could be quoted of this considered or intuitive interdependence of the component factors of Stravinsky's work. I shall point out several while discussing his works in detail. If I quote no others for the

Creative Typology and Craftsmanship 75

time being, it is because here I intended chiefly to point out a general phenomenon, and merely to illustrate it with a typical example.

The very structure of a melodic phrase in Stravinsky's work is so closely connected with its rhythmic treatment that the same component element sometimes fulfills both functions: linear patterning and movement. The melody, as it turns around itself and changes its point of departure by displacing the accents, thereby changes the point at which it resolves itself cadentially. Broken by caesuras that throw it back upon a different beginning and create for it a new starting point, it is the basis for a perpetual rhythmic activity, whose frame it often determines, while its continual renewal and displacement in time result in a point that gives rise to new possibilities of harmonic modulations as well.

This perpetual rebounding of the musical material, unified in its components, which feed one another, gives Stravinsky's works their constant aspect of immanent life, presence, and unremitting orderliness. His genius organizes a sort of organic unfolding of movement while he himself remains, so to speak, on the outside, like a "Sorcerer's apprentice" who would know the key with which to begin the movement, but who would also have made certain of that with which to stop it.

Anything that might be intuitive seems indispensable, for in whatever is not intuitive, nothing is left to chance. The work lives a life of its own, like a being apart from its creator, while yet remaining under his guidance at each step along its way.

Thus we always find the presence of Stravinsky's "musical" personality in this synthetic craft—but we would seek in vain for Mr. Igor Stravinsky's personal joys or sorrows.

The man here is subordinated to the creator. The desire for personal exhibitionism makes way for that of perfection in the work itself.

It would be useless to insist upon the fact that, in spite of its relationship with the other component factors of Stravinsky's work, each factor bears the mark of a personality unmistakable among so many others. Although these elements acquire their final significance from their relationship one to the other, or to the others as a whole, and although none of them ever becomes an autonomous goal in the composer's intention, all of them conform to a determinate principle, all have peculiar features and bear a characteristic trade-mark. There is that about them which is necessary, indispensable even, so that a Stravinskyan chord not only takes on value as a result of its proper placement, but turns out to be exactly the chord that, upon hearing and analysis, we find to be desirable in that particular place, so much so that no other could have fulfilled its purpose so effectively or with such justification.

II

Whether it feeds upon the source of Russian folksong or finds its inspiration in the great German polyphonists or in the Italians (Rossini, Donizetti, or Bellini), Stravinsky's melody always follows a characteristically preferred curve.

As we well know, Stravinsky retains only those elements in his concrete source of inspiration which fit into his own conception of linear design.

Stravinsky's melodic themes usually are clear cut and direct, well scanned as to their rhythm, lively, plastic, and strictly delimited.

Creative Typology and Craftsmanship 77

Their morphology follows, for the most part, two conceptions:

1. The phrase is made of the adjacent tones of a scale or of a mode, or of fragments thereof. Their meter determines the pattern. ("Russian Dance" in *Petrouchka,* the "Rival Cities" of the *Rite of Spring,* most of the themes of *Les Noces, l'Histoire du Soldat,* the beginning of the *Danses Concertantes,* etc.) (examples 5 and 6).

2. It consists in the unfolding of a harmonic complex or of a simple tonal arpeggio, particularly with an ambiguous play of the third, acting as a thematic balance between major and minor (*Apollon-Musagète, Capriccio, Danses Concertantes, Scènes de Ballet, Symphony in Three Movements,* etc.).

Most of the wide intervals frequent in Stravinsky's melody are the result of inversions to the octave of adjacent intervals (such as the minor second to the major seventh, or major second to ninth), but also, at times, of the necessities of a peculiar polyphony. Stravinsky's thematic invention or choice is nearly always diatonic with a surprising manner of using passing tones and alterations. The use of partial chromaticism, however, is not lacking in Stravinsky's melody, but it is always grafted upon a real or implicit basis of diatonic tonal material.

As we have already seen in his æsthetic, Stravinsky considers tonality (I mean the diatonic element in it that resolves itself in the cadence) as a restraint attached to the component parts of the melody. He does as he pleases with it, but even when he fights against it, he does not ignore it. He never loses sight of its existence, of its presence. The chromaticism that can be perceived in Stravinsky's work is most frequently harmonic in origin, and not thematic, as we see, for example, in the *Nightingale* (not to mention the *Firebird*, where, as we shall see later, the personal style of the composer had not yet found its final direction).

Even in the development of the first movement of the *Ode,* the chromatic patterns of the strings never result in melodic chromaticism. They are superposed upon the real presence of a diatonic polarity. The same phenomenon also determines a certain amount of chromaticism in the *Rite* or in the recent *Symphony*. We shall discuss them in greater detail when we come to the composer's harmonic language.

Stravinsky's attachment to the tonal system in his melody, as well as the plastic, direct, and relatively short character of his thematic design, corresponds exactly to the constructive exigencies of his work. A long-drawn-out theme, the "infinite melody" such as Wagner and his

Creative Typology and Craftsmanship 79

followers understood it, is not entirely suited to formal treatment. His unprecise, "chronic" caesura (not asymmetrical, as is often the case with Stravinsky) prevents an organized interplay with the opposition in the development, and here Stravinsky is closer to Beethoven's thematic conception than to that of other composers of the so-called romantic period.

It is, then, an architectonic, tonal reason, as well, that dictates Stravinsky's preference for diatonic, tonal melody, its plastic, clear-cut aspect, its linear, horizontal character, and, finally, its quality as an "inexpressive" factor, as well as his hatred for everything lacking in precise limits.

His melodic phrase usually is concise and precise, while its linear flexibility makes possible rhythmic transformations as well as contrasts in the polyphonic interplay.

His meter is frequently asymmetrically orderly, which is the result of displacements on the strong and weak beats of the measure, of the prolonging of a tone overlapping its ulterior point of departure or anticipating it. As we have already noticed, the melodic element in Stravinsky is always closely connected with the metric caesura, the internal pulsation of a rhythm that constantly revitalizes its linear flow in time.

III

Stravinsky's harmony moves in a vast and spacious domain, in accordance with a stylistically determined course. As is the case with his melody, the axis around which the composer's harmonic writing revolves is always determined by a clearly tonal order.

This harmonic tonal basis is for Stravinsky an obstacle with a framework both fixed and flexible. As we shall see later on, he feels bound to no formula or system, but considers the harmonic restraint of tonality as an essential factor in his writing.

Of course, when we discuss Stravinsky's technique we cannot consider it as an object acquired in its final form with his first work. A general principle is involved, manifesting itself gradually from one work to the next—a sort of general method that this technique approaches little by little, in its evolution, before it becomes fixed in a general dogma.

The writing in *Petrouchka* and that in the *Danses Concertantes* are indeed very different, but everything on the path from *Petrouchka* to the *Danses Concertantes* leads, in perspective, to the present predominance of the melodic factor, the polyphonic horizontalism of his conception, the purification of the harmonic language and the doing away with the latter's significance by and for itself. The same is true of the component element of rhythm or timbre. Each work contains the seeds for a fertile renewal of his method, seeds that sometimes manifest their presence only intermittently in the course of several works. But in spite of skips and zigzags, the integrity of the stylistic evolution they reveal is beyond dispute.

We shall follow this technical evolution more closely when we discuss the works of Igor Stravinsky in themselves. We shall use, above all, the more recent works, and particularly the *Symphony in Three Movements*, for the quotations illustrating Stravinsky's style in its present state, except for a few examples that we shall take from earlier works to show the autonomous sources of this style throughout its evolution.

A work like the *Firebird* already reveals genius in certain of its episodes, if one considers them in perspective. But it does not as yet bear the characteristic marks of Stra-

Creative Typology and Craftsmanship

vinsky's harmonic language. In spite of harmonies that are new and original in themselves, of novel chord progressions and surprising modulations, the harmonic language as such does not as yet have the clearly asserted personality that it assumes in later works.

I am not thinking now of the passing influences Stravinsky may have come under at the time, such as those of Wagner, Rimsky-Korsakoff, Dukas, Ravel, or Scriabin. Influences are a natural thing in any creative evolution, but remain very secondary in their importance when such a powerful personality is involved. They may interest the musicologist from a documentary point of view. But the musician during his lifetime is interested only in the value of the work itself.

It is from *Petrouchka* on that Stravinsky's harmony began to use tonality as a regulating principle. A kind of "knot," toward which each well-defined horizontal line converges, serves as a stable harmonic point of attraction. Each point, each thread in this knot makes it possible to take a new tonal departure, and this is how the inexhaustible richness and the novelty of Stravinsky's modulation are created.

Most of the lines converging toward this magnetic pole, this center of radiation and attraction, are in themselves harmonic, each one developing in its own framework of tonal cadence, so that their progression is always attracted by a tonal or modal polarization.

This is how the superposition of several transition tonalities is established, each one subordinated to its own respective tonal cadence, and all of them subordinated to that of the axis and to its resolution. From the traditional harmonic point of view, the "transition tonality" gradually replaces the idea of the transition tone and common or enharmonic note, which had until then been used as the pole of attraction or of projection.

This treatment of the superposition or of the multitonal modulation brings, in spite of its complexity, the possibility of a new method, without its becoming an unconditional system. Igor Stravinsky is thus the inventor of polytonality (unconscious traces of which are already to be found in Beethoven, who superposes in the first movement of the *Eroica* the tonic and the dominant of the same tonality, and even in Mozart, in the *Musical Jest,* without mentioning Bach, in whose work one could find numerous examples). However, Stravinsky never becomes its slave. He never uses it as a new and exclusive harmonic language, but only as a means of musical expression to be employed whenever he requires it. Thus one should not consider Stravinsky as devoted to harmonic polytonality because he made use of that device in *Petrouchka* and more especially in the *Rite of Spring,* for that is only one aspect of his craft, one of its component elements, but not the substance of it.

The use of harmonic polytonality is only one of the consequences of Stravinsky's devotion to the tonal, diatonic principle. He never considers it as the modern idiom *par excellence.* It anticipates the future predominance of the melodic factor in the composer's evolution, for only the melodic factor can be treated in a lively polyphonic manner and become the basis for constructive work.

Harmony here is already the subconscious servant of melody, despite the appearance of autonomy, which the latter owes to its complexity. Stylistic polyphony shows itself in these works on the level of the unifying tonality as well as on that of the superposition of the transition tonalities, clearly defined by their own attributes of cadence and resolution.

Creative Typology and Craftsmanship

I do not, for my part, consider as a bitonal passage the episode of the two clarinets in the "Cercle Mystérieux des Adolescents" in the *Rite of Spring* (example 7).

Ex. 7 The Rite of Spring
Mystic Circle of the Adolescents

At first the second clarinet plays in D flat minor, whereas the first one, with its chromatic trills, forms a counterpoint turning upon three notes, of which the A flat is rhythmically displaced, thus making a diversion of the binary measure by a ternary intervention. From the fourth measure on, the parallel movement of the design excludes every intent of bitonal polyphony; we are dealing here, quite simply, with a tonal theme exposed in parallel major sevenths, as it might be in thirds or sixths. A parallel movement of the voices is not counterpoint, contrary to what certain critics of Stravinsky's technique assert. But how bold nevertheless to double a theme in major sevenths!

On the other hand, polytonal passages abound in *Petrouchka* and in the *Rite,* as well as in numerous later works: the episode of the "Barrel Organ," with its two themes in D minor and in B flat major, the "Dance of the Nurses" in *Petrouchka,* the "Auguries of Spring," the "Dance of the Earth," and the "Sacred Dance of the Elect" in the *Rite,* and many passages in *L'Histoire du Soldat,* etc.

But we are always concerned with several tonalities, superposed about a pole of attraction that determines their interweaving, gives them a provisional liberty, a surcease, then finally integrates them into the principal tonal cadence. As we have remarked, despite the diatonic tonal predominance, Stravinsky in no way denies himself the use of chromaticism when it is needed, as in the admirable "Sleight of Hand Trick" of *Petrouchka*, the only example, perhaps, in the entire history of music in which a chromatic polyphony makes for such a musically and emotionally lucid effect.

The second "Prelude" of the *Rite,* an astonishing page of music in which the mystery is in the notes and not in the evocation, a large part of the *Nightingale,* and the *Song of the Nightingale* (not to mention the *Firebird*) also contain abundant chromatic material. But here, chromaticism is used in relation to the fundamental diatonic principle that is always present, and that remains "basic" in Stravinsky's harmonic conception.

In spite of a vertical, rough, complex, and merciless harmonic end result, the *Rite of Spring* remains clearly polyphonic, that is to say, melodic, in its workmanship. The harmonic effect is the result of a thought that moves horizontally; its superposed elements are endowed with their own harmonic attributes, thus asserting that they, too, are tonal and melodic.

IV

Although harmony here is the result of melodic interweaving, it is also a factor in the rhythmic outline, as is the case in *Le Jeu des Deux Cités*. Often the tones that go into the composition of this particular harmony give birth in the course of their development to a new melodic epi-

Creative Typology and Craftsmanship 85

sode, as a result of the composer's borrowing an interior tone from each progressive chord. There thus comes into being a melodic design issuing from the harmony and the rhythm, which themselves originate in superposed melodies.

This method, which excludes any arbitrary moment, is put to use with equal effectiveness in the powerful aggregates of the *Rite* and in the surprising "tonality transitions" that are the result of a simple crossing of two transparent lines, as in the *Ode*, the *Sonata for Two Pianos*, the *Symphony in C*, the *Symphony in Three Movements* and, between the two periods, in the first movement of the *Concerto for Piano*, the *Capriccio*, *Apollon-Musagète*, and the *Concerto for Two Pianos*.

Curiously enough, this horizontality in his thought, this predominance of the melodic factor, does not manifest itself only on the plane of polyphonic superposition, but sometimes on another plane as well, when harmony is reduced to its primitive part as chords supporting the melody. Everything remains subordinated to the actual problem, for the use of an arbitrary system is excluded. In *Oedipus-Rex*, for example, the melodic conception of several arias remains definitely homophonic. Harmonic verticalism acts the part only of a support for the melody, of an accompaniment which directs the tonal flow. It merely buttresses the angles of the moving line.

The *Three Pieces for Solo Clarinet* are monodies in which a melodic line often functions so that by the unfolding of a tonally defined center, modulation is made possible by the mere fact of spreading out the notes that would correspond, in an implicit chord, to a cadential harmonic idea.

On the other hand, harmonic superposition is often used by Stravinsky within a single tonality, such as that of the tonic with its own dominant (thus continuing the traditional conceptions of suspension and anticipation so dear to Mozart and Haydn), that of the major with its relative minor, arising from Stravinsky's devotion to the ambiguous mode, and from his surprising ability to "play" with thirds. We will cite examples when we analyze particular works.

This ambiguous major-minor tonality manifests itself in Stravinsky's writing either on the harmonic plane, as in the *Rite*, when a tonal chord contains at the same time the major and minor third (G sharp, E, G natural, or G natural, E, G sharp), or on the melodic plane, as is the case in many recent works where the same theme moves between the two modes as in *Apollon-Musagète, Danses Concertantes, Scènes de Ballet,* and the two *Symphonies*). Often the two modes are not merely maintained in a precarious sort of balance; they are crudely superposed in a simultaneous exposition, as in the slow movement of the *Symphony in Three Movements* (example 8) where the second violins and the violas clearly play in D major while the violoncellos and the contrabasses play in D minor.

Ex. 8 Symphony in Three Movements, Movement II

It is not here, as in Ravel, a harmonic "friction" of the second, but real major and minor thirds, each one fixing a precise, clearly determined mode.

Creative Typology and Craftsmanship 87

The same element is used with the same consistency in the trio of the final movement of the *Sonata for Two Pianos*.

Since the chronological method is not necessarily applicable to the psychological analysis of the creative process, which always remains an impenetrable mystery, it would be difficult for us to define (and I am thinking here of the composer himself as well) when his melody—especially in recent works—has a harmonic origin (unfolding of the chord) as the result of the interplay of major and minor thirds, and when this characteristic of his harmonic language is the result of a sort of condensing of the thematic idea.

Most probably, and as is always the case with Stravinsky, we have here an active synchronization of all the components of his musical material, projecting themselves on the melodic, harmonic, and rhythmic planes in common interdependence.

Stravinsky's modulation, even when it seems sudden and unprepared by the cadence, leans upon a "quasi-cadential" sort of conclusion, which, although unexpected, does not seem in the least constrained. The *poco a poco rallentando* leading back to the *tempo primo* in the slow movement of the last *Symphony* is a characteristic example.

The movement of the second cellos, in spite of the F natural, leads back to the major-minor D of the beginning in a manner as logical as it is ingenious, thanks to its descent to E.

This modal ambiguity in Stravinsky is never thought of as a sonority effect in the sensualistic acceptance of the phrase, but as a true and conscious opposition of the major to the minor with all the purely harmonic implications thereof.

Some sudden modulations, more especially in recent works, have an almost Schubertian freshness and ingenuousness in their musicality and simplicity. The *Danses Concertantes,* the *Scènes de Ballet,* and the *Sonata for Two Pianos* are replete with them. I shall only cite as an example the transition from E flat major to C major in the very serene and tender fragment of the *"pas d'action"* in the *Danses Concertantes:* B natural is enharmonically substituted as a leading tone for C flat (alteration of the sixth), which is part of the preceding harmony (example 9). Of course, the "modulation of the third" could have

Ex. 9 Danses Concertantes, Movement II, Pas d'Action
(Arranged for two Pianos)

been accomplished by less devious and more orthodox ways (all the treatises on harmony offer us many methods), but never in a more natural one.

In the *Symphony in C* we often see realized the particularly effective use of Stravinsky's method of operating a transition to a different tonality without any harmonic

Creative Typology and Craftsmanship 89

modulation, by the simple substitution of one tonality, already resolved by its cadence, for another merely by "holding" the tonic degree or the dominant as a common tone long enough to destroy the previous polarization. This "forgotten" tone then finds itself inside a harmonic aggregate, which the latter tonality determines with perfect ease.

It is impossible to exhaust the variety of means of Stravinsky's modulation, its wealth, and its musical importance. This modulation, like all the rest and in spite of its complexity, precludes anything arbitrary in its method and is founded upon the harmonic principles of traditional modulation. It is accomplished with equal effectiveness in complex harmonic superstructures and in the outlining of simple contrapuntal designs, for Stravinsky's language is more and more subordinated to the principle of the means available, and loses more and more, in the composer's stylistic evolution, its value as an autonomous device for immediate and unexpected effect.

The composer considers experiments as his own personal affair: he has too much discretion to disclose any of his research when he offers us the "finished product." Stravinsky has no desire to claim an exclusive technical system that would be worth nothing in itself, except in so far as it is part of an integrated whole, whose component factors are co-ordinated by thought.

His technique has a favorite method for certain means of expression—a method that is all his own, liberal, but clearly circumscribed, and that never leads to a narrow formula or to a pedantic system of writing.

His harmony, for example, always remains, like the other component factors of his work, an element at his disposal, that he uses in accordance with the needs arising from a particular problem. That is why it is impossible to assign Stravinsky a place in a given harmonic system of writing, such as the polytonal, for example, although he has demonstrated its resources to us.

He does not always draw his melodic line in sevenths or ninths; sometimes a succession of thirds and sixths is enough to express his musical thought. He is far from scorning the perfect cadence. He uses the good old dominant with no shame whatever, and honestly resolves it to its tonic. It is with the same conscious method, unprejudiced and appropriate to each different case, that he uses superpositions of complex harmonic aggregates—each one of which resonates with its entire series of overtones which converge, with their harmonic and tonal covering, toward the final pivot from which a new projection of melodic lines can begin once more.

Cuique suum—to each his own: a harmonic skyscraper, if need be, or a unison of diatonic design, but always according to the needs of the subject at hand.

It is by studying the application of the harmonic means through Stravinsky's work that we can clearly understand the profound difference separating a method from a system. How is it that an ordinary diatonic theme, frequently harmonized in parallel thirds or sixths, carries with it, in Stravinsky's case, an immediately recognizable mark, whereas, in the case of so many other innovators, the boldest excesses of language often remain unimpressive and without the slightest effect of genuine originality? It is because in the case of the former we are dealing with the co-ordination of elements economically distributed toward an abstract end that is clearly assigned to them, and in the case of the latter with a cerebral fabrication whose only aim is to accomplish something unheard of.

Stravinsky is concerned with composing, while so many

Creative Typology and Craftsmanship 91

others are concerned with astonishing or with blindly following an idiom that happens to be in vogue.

The essential aim of our argument was to emphasize the importance of the fact that, with Stravinsky, we always deal with a personal stylistic technique, and never with a restrictive and individualized system of language or of musical style.

The purely rhythmic disposition of a melodic line frequently intervenes, with Stravinsky, to determine a new elaboration of the musical material. There is an astonishing example of this in the first allegro of the *Symphony in Three Movements*, previously cited: the end result is comparable to that of Beethoven's style in the last string quartets and the last piano sonatas, in which all the expressive factors of the music contribute to a monumental construction—in the sense, of course, of spiritual grandeur, and not of volume.

Despite the uniformity of the thematic design in the basses (one revolving around three notes of a tonal arpeggio in which the beginning is displaced upon various beats of the measure), the development always remains organic and alive, has nothing in common with the facile and blunted effect of the usual moving pedal point, in which a dynamic result is achieved by the static process of the persistent repetition of the pattern.

In this moving and irresistible development, everything stirs with controlled freedom, everything revolves about a square and direct framework, formed by the rhythmic play of three notes (tonic, third, tonic) driven, in their turn, by the movement of the superposed material toward modulations as smooth as they are uncommon.

It is extremely interesting to follow, in this allegro, the "linking" of Stravinsky's modulation, about which we have already spoken. Sometimes, he fishes out some lost interior note from within its converging axis of tonal polarization, and sustains it: this note is then used by him as a new point of departure, as the internal element of another chord, and he brings it, implacably, toward other pivots, with the same ingeniousness.

V

It is natural that new thoughts should appear on the way, in the course of realization, just as smaller streams contribute to a river that has already broadened its course. These ideas are integrated by Stravinsky into the original stream as they appear, after they have been filtered through, polished, verified as to their utility and even their necessity, in the general scheme.

This explains why any one of Stravinsky's manuscripts can so clearly reflect the man and the artist. On the one hand, it gives us an impression of rare precision, while on the other, it reminds one of a geographical or hydrographic map, or of a meteorological bulletin. Secondary lines are superposed, as they appear, on several additional staves that he draws with a sort of "staff-stencil-ruler" (invented by the composer) in the particular spots where they integrate themselves in the work as a whole. And how significant and revealing of Stravinsky's art that he should prefer the use of blank paper with no staves on it whatever, making staves on it with his stencil: he can thus clearly establish on paper the course of each instrumental voice, indicate the plane on which each harmonic combination is resolved, group his conception of sonority, and decide upon the location of each note in a precise and logical manner.

VI

Rhythm is what has usually been emphasized as the most powerful factor in Stravinsky's art, the most easily identified characteristic in his idiom, for it is rhythm that quickens all his creations with inexhaustible life.

Indeed, no other composer has been able to order the flow of musical material through time in such new, rich, and varied ways. No one has as yet been able to extract so many living possibilities from the relationship of measures to each other, the interplay of strong and weak beats and of their elements within the measure itself, from the displaced accent or the opposition of the meter to the barline.

Now, in the course of his evolution, Stravinsky adopts little by little the same attitude with regard to rhythm as to the other components of his musical craft.

The huge complexity and diversity of Stravinsky's rhythm is never the result of a desire to be novel or to create a spell. It is a particular means of expression, whose most striking characteristic is its originality.

Rhythm, which acts partially upon our nervous sensitivity, is naturally the musical factor whose variety is most easily perceived. But as we have already observed, rhythm for Stravinsky is not an autonomous entity. It acts as an internal pulsation of his music, to which the composer seems, in addition to brains and a heart, to have added lungs, so to speak, as another productive organ.

For the rhythmic course of Stravinsky's music, whether dynamic or static, always seems to be of a clearly respiratory nature. The frequent asymmetries in its outlines are always organized infallibly with regard to the generating idea and with a strictly musical end, without any desire to surprise, to stir physically, or to fascinate by diversity or obsession.

It is almost always closely related to the essential melodic element, whose outline it defines, or to which it forms a contrast in time.

No one has understood and solved in his work the positive action of silence and interruption better than Stravinsky. A pause for Stravinsky is not a gap, a void, but an implicit interval in organized time, a sound the seeming absence of which is a perceptible presence, not only in the pattern of the phrase, but in its basic framework as well. In Stravinsky's rhythm there is then not only a feeling for the concreteness of sound, but also the plasticity of that sound in its relation to the intervals of silence, its real organization in time.

Except for a fragment of *L'Histoire du Soldat* and the *Ragtime for Eleven Instruments or for Piano*, it would be difficult to find in Stravinsky's work a case where rhythm is considered as an autonomous entity.

A piece such as, for example, the "Auguries of Spring" cannot, in my opinion, be considered without arbitrariness as pure rhythm, in spite of the percussive quality of the strings, their obsessive hammering, and their asymmetrical accentuation. This hammering, isolated for a few measures only, as an introduction to a determined framework, defines such a complex melodic, rhythmic, and harmonic development that it loses its autonomous function little by little and becomes a source of nourishment for the entire fragment.

The musical idea, then, probably comes to Stravinsky with its real or potential rhythmic framework. His rhythmic achievements are connected with the same imperative clarity and the same ingenuity with which he ties

Creative Typology and Craftsmanship 95

together with harmonic modulations the tonalities that are furthest apart.

Just as tonality represents in his eyes the melodic or harmonic obstacle to be overcome, the barline plays the part of a rhythmic restraint. Apart from one or two exceptions, Stravinsky never loses sight of it and never ignores it. As is the case with the tonal framework, he imposes upon the barline every conceivable form of violence, varies the cadence and the meter, dissects it into slices—but recognizes the beneficence of its tyranny the more he struggles against it.

His genius for rhythmic invention, his "lungs," and his intelligence as an architect, offer him the clear vision of everything a musical idea can contain in the way of metrical diversity with which to hollow out doors and windows in the edifice of sounds; thus he makes sure that air circulates freely through these apertures, and that his music breathes by itself, without "evoking," "expressing," or "meaning."

Thus with Stravinsky we are far from evocative reconstitutions, from "tomtoms" and "Chinese gongs." Even in the *Nightingale* and in *Ragtime* he never tries to create a mysterious or hallucinating "genre" with his rhythms. His rhythms move through his music the way blood circulates in an organism. They fulfill a function, and do not try to be effects in themselves and for their own sake.

It matters little whether this admirably fulfilled function is the effect of intelligence alone, which in itself is highly debatable and improbable! It is the result only that interests us in its aliveness. The most powerful of intellects could not have achieved it alone. It must have been applied by a creative faculty that fertilized it and gave it an object to work upon. It certainly pertains to the intelligence to realize a thing, but the "idea" of the work, the desire to realize it thus and in no other way, belongs quite obviously to creative genius, with all the postulates of gift and invention which it implies.

Rhythm as an isolated entity is to Stravinsky as vain and empty of musical significance as harmony in itself, or timbre for its own sake.

The composer's treatment of rhythmic material escapes analytic classification because of its diversity. We have here a latent technique, whose renewal seems unlimited, a component factor closely bound to all the others: melody, harmony, architectonics, timbre—a factor that quickens, stops, or animates all of the sonorous material of a Stravinskyan work, while feeding upon the other factors that participate in the general action.

We can therefore only cite some characteristic rhythmic applications, without attempting to cover completely this inexhaustible subject, so difficult to grasp:

1. A very particular use of the syncope, owing very little to jazz, except in *L'Histoire du Soldat, Ragtime,* and the *Piano-Rag-Music.* With Stravinsky, the syncope is not exclusively the accenting of the weak beats of a melodic pattern. With its appearance, it often displaces the very idea of weak and strong beats. We often have, then, a fixed accent upon a beat whose metric function varies in accordance with what follows.

2. The displacement of the accents of a rhythmic design, which starts again, each time on another beat, and thus acquires a linear asymmetric form.

3. Extension by sustaining or omitting a beat of the measure, resulting in the same effect of rhythmic caesura.

4. The altogether new means of opposing the binary and the ternary measure, already observed in the first scene of *Petrouchka.* It is the result of the independent

Creative Typology and Craftsmanship 97

action of two melodic designs of different meter resulting in a rhythmic effect of melodic origin.

5. The revitalization of the meter by the introduction of the "interpolated measure," most often by the use of an odd, irregular rhythm. This is the method to which Stravinsky has remained faithful since *Petrouchka*, even while simplifying the graphic expression.

6. The pulse of a symmetric character with the superposition of asymmetric accents (as in the "Auguries of Spring" of the *Rite*, many fragments of *Les Noces*, *Le Renard*, etc.).

7. The simultaneity of several rhythmic designs clashing against each other in the independence of their logical development (as in the *Rite*, *Mavra*, *Danses Concertantes*, and the *Symphonies for Wind Instruments*).

8. A pulsating phrase, opposing the cut-off triplets of an eighth note to the regular, binary eighths (as in the development of the first allegro of the *Symphony in Three Movements*).

9. A percussive caesura, partially harmonic, which brutally interrupts one phrase for a new departure, like a snap of the whip (already used in the "Danse de Kashtcheï" of the *Firebird*, reappearing in the "Jeu des Cités Rivales" of the *Rite*, and resulting in *Les Noces* in a definite effect): it is a stopping and a starting point, a stroke that puts everything in question, while at the same time it creates a new order of things.

10. A rhythmic accentuation obtained by emphasizing certain beats of the measure with the help of an instrumentally opposed group, from which a subsidiary rhythm arises (a device that has always been a part of Stravinsky's rhythmic technique and from which he drew an extremely new effect in his latest *Symphony*).

11. Last and above all, the respiratory character of the composer's melodic phrase in itself, its discursive fluctuations, its particular rhythmic cut, its hiatus, its breaks, its direct, lapidary atmosphere, and the changes in its pulsation.

As was the case with the polyphonic horizontal superposition of several tonal melodies, each one having its respective harmonic attributes, Stravinsky treats polyrhythms as a contrast of sharp edges, instead of linking them by what they have in common. The rhythms clash, hurl one against the other, but are not blended in a monochromatic amalgam. For, even while allowing the metric indentions of each component rhythm its implacable individual freedom, the rhythmic forms are always conceived in a plastic and direct manner. Their construction in time is based upon values differing one from the other in their respective duration, their pattern and their disposition one with regard to the other.

Thus, to a rhythmic movement of eighths or sixteenths, he will oppose a pattern of sixteenths with sustained points of caesuras in each pattern, so that nothing is lost of their horizontal relief in the vertical, crossed impact.

These patterns, components of the rhythm, can go their way freely, for each one of them is endowed from the start with a "guide," making it possible for it to remain intact, instead of blending with the others when it clashes with them.

Of course, this rhythmic plasticity, while it makes it possible for the composer to superpose several different cuts, each one of which remains independent of the others, is itself made easier by the diatonic character of the melodic pattern, which these cuts either support or contrast with.

So that this diatonic character of the melody becomes,

with Stravinsky, an essential condition for any true polyphony, polyharmony, and polyrhythm, all of which assume reality on an acoustical plane, and not on the optic plane, as is often the case with atonal music.

We observe numerous examples of this polyrhythm, based upon clear cuts in the component rhythms, in *Petrouchka*, in the *Rite*, and in later works as well.

VII

The novelty and originality of Stravinsky's rhythmic conception does not, then, depend so much upon changes in the meter as upon the perpetual vitality of his musical work as a whole, in the spaciousness of his dynamism, in his gift both intuitive and lucid of knowing just when a movement once begun has reached a point of saturation, and when the time has come to modulate or authoritatively to compose another.

This rhythmic multiplicity, then, is more a factor of unity than a series of arbitrary changes—which explains why, in Stravinsky, an obsessive rhythm never casts a spell on the nervous system. One does not yield to a Stravinskyan rhythm for lack of resistance: one follows it while submitting to it, one lives with it, participating in its intense development, for it is human and natural in spite of the great complexity of its action.

The composer imparts life to his rhythmic framework. He does not express himself in it, he expresses in it nothing else. The rhythm is present for the same reason as the other elements of his musical material: it is a factor in the homogeneous whole of a music that continues with a motion of its own, once the composer has started it going at a given point, and that stops at a point predetermined by its own development.

The graphic notation of Stravinsky's rhythms has become much simpler in the course of the composer's evolution. Although changes in the barline are nearly as frequent in the first movement of the recent *Symphony* as they were in *Les Noces,* their internal metric cut is obtained more often by the use of displaced accentuation than by measures of seven, nine, or eleven sixteenths, as in *Petrouchka,* and the analytical action of the meter often takes place within the measure itself.

One of Stravinsky's favorite devices is to impart new life to a cut by the introduction of a measure with a double odd meter. It is part of his rhythmic idiom from *Le Feu d'Artifice* to his most recent works, and its appearance reacts upon the chronic meter as well as it does upon the melodic delineation (see the *Symphony in Three Movements*).

VIII

No contemporary musician has contributed more wealth, more variety in the instrumental combinations, and more novelties in the choice of timbres than Igor Stravinsky.

From *Petrouchka* onward, and already to a large extent even in the *Feu d'Artifice,* Stravinsky considers the timbre as a participating component, and not as an effect in and for itself.

Although the *Firebird* is still *orchestral* in its conception, with the whole magic apparatus and sonorous mass from which Stravinsky knew how to extract unexpected discoveries, the *instrumental* plasticity of the timbre took on more and more importance in his technique. The timbre was to be considered, with regard to the musical idea

Creative Typology and Craftsmanship 101

and of the whole work, as a messenger, and not as the "hero" of the transmission.

The rough and somewhat arrogant orchestra of the *Feu d'Artifice* already contained, when one looks at it now, the promise of an instrumental conception different from that of the period. The timbres try to contrast in their independence, to bring out their sonorous personalities, instead of blending themselves into color combinations.

The *Firebird* and parts of the *Nightingale* show a momentary return to the conception of the chromatic orchestra. As for the melodic, harmonic, and rhythmic elements, the orchestration of the *Firebird* is full of finds, of rare sonorities, of sparkle and sheen, and of magical boldness. Probably no one before him would have dared to give the tender theme of the "Lullaby" to the bassoon—ordinarily used for less delicate work.

However, when taken as a whole, the orchestra of the *Firebird* does not as yet contain the *instrumental* principle of Stravinsky's future orchestra as it was to develop later. Here the instruments try to combine into a blended, compound sonority rather than to contrast either individually or in groups. As we shall see for the other elements of the *Firebird*, it is the "Infernal Dance of Kashtchei" that is an exception, and that points to the future while continuing the style of the *Feu d'Artifice*.

This evolution is part of his general development, and should be judged, therefore, in its relationship to his technique as a whole and to the decline in the autonomy of its particular components.

The appearance of *Petrouchka* determined Stravinsky's orchestral conception. He returns here to the classical attitude, restoring to the timbre a plastic function related to the melodic idea—that is to say, making it above all the "sonorous bearer" of a theme, instead of a color to be chemically integrated into a many-colored palette, by means of a linear pattern.

The timbre is extracted, and no longer assimilated. The timbre of each instrument is emphasized at the expense of the *orchestral* timbre, of sonority in itself and for its own sake. So that the instrumental timbre, in its clear-cut individuality, now puts the orchestration at the service of the musical whole. The problem was to restore to the theme its concrete value, its plastic relief, presented raw, instead of submerging it in an overladen atmosphere.

From *Petrouchka* on, this instrumental conception makes itself more and more evident, throughout a whole series of works for chamber orchestras that vary in their composition with each work, and finally, it results in the present linear idiom, where groups tend to oppose one another by their particular timbres, instead of forming a new and unifying sonority by their combination.

This liberation of the individual timbre, the restoration of its melodic function, and the suppression of its part as an autonomous entity (resulting in the shifting of attention from the "musical" to the "derivative" and secondary factors) all follow on Stravinsky's æsthetic evolution as well as, and even more than, on his purely technical and melodic development.

The orchestral conception of timbre for its own sake, as an autonomous effect, resulted in the introduction of an extramusical element with an expressive significance or an indirect action into a harmonious structure, a constructive whole, in which timbre should have been only a component factor, instead of a determining element.

The quest for orchestral color, however interesting from an experimental point of view, and with an appropriate use in mind, brings into the composition a foreign factor

Creative Typology and Craftsmanship 103

of imaginative correspondence, of imitation, of concrete, realistic, or affective significance.

The interest in timbre also results in an "expressive" conception. The circumstances surrounding the work take on a predominant importance by separating the perceptive reaction from the essential goal, which is the abstract understanding of the work as a whole.

Now, it seems to Stravinsky that by giving his music a significance other than that which he æsthetically attributes to it, one taints the purity of his art, in which, as we know, all factors are subservient to the abstract and purely musical structure.

Although Stravinsky carefully measures the range of his orchestral timbres and their peculiar effects, it is not with the intention of exhibiting them as ends in themselves; it is to "place" them, whenever necessary, and not to give them an autonomous significance.

It is, then, the whole work that is offered to the listener —as is the case with all the other components of his music —not the details and circumstances of its birth.

Unfortunately, we have contracted the inveterate habit of insisting upon being present at the delivery, and of knowing the father, the mother, the aunts and uncles, in addition to the midwife, instead of simply being content with admiring the handsomeness and good health of the child. All questions such as "What did he *mean* by this music?" or, "What does it suggest and signify?" are completely gratuitous, if one asks them of a work by this composer.

IX

It should be said once and for all: music for Igor Stravinsky means nothing but what he has written with all possible precision on the staves of his music paper. Music hides nothing under a sonorous wrapping. Timbre remains a direct factor of its truth, but without concealing or camouflaging anything essential.

As we have said, the autonomy of the individual instrumental timbre or of the ensemble is then clearly substituted for the autonomous orchestral timbre in Stravinsky's technique. The timbre is used to bring out a thematic line, and does not seek to create an atmosphere or *ambiance*.

Its function is to lend the musical material plasticity, without drowning it in a mass of magical sonorities, thought of in terms of their own individual effect.

This is why, since *Petrouchka* (and *Petrouchka* included, despite the opinion prevalent with regard to its musical conception), Stravinsky has sacrificed every element of picturesqueness and virtuosity in the use of the orchestral palette to the direct, raw, and logical timbre and to the individual virtuosity of the instruments, thus arriving in *Les Noces, L'Histoire du Soldat,* and *Le Renard,* at a final statement of his doctrine. Despite the current belief to the contrary, neither the *Rite* nor *Petrouchka* is colorful or picturesque in its orchestration, and the works that follow them are even less so. As we shall later try to prove, that is precisely what another element of Stravinsky's "reactionary" revolution consists in: he restored to the timbre its traditional function in a work like *Petrouchka,* establishing the instrumental principle of the direct conception of an orchestra that became analytical from that time onward. And that, while the use of blurred, magical, colored, and composite sonorities was in full vogue. The superficial picturesqueness in *Petrouchka* is chiefly due to the contrast of raw timbres, each one of which follows its own musical path, refusing to participate in a general mixture, and retaining its clear-cut color. In

Creative Typology and Craftsmanship

the same way, the aggressive sonorities of the *Rite* have their origin in the sharp contrast between instrumental groups, and not in a blend intended to create "color" or "atmosphere."

Les Noces, with its mass of "instrumental choirs," the four uni-sonorous pianos, and the percussion, precludes any attempts at autonomous timbre, because of the common characteristics of its metallic, percussive, and resonating sonorities. *L'Histoire du Soldat* makes use of an ensemble of seven instrumentalists, all of them virtuosi, wherein even the combination of dissimilar timbres results in the creation of a new *individual, polyphonic* timbre, rather than in a blended sonority.

When Stravinsky "doubles" one timbre with another, it is not to create a blend, but because this doubling results in the creation of a particular sonority, created by the *co-operation* of two instruments, and not by their fusion.

For example, when the two clarinets in the conclusion of the first movement of the *Ode* perform an identical melodic phrase, the first one legato and the second one staccato, the perceived effect is that of a single instrument with a double emission, having a single timbre. The result obtained is the same in the case of the piano and the xylophone in *Les Noces,* or the cymbalum and contrabass in *Le Renard.*

X

In his instrumental and melodic conception of the orchestra, as well as in his ever increasing preference for an interplay of clear-cut timbres at the expense of the blended timbre, Stravinsky's technique has resulted in astonishing mastery and a striking originality.

His knowledge of all the technical possibilities of each

instrument, the sonorous value of each register, the relationships between instruments, whether united or contrasted, the emotional value of their mode of emission, joined to an admirable gift of intuition and divination, are made use of by the composer with rare and infallible success.

We already quoted the case of the bassoon at the beginning of the *Rite*. Stravinsky's use of a deliberately created difficulty is also manifest, for example, in the high trumpet passage at the end of the third scene in *Petrouchka*, where the very effort of the performer, his tension, go into the making of the harrowing climate characteristic of that movement.

It would take an encyclopedia to try and dissect the orchestral cuisine of Stravinsky, for each work, each phrase exemplifies a different problem, a new restraint, an *ad hoc* solution, a particular object of study.

We have tried to isolate the very principle of his conception, such as it developed logically from *Petrouchka* to the most recent of his works, his general discipline of the sonorous treatment of musical material, his use of individual plastic timbres contrasting with the blends of the autonomous sonority of timbre for its own sake.

However, we will have to call the reader's attention to a few characteristic features of his orchestral idiom, when we discuss his particular works in detail. It is useless to say that this orchestral technique is governed by the method he uses to realize his work generally, and that in turn is governed by his general æsthetic discipline.

The component element of sonority, then, is treated by Stravinsky with the same lucidity and perspicacity, the same careful distinction between the essential and the superfluous, the same economy of means, as all the other elements of his work.

Creative Typology and Craftsmanship 107

His treatment of timbre leaves nothing in a hypothetical state. He foresees exactly the actual sonority as it will be revealed at the performance, and it certainly is not Stravinsky who could be surprised, pleasantly or otherwise, at the first rehearsal of a new work.

XI

Thanks to this instrumental conception of scoring, Stravinsky ventilates the scoring, clears the space around the various instrumental groups, and particularly that of the woodwinds, thus emphasizing their importance.

The function of the woodwinds had been sacrificed in symphonic music since Beethoven, particularly by Wagner and the schools that derived from him, while the strings had been emphasized because of their expressive and vibrant character, better fitted for a romantic and individualistic conception of music—not to mention their variety of timbres.

Already the French school, and more particularly Debussy and Ravel, had tried to restore a balance between the groups, but they treated them more by balancing them against one another than by contrasting them directly. Stravinsky restores to the woodwinds their individuality and their importance as a homogeneous group. He makes use again of the abandoned formula of an independent sonority of the "woodwind ensemble." He extracts from it all its possibilities for timbre. He opposes them to the other groups without integrating them into the orchestral mass as partial factors.

At the same time, he enriches the orchestral use of the strings, makes use of them in ways that are often novel, and finds in them, not only expressive and vocal qualities, but percussive, resonating, and burlesque qualities as well.

Even the percussion group takes on broader functions; it becomes a homogeneous group, and serves not only to scan the rhythmic framework or to prepare a climax by a dynamic progression, but to participate in a musical fashion to the movement, to which it imparts a living outline; it contrasts as an individual ensemble, contributing sound instead of mere noise (as in the *Rite, L'Histoire du Soldat,* the *Symphony of Psalms,* and the *Symphony in Three Movements*).

The introduction into the orchestra of the percussive sonority of the piano contributed new possibilities. The manner in which it contrasts with the other instruments or orchestral groups results in a specific timbre in the sonority of the orchestra as a whole.

Stravinsky, in his treatment of orchestral technique, is not concerned with knowing whether or not a process is new: the only thing that interests him is to know whether it will prove useful in the particular case under consideration, and whether it corresponds to the intentions and postulates that it is expected to solve. He often innovates by using a traditional device, whose frequent use should have dulled its effectiveness, as for example the tremolo, which no "serious" symphonic composer would have dared to put back in circulation. Now, Stravinsky uses it in the ending of the *Scènes de Ballet* and in the last *Symphony* and obtains surprisingly novel and significant effects. These innocuous tremolos, developing within struck and accented chords, which are stressed by a movement of the basses, create a striking impression of freshness and power. We shall discuss it again at the proper time.

Again, Stravinsky renews the use, not only melodic or

harmonic, but instrumental as well, of the trill and of the appoggiatura. We all remember the admirable use he makes of the latter in the *Rite*, *Les Noces*, and *Le Renard*.

And by initiating the use of human voices as instruments with a soloist timbre, in the *Pleasant Songs*, the *Berceuses du Chat*, *Four Russian Songs*, and *Le Renard*, and as a choral instrument in *Les Noces*, the composer opens a new field with infinite horizons.

XII

Stravinsky, faithful to his æsthetic preoccupations, does not seek for expressive quality in the sonority of his orchestral conception, but only for a purely musical one. Once more, the strength of his spiritual conviction predominates over the use of latent and easily exploited riches. What a wealth of timbre coloration this astonishing man could have achieved, who at twenty-eight displayed the myriad iridescence of the orchestral palette of the *Firebird*, revealing here a surprising mastery and virtuosity, an unprecedented intuition for sonorities! Stravinsky gradually gave up what he came to consider as deceptive appearances, the very opposite of musical truth as he understands it in his art.

The orchestral chemistry, whose essential aim is a composite and blended effect in the sonority, interests him less and less; as is the case with his genius for novel harmonies and the invention of autonomous rhythms, he sacrifices the use of his own discoveries to the quality of the musical ensemble, the abstract construction of the work.

A man would have to possess an unshakable faith in his own wealth to impoverish himself deliberately and consciously, to economize on means to the point of artistic asceticism. It is indeed a mark of quasi-religious faith in the indispensable purity of art, which he serves only by "delegation."

The conception of *Apollon-Musagète* is extremely significant as an illustration of this conscious frugality. It is easy to imagine what sonorous virtuosity a Stravinsky might have extracted from the instrumental ensemble at his disposal. But the instrumental idiom of *Apollon* is of a quasi-congealed austerity and coldness. The pure melodic lines are traced polyphonically, renouncing all ornamental character or seeking after timbre. No iridescence, no harmonics interrupt this bareness of the unadorned melody, "carried" on the surface, so to speak, by the strings.

So arid a conception is necessary in this music because it adds relief to the horizontal lines with complete plasticity, and gives the musical material, with its appearance of coldness, of expressive neutrality, a basis of tenderness: the "Finale," of a sublimated serenity, touches us much more deeply than so many pseudopathetic effusions.

The same attitude of musical restraint results in the same effect in the slow movement of the *Octet for Woodwinds*. The deep and heavy chords of the chorale of the *Symphonies for Wind Instruments*, in their dark grandeur, achieve an extraordinary effect of "inner climate," and that only by a peculiar instrumental arrangement, and in spite of a general and obviously neutral and simple use of the brasses.

The perfect success of the little concertini in the *Symphony in Three Movements* owes its richness and freshness only to its seeming poverty in color, its presentation as a group independent of the sonorous mass, as in the old *concerti grossi*—that group being treated as a soloist and introducing an element of chamber music into a symphonic conception.

Creative Typology and Craftsmanship 111

As to the solo instruments, Stravinsky has been remarkably concerned with the piano, whose idiom he has at the same time enriched, while trying to restore to it some of the qualities blunted by long use.

Although the aspect of instrumental virtuosity was somewhat overemphasized in the four *études* of his youth, it reappears in the *Capriccio* in the form of a game, rather than as an exhibition. Stravinsky never sacrifices the musical idea even to virtuosity, although he does try to bring out all of the concrete individuality and musical possibilities of the instrument.

In the *Concerto for Piano and Wind Orchestra,* in the *Sonata,* the *Serenade,* and the *Concerto for Two Pianos,* the instrument becomes a polyphonic musical entity, a bearer of melodic phrases, rather than of passages, and also the instrument of discursive movements, either dynamic and percussive, or lyrical and capricious.

This technique of writing, always exploited in a lively, often-renewed fashion, is the fruit of exhaustive study, of a careful weighing of the instrumental possibilities of the piano, of its peculiar qualities, and never of the faculty its timbre has of evoking that of another instrument. Stravinsky, then, does not use a piano so that it will sound like a celesta; he uses the latter itself, whenever he needs that sonority.

We shall discuss this question of instrumental writing when we study individually the works composed for the piano.

The same ingenuity, the same sure craftsmanship, are to be found in the composer's treatment of the piano in combination with the voice or another instrument. We have already mentioned the effect resulting from the introduction of the clear-cut sonority of the piano in the orchestral mass.

In the *Duo Concertant* for violin and piano, Stravinsky tried to solve the difficult and seldom happily solved problem of the co-ordination of two instruments that usually do not combine in a satisfactory and homogeneous manner. Now Stravinsky, by a skillful opposition of registers discriminately chosen for their contrasts, and by distinguishing the respective idioms, achieved real success in the composition of music that seems to be born of a unified group with a homogeneous timbre.

The *Concerto for Violin*, very difficult to perform, solves the problem of musical timbre and instrumental virtuosity with rare success, by adopting a violin idiom which is discursive in character and thus related to J. S. Bach's sonatas for unaccompanied violin.

We shall later discuss again in detail the instrumental treatment by examining particular works, and especially musical ensembles, with regard to their "group timbre"— by considering *L'Histoire du Soldat*, the *Ragtime for Eleven Instruments*, *Le Renard*, the *Symphonies for Wind Instruments*, the *Octet*, *Mavra*, *Dumbarton Oaks Concerto*, the *Danses Concertantes*, and the concertini of the *Symphony in Three Movements*.

XIII

We shall now consider the problem of constructive form, which, with Stravinsky, and considering his particular production, is closely connected with his lyric conception. Corresponding to his æsthetic discipline of pure music, the constructive element in Stravinsky's work assumes an increasingly controlling importance and becomes the very center of his present preoccupations.

The simple fact of having written such a considerable number of ballet works (*Firebird, Petrouchka, Rite of*

Creative Typology and Craftsmanship

Spring, Pulcinella, Apollon-Musagète, Le Baiser de la Fée, Jeu de Cartes, Scènes de Ballet, and, recently, *Orpheus*) and works upon which a choreographic realization has later been grafted (*Les Noces, Danses Concertantes*), as well as works lyrically conceived (*Nightingale, Le Renard, L'Histoire du Soldat, Mavra, Oedipus-Rex,* and *Persephone*), has given Stravinsky the reputation of being above all a "musician of the theater."

There are even those who assert that each time the composer does not have before him a realistic idea to absorb into his musical work, the thought of a scenario, or a fixed idea of dramatic or lyric action, his work shows a certain defectiveness.

We have already touched upon this question in the analysis of Stravinsky's artistic attitude, but in a study of the constructive character of his art, it is indispensable to discuss it anew.

It is a paradoxical fact that the musician who, by his æsthetic discipline and craftsmanship, has been most instrumental in restoring to music its function as an independent art, should have remained misunderstood, and appreciated in a sense diametrically opposed to all of his artistic aspirations! This phenomenon may be explained by the fact that, for certain listeners, the need for an imaginative and evocative stimulant remains an indispensable factor in their perceptive reaction, even in those works where it is not really present (as in the symphonies of Beethoven, all the works of Chopin, etc.) and apparently even more so in the works in which a poetic text serves as a point of concrete departure, as is the case with Stravinsky for those of his works based upon a lyric conception.

Now, we know that in all his scenic works the composer aims at and obtains a purely musical result. These works are sufficient unto and by themselves, not according to the composer's good intentions, but as a matter of fact.

All of Stravinsky's ballet music is played in the concert hall, in symphonic form, much more often than as choreographic performances. Some of it has momentarily or definitely passed to the purely musical plane, as *Les Noces, Scènes de Ballet, Rite,* etc. It all gives the same complete pleasure and the same complete satisfaction to the listeners, of whom many have never known a visual, lyrical, or dramatic version.

With the exception of the *Firebird,* this has nothing at all to do with suites or extracts taken from these ballets or concert arrangements, but rather with the complete work as it is performed at the theater.

Whether the ballet remains the basis, the concrete point of departure, of the musical organization is a matter of no importance. Once the music has begun, it develops of itself, brought into being by the laws of music alone and without any descriptive, literary, or active influence. It is the music that by its development alone determines the action. It never follows it, never subordinates its constructive quality to it, and never seeks blindly to illustrate it.

Its evolution remains independent of everything that does not constitute a part of its particular elements.

It is rather curious that a dancer and choreographer like Serge Lifar should emphasize, in the opposite sense, the "too musical" character of Stravinsky's ballets, their too great independence with regard to the scenic action, the wrong which this abuse of the power of music does to the evolution of the dance itself.

In an article that Mr. Serge Lifar devotes to "Igor Stravinsky, Legislator of the Ballet," in the special issue of the *Revue Musicale* of May-June, 1939, he expresses himself upon this subject with complete frankness:

Creative Typology and Craftsmanship 115

"Igor Stravinsky was the man predestined for Diaghileff and the Ballets Russes, their good genius. He was also the tyrant, the despot, the 'bad genius' of the Ballets Russes and *of ballet in general.* [These are Mr. Lifar's italics.] The music of Stravinsky evokes nothing of the dance. Rather to the contrary, it destroys the dance . . . A score of Stravinsky impoverishes, weighs down, and binds the dance rather than enriches it. . . .

"Stravinsky's music is so beautiful in itself that it is self-sufficient, has no need of any dancing accompaniment, and the dance only serves to distract the listener's attention."

And further on, "Mr. Stravinsky committed a fatal error in becoming a composer of ballets."

An opinion like this, by its absolute opposition to the thesis affirming the essentially scenic character of Stravinsky's genius at the expense of his faculties as a constructor, is extremely significant in its forcefulness.

It confirms our opinion that, for Stravinsky, music is too sublime an art to be placed at the disposition of the other arts. The ballet, for him, comprises movements having their own æsthetic and their own logic, and the moment of visualization of the movement plays the same role, according to him, as "the guitar in a still life of Picasso."

"The dancers have nothing to recount any more than my music has. Even in the old ballets, like *Giselle,* the descriptive character was eliminated from it by the very fact of its naïveté, its unpretentious traditionalism, and reduces the objectivity to the pure rule of the game. My ballet music, consequently, never seeks to explain the action, but rather to live side by side with the visual movement, in happy combination, like two distinct individuals.

"In the *Scènes de Ballet* the dramatic action was determined by the evolution of the plastic problems; both dance and music should be established on the basis of the constructive feeling of contrast and similarity." *

For Stravinsky, then, the choreographic problem remains purely architectonic or deductive and nonillustrative in nature.

"It must go back to the roots of the musical *form*, of the musical game, and re-create them in the forms of movement." †

XIV

The same conception of the absolute independence of music reappears with regard to poetic action, and presides over Stravinsky's vocal works as well as his dramatic creations. The final result for *L'Histoire du Soldat* was obtained, not by an effort to write background music such as would explain the dramatic action, or descriptive music to stimulate the action, but rather by making the action, the narration, and the music simultaneous, thus contributing to the dramatic power of the work as a whole.

"Let us put the music and the drama together like two individual entities, allowing them to live their own lives without forcing the one to explain the other or to react against it.

"My ideal—to use a term borrowed from chemistry—is that of the chemical *reaction*, where a new element, a third body, results from the union of two different but equally important bodies: the music and the drama. This is not the same as a *mixture*, in which the new ingredient of a music representing nothing new or creative is added to a preconceived whole." ‡

---

* Interview on music and films in *Musical Digest*.
† *Ibid.*
‡ *Ibid.*

Creative Typology and Craftsmanship

We shall discuss again certain of Stravinsky's achievements when we analyze his lyrical works, but we consider it important, even now, to insist upon the fact that all of them are governed by a clearly established attitude of complete predominance of the music whereby they avoid anything like subordination to the dramatic action motivating them. The parallelism of their development is planned to be independent of any synchronization with the visual or scenic element.

Their strength, then, is above all of a constructive nature. They are planned and realized as works of pure music.

To those who know them from having seen them on the stage, they may evoke the episodic action that they follow in their parallelism; but this visual element is not what determines their essence, their true value, or even their action, which remains purely abstract.

The spectacle on the stage remains the concrete basis for the music, but never becomes the condition of the work once it is achieved.

This conception, especially with regard to the relationship of dance and music, explains, at least partially, why, until he collaborated artistically with Georges Balanchine, Stravinsky was seldom satisfied with the choreographic representation of his ballets. Only in Balanchine did he find this abstract vision of the dance as plastic movement, as an agent in a chemical reaction, instead of an element in a mixture. In their abstract conventionalism, inherited from the classic ballet, *Appolon-Musagète* and the *Danses Concertantes* are much closer in their choreography to Stravinsky's ideology than to the scenic realizations of Michel Fokine or of Waslaw Nijinsky.

XV

It seems perfectly natural, then, that Stravinsky's ballet music, separated from its point of departure and its scenic destination, should find a place in the universal symphonic repertory, thanks to its architectural qualities, and thus live a life of its own.

All of these works, like his compositions that are purely musical in origin, demonstrate an admirable mastery of construction, an infallible treatment in the renewal of traditional forms: sonata, rondo, three-part song form, large variation forms, and fugue.

Stravinsky could not, then, be seriously reproached for a lack of the faculty for organizing musical material constructively, since that is one of the essential aims of his work. Whether in the *Symphony of Psalms*, in his two recent *Symphonies* (without mentioning the one that he composed in his youth, and in which, in spite of an academic craftsmanship, a gift and attraction for the treatment of abstract forms already manifests itself), in the *Concerti*, the *Octet*, the *Sonata*, the *Ode*, the *Dumbarton Oaks Concerto*, the *Danses Concertantes*, or in any of his works for the stage, his preoccupation with architectonic realization always remains the chief aim of his works. It is, as we have said from the start, at once a general discipline and a technical realization that gives them their purely musical unity.

Petrouchka, as we have already seen, took for a concrete point of departure the idea of a concert work for piano opposing itself to the orchestra. Upon that musical point of departure was later grafted the idea of a poetic and choreographic action.

Creative Typology and Craftsmanship 119

In my opinion, each scene in that "suite of burlesque scenes in four movements" is not, as Mr. de Schloezer would have it, a sonata movement—not, at least, in the precise meaning of the form as it was created by Philip Emanuel Bach and continued by Mozart, Haydn, Beethoven, and Brahms. However, each one presents a complete architectonic form: the movements balance each other and the form is pleasing in itself, independent of any literary guide.

The *Rite of Spring* is a suite in thirteen episodes, which, separated from their scenic titles, are so many symphonic pieces in rondo or song form, unified by a common stylistic method.

Les Noces is a profane cantata to which was added a choreographic representation in four movements, parallel to the four musical movements, and strictly constructed, as we shall see, on the opposition of themes decided upon for each movement.

Musically speaking, *Pulcinella* is an orchestral suite, as are *Apollon-Musagète,* the *Danses Concertantes,* and even the action ballets, such as the *Jeu de Cartes* or the *Baiser de la Fée.*

Each one of the component episodes has its particular construction, firmly realized, and respectful of all the rules of the classical abstract form or of a dance movement in a suite.

It is significant that so far, of all of Stravinsky's scenic works, the ballet given the most successful choreographic representation was the *Danses Concertantes,* a work composed for chamber orchestra without any dramatic intent, and used by Balanchine as choreographic music a few years later.

Again, all that Stravinsky knew when he was working on the *Scènes de Ballet* was his intention of composing a ballet in the classical style, without paying attention to any scenario.

In *Mavra*, with its detached arias, as well as in *Oedipus-Rex*, which he conceived as a Handelian oratorio-opera, the preoccupation with musical construction indisputably dominates any interest in synchronization with the visual action. Sometimes it goes so far as to be opposed to it in its expressive delineation.

We have already discussed the lyrical conception of *L'Histoire du Soldat*, and we shall discuss it again, as well as that of *Le Renard*, when we study these works. Such conceptions are always subordinated to traditional discipline, while at the same time they evidence a personal æsthetic attitude. We have noticed that, in works like *Les Noces* or *Le Renard*, the musical components are independent, not only of the poetic subject, but also of the text sung, which, in itself, is but a phonetic, syllabic accessory, and, so to speak, an auxiliary music.

We already mentioned such a conception with regard to the dramas of *L'Histoire du Soldat* and the Latin text of *Oedipus-Rex*, even the prosody of which does not disturb the composer in his constructive preoccupations. But how wonderful the intelligence that presided over the fine achievement of the finale of *Mavra*, where the sung drama and the "music," after proceeding in two opposite directions, finally unite in a manner as unexpected as it is natural! The incredible crescendo of the one here opposes itself to the progressive diminuendo of the other, and they neutralize each other in an orderly disorder, with infallible precision and care. As usual with Stravinsky, nothing is left to chance or to a lucky coincidence in this improvisation of geniuslike and lucid buffoonery, where everything works, not toward *one* effect of paradox or shock by surprise, but toward the *general* effect desired.

Creative Typology and Craftsmanship 121

It is with his intelligence that he succeeds in achieving the effect, but it is his gift of sensitivity and intuition that *creates* the necessity for it, and presides over the *will* to realize it.

No Pygmalionesque ability would be sufficient to achieve it, were it not applied to a vital idea, born of the latent gift only. We have insisted a good deal upon the formal side of Stravinsky's art. That is because his composing so many works with apparently theatrical subjects had created a sort of a misunderstanding in the classification of the composer as a creator of symphonic or chamber music.

Experience being stronger than arbitrary deductions, reality itself disproves the theory of the descriptive or applied quality of Stravinsky's music, since it is being transferred more and more from the theater to the concert stage.

XVI

It is obvious that Stravinsky does not follow a fixed form, just as he does not, while borrowing from tradition, follow the melodic, the harmonic, the rhythmic, or the orchestral conception as a *ratio scripta*. When he innovates, he always takes a traditional guiding line as a point of departure, and eliminates outmoded elements by creating in accordance with unifying methods of his own, by increasing the importance of certain factors, or by decreasing that of others.

His organization of musical material, in the unity of its movements and the superposition of its episodes, refers to that of J. S. Bach, whose discursive style of development he renews—and he manifests but seldom a particular preference for the opposition of two themes with their expressive characters, since he prefers the unity of the movement to the interplay of thematic contrasts. However, his form always remains precise in its construction.

A perfect form demands above all an organized unity, a proportionate and symmetrical distribution of the elements. This constructive perfection constitutes one of the chief qualities of Stravinsky's art.

Considerations of a totally different order often interfere with the study of Stravinsky's melody, which, from a thematic point of view, is objected to for not being sufficiently "symphonic," and for being unfit because of its cut for an easy adaptation to the demands of the development as it was conceived in the traditional sonata-allegro form. The remark is often passed that the concise character of his melody is more fitting for stage music than for the more abstract forms of the art.

A truly paradoxical reproach, if one opposes it to the other criticism, that of a so-called lack of expressiveness in the nature of his themes! Only a complete misunderstanding of Stravinsky's whole work can account for such a display of incomprehension and such flagrant contradiction. For only expressive, individualized melody lends itself to purely theatrical treatment, or rather, that is the sort of melody that is considered most fit for it, while a so-called inexpressive melody potentially corresponds to the elaboration of the abstract music form.

Let us come back, then, to the question of thematics in its relation to pure music.

Let us first of all agree upon an exact definition. What, theoretically, constitutes a symphonic theme? If one takes as authorities the great classical masters—for that is where we should seek stylistic purity before the anarchy of expression led to a Babel of individualistic languages—a

Creative Typology and Craftsmanship 123

theme is a melodic pattern composed of intervals arranged in a determined metric order, regulating their flow in time.

The question of the length of the theme, of the "melodic breadth," acts somewhat as a particular quality of the composer, but does not determine the value of the work itself.

In many cases, the shortness of the theme is considered an essential condition of its ultimate effectiveness: it is a victory over an obstacle, over constraint—a feat.

How often has it not been said that one example of Beethoven's constructive genius was the fact that he built the entire first movement of the Fifth Symphony upon the simple pattern, more rhythmic than it is melodic, of a third—a pattern whose rhythmic cut takes on an indisputable primacy over the musical material.

Is it possible for a theme to be more lapidary, less expressive, and less inclined toward a distended melodic breadth?

We know very well that, in other cases, Beethoven manifested a long-sustained thematic creativeness, but the point here is to observe that the shortness of a theme has nothing to do with its structural possibilities. Is not the theme of the first allegro of the *Eroica* a simple rhythmic unfolding of the tonic chord of E flat major, and does it not govern the entire monumental structure of this movement?

Why then should the laconicism of Stravinsky's themes be more troublesome than Beethoven's, so long as the author achieves an abstract construction in a determined form, in accordance with an appropriate framework which at the same time satisfies all the demands for proportion and logical organization of its components?

The composer uses for each given problem the themes he deems necessary, and it is the solution of these problems, in their final form, that interests us.

This limitation of the melody is to be explained above all by Stravinsky's attachment to unity of style and his scorn for everything unprecise and nonconcrete in the development, by his hatred for prolixity, which sometimes camouflages a lack of clarity in the design.

XVII

The neoromantic period, whose enormous contribution I do not intend to dispute, and whose musical genius I acknowledge in some of its representatives, created a false sort of thematic convention and routine by imaginative and illustrative means. Little by little, habit and facileness changed this convention into a dogmatic rule of the game.

For example, a certain tormented chromaticism is often considered as a somehow "profound" symphonic quality; slow passages of the cellos and basses are looked upon as mysterious, while a crescendo is a manifestation of "exalted passion," a tremolo the expression of "anguish," etc.

What disturbs some in Stravinsky's melody is the absence of any kind of mystery. His themes are neither tormented, insinuating, nor ambiguous in their expression. In addition to being brief and plastic, they usually are tonal, diatonic, and, in a word, simple.

Another sort of melody might be preferred, since no conception is exclusive of others. Stravinsky's conception is what it is. It is, above all, what Stravinsky needs it to be to offer us an uninterrupted series of masterpieces. Let us not reproach a brunette with not being a blonde when, and above all because, we prefer blondes.

XVIII

In the organization of his materials, Stravinsky prefers to deal with solid, concrete matter, with a "style," and therefore a language that has proven its universality before it became divided into numerous dialects.

That is why, thematically, he renews the tie with the tradition of the eighteenth century and the beginning of the nineteenth—a tradition to which he imparts new blood, thanks to his stylistic renovation.

But it is in no way his language in itself that makes Stravinsky a classic, as we have abundantly proven. What matters above all are the *reasons* why he insists upon returning to it: These are objective reasons, pertaining to his doctrine, as well as his own individual reaction before the work to be accomplished.

When the æsthetic personality of Stravinsky is under discussion, that absurd term, "neoclassicism," is often introduced. What has not been written about this so-called "neoclassicism" of Stravinsky! As usual, similarities in the "idiom" have been emphasized, while the deep reasons for the "style" are neglected.

Pulcinella and the famous forsaking of the Russian manner, seem, according to some, to have inaugurated the so-called neoclassical period of Stravinsky's art, his so-called cosmopolitan manner.

But in reality, it is *Petrouchka* that inaugurated, not Stravinsky's neoclassical manner, but his classical discipline. Stravinsky's treatment of the materials taken from Pergolesi fits in rigorously with the same postulates as his work in the period of Russian popular inspiration, as well as in the middle and later periods: that is to say, a lucid balance of the stylized materials (filtered in accordance with the demands of style) and of technical achievement, without the interference as an act of the will of the creator's intimate and expressive individuality.

This attitude, discussed at length in another chapter, has absolutely nothing "neo" about it. It is but the manifestation of the type to which he belongs as an artist. Only the spiritual attitude of the artist determines his æsthetic direction, to the exclusion of the linguistic elements of his art.

For example, a work like the *Rite of Spring*, in spite of its aggressive language and the shocks between sounds and contrasting tonalities in its harmonic blocks, in spite, also, of the personal novelty of its idiom, is no more romantic than *Oedipus-Rex* or *Apollon-Musagète* are neoclassical.

Although the ends that the composer assigns himself in these various works differ one from the other, his creative process and his craftsmanship remain identical. His presence in the inception of the work remains invisible. The work, once it starts moving, develops independently of his physical and psychological personality.

Shall we hesitate then among the definitions of classical, objective, or Apollonian art? It matters little! Stravinsky achieves plain and simple art, the art of music in and for itself, which needs no "ism" to assert itself.

It is thanks to this detachment, this elimination of the expressive ego, that Stravinsky proves that he belongs to the type of the order-creating Apollo. The composer does not like to take his hair down in public (a certain public, alas, relishes that brand of exhibitionism). He offers us the lyricism of his work in its final achievement, and not that of his intimate personality. He considers it a lack of taste and modesty to display his ego, and desires to be judged only by his "composed" work.

XIX

This tactfulness and personal reserve disturbed some of the readers and critics of his *Chroniques*. This autobiography even disappointed some of his habitual admirers by the simplicity of the narration and by the absence of any sort of expansive lyricism and anecdote.

They expected some sensational revelations on the little tricks that are supposed to explain the formation of genius—how was the *Rite of Spring* composed, what did Stravinsky intend to express in this or that passage—a whole mass of information that, to him, would have been pure and simple indiscretion.

Instead of all that, here was a bare and precise, almost austere recounting of the facts, year by year, and a direct exposition of his æsthetic and technical preoccupations, as they evolved from one work to another.

"From such and such a year to such and such another, I worked at the composition of the *Rite of Spring*," Stravinsky tells us, without exposing the mysterious and allegorical trickery some would have liked to discover in it, and without explaining to us the "hidden meaning" of a work that revolutionized the music of our time, and that *should* have had a hidden meaning.

Is it pride or humility on Igor Stravinsky's part?

Since the composer is a complete man, and therefore an artistic man and a human artist, this problem is not without bearing on the knowledge we have of his work.

For one who knows Stravinsky intimately, this reserve, this restraint, this attitude of a classic, is neither pride nor humility.

Stravinsky is conscious of his ability, but he is not the least bit vain about it, and manifests no false modesty for which he might expect to be outbidden. He considers his ability (his gifts) as an acquired fact.

He is humble only in his attitude toward that which involves a dogmatic hierarchy of a universal kind: his religious faith and his musical faith.

He is neither distant nor exuberant. He feels that life, which is so short, is too precious for him to waste his time on people or things of no interest to him. But with those who have become his friends, and whom he numbers among his intimates, he is trusting, affectionate, even tender. As is the case with his art, he economizes on the superfluous in order to enjoy completely that which is useful.

In a being organized like Stravinsky, every thought comes from within, no thought speculates upon facile effect. However fond this epicurean may be of earthly comforts, he would never commit an act or create a work if these were contrary to his principles or opinions as an artist.

This seems to me an opportune place to discuss Stravinsky as a religious musician, in a short anticipation of the chapters that we shall devote to his individual works. It is difficult to ignore this aspect if one wishes to understand Stravinsky's spiritual background as a whole.

Moreover, considering the large number of works—religious, mystical, and liturgical in inspiration—now being composed, it seems important to define his convictions, so attractive in their purity, on the plane closest to us—that is to say, the human plane.

For beyond the æsthetic discipline and the technique, a new aspect then manifests itself; the attitude of the man, as well as that of the artist, with regard to the Divinity.

Apart from the "Gloria"—so moving in the simplicity of its main lines (the only fragment of the *Mass* finished

Creative Typology and Craftsmanship 129

before I left the United States in 1946), two works present themselves for æsthetic criticism from that viewpoint: the "Tower of Babel" episode from the *Genesis Suite* (a work for which each of several composers who had lived in America was commissioned to write a movement), and the *Symphony of Psalms*, which was written earlier.

Stravinsky is a man of profound religious faith. He observes rigorously the precepts of the Orthodox religion. He is a believer in the full sense of the term.

Stravinsky's attitude toward the mystery of the Divinity remains hidden in the very depths of his soul; it would never occur to him to display it in his everyday living, and even less so in his art. Music stops where prayer begins.

His faith is at once spiritual and dogmatic, for he is temperamentally responsive to every manifestation of the universal dogmatic order, the great order presiding over creation and the unfolding of life.

His mysticism, in so far as it exists, is never exalted, ecstatic, or hysterical, and he never uses it for the outward expression in music of his religious faith. Stravinsky's religious music, then, should be considered as a sort of professional offering from a musician for the purpose of glorifying the Divinity, a sort of musical *ex voto;* yet it has no illustrative or literary relationship with the great order of things, it is not a transcendental and exalted transcription in sound by a mystic describing his vision.

Stravinsky's respect for and humility toward the Almighty remain too great for him to dare to touch upon it by a realistic or imaginative conception. He prefers a direct convention, thus avoiding any suspicion of consciously representing the Divinity.

I shall cite as an example of this attitude of humility, based upon unshakable conviction, his musical treatment of the "Tower of Babel" cantata. Since I was present at the conversation between the composer and our patron, and since I rather frequently discussed with Stravinsky the manner in which he had defined his problem from an æsthetic, religious, and technical point of view, I consider myself qualified to discuss this subject.

The work includes, in its technical realization, a large orchestra, mixed chorus, with or without soloists, and a narrator. Now, contrary to the thought of our friendly Maecenas (who had inspired this whole suite), Stravinsky's conception of his work immediately revealed his views on faith, and on music as a function of faith. Instead of the chorus relating the epic action while the narrator speaks for the Eternal, it is the latter who relates the events of the biblical episode while the chorus sings the divine words. This conception avoids any sort of ambiguity, any suspicion of imitation of the divine voice by the human voice. This word, spoken by the chorus, remains, so to speak, in quotes, and retains for that part its function as a quotation.

The divine word has no musical background that would create a suggestive atmosphere. The same is true of the episodes of the construction and destruction of the Tower; everything remains on a purely musical plane, without any descriptive evocation.

The religious mystery, original source of the creation, made room for the technician intent upon his musical material, while imposing upon himself an added restriction: to avoid the profanation that would consist in visualizing what must remain a mystery and is accepted as dogma.

The discussion with our patron, who saw things quite differently, and almost cinematographically, as an external synchronization of the text with the musical atmosphere, was interesting in its very liveliness. Stravinsky,

Creative Typology and Craftsmanship 131

a believer and a musician, would have changed his conviction for nothing on earth. He would rather have refused the commission. The Divinity should be illustrated in no way whatsoever. He is too great. Music should illustrate nothing whatsoever. Such is not its function, and in this case less than ever.

Fortunately, our friend had sufficient admiration for the composer and respect for his spiritual conviction and his artistic principles to let him have his own way.

Was it a triumph of spirit over matter, or was it simply that Stravinsky's name was too attractive for the program to do without it? That is another mystery, a human mystery this time, and it is useless to insist upon it too much.

XX

It is this same attitude of spiritual integrity and abstract objectivity that we find in that monument of contemporary religious music, the admirable *Symphony of Psalms*, a work that can be placed, without the slightest hesitation or fear, side by side with the *Passions* of J. S. Bach and the *Missa Solemnis* of Beethoven. It is a work altogether profound, and Stravinsky's lyricism is manifested in it with all the brilliance of his musical genius.

It is a symphony with chorus, which makes use of the text of the psalms: a purely musical symphony, composed according to the laws of our art for the purpose of glorifying God.

We are not dealing, then, with a work buried in the rubbish of a false mysticism or of an equivocal and indiscreet literature. Stravinsky never "speculates" upon his faith; he does not use it as a means of expression. He dedicates his music to it in the objective manner of a medieval artisan, who might consecrate a work of his craft to God.

It is an homage, but never a public prayer or an externalized mystery like *Parsifal*.

The religious mysticism that might enrich a nature as profound as that of Stravinsky certainly puts him, in a way, in relationship with the Divine, but the author never manifests this relationship in his contacts with the public. He does not confuse the two levels; he writes a purely musical work whose emotional origin remains a secret with him. What he personally pours out in the work concerns no one.

In the *Chroniques de ma Vie*, Stravinsky clearly and with rare frankness exposes his views upon this delicate subject.

Speaking of the impression that his first hearing of *Parsifal* made upon him, he tells us: "What revolts me about this whole undertaking is the elementary attitude which dictated it, the very principle of placing a spectacle upon the same level as the sacred and symbolic action constituting the religious service." And further on: "It is high time to do away, once and for all, with this inept and sacrilegious conception of art as religion and the theater as its temple."

Faith is based upon a dogmatic order, allowing neither for discussion nor for criticism, but demanding, rather, a total submission, whereas a work of art presumes freedom of judgment, the possibility of accepting or rejecting, in short, a work of art is subject to every manifestation of human weakness, and finds itself, consequently, submitted to the critical faculty. This very fact definitely precludes for Stravinsky every possibility of a synthesis of these two elements: "To confuse these two orders is to show an absolute lack of discernment and unmistakably bad taste."

Creative Typology and Craftsmanship 133

Others may prefer a more externalized and materialized conception of their faith, and that certainly is their right. Stravinsky retains his personal side undisclosed. He shows only his work. This entails the sacrifice of a possibly greater popularity, but that is the way it is; the composer remains impervious.

Stravinsky's work is not modern; it is not intended to respond to some particular present need, but rather to a universal one, that has its place apart from any concept of a fixed period. He therefore remains indifferent as to whether each new composition is immediately understood, or whether its significance will ultimately be revealed. He is sure of always coming into his own, despite the reservations and the polemics of the moment.

Before we go into the life and musical works of the composer, I therefore consider it useful, at the risk of repeating myself once more, to restate my views upon his creative personality, as I have attempted to develop them in the course of this work. This general synthesis, coming as a conclusion of the æsthetic and technical analysis of the body of his work, will serve us as an introduction to his personal life and to the linking of his works.

XXI

Some types of music come to us directly, because their message is so clear. Others require a certain spiritual effort (I do not mean a personal effort, but a certain abstraction from reality, and detachment from perception).

Despite its direct and precise, sometimes even explosive, character, Stravinsky's work certainly should be numbered among these—especially his recent works, which seem more and more purified of any foreign, adventitious matter,

This has nothing to do with an esoteric doctrine or with an ivory tower, but rather with a tendency toward the sublimation of the musical phenomenon to an increasingly high degree of independence and self-sufficiency.

One should make the effort to penetrate a seeming coldness to find, in the absence of pathos or individualized outpourings, an infinite tenderness and serene humanity.

Stravinsky never gossips in order to say nothing. He detests padding, and is gifted with a particularly keen sense of what is effective. He works with the same finesse of observation as, for example, Maurice Ravel, but in a totally different direction: Ravel perfected his work like a watchmaker; Stravinsky, like a polisher of glass. Ravel *adds* what in his opinion would be useful or valuable; Stravinsky *eliminates* what he considers nonessential.

Ravel was a sensualist; he loved the action of sound, its repercussion, its autonomous interplay of timbre or harmony: he enriched it. For Stravinsky, sound is only a material with which to build, measure, circumscribe: he knows how to impoverish it for the benefit of the construction itself.

It is interesting to notice that the last phase of Ravel's evolution seemed to manifest an æsthetic tendency toward that same conception. A work like the *Concerto for the Left Hand* may be considered as an indication in that direction. But the technical postulates of Ravel's musical nature, his innate preference for rare harmonies, a vertical conception of writing, the magic, spellbinding effect of his orchestral timbre, make it difficult for him to take the final steps in a direction that leads to achievements so dematerialized, so far from sensualism of any kind.

Artifice, the rule of the game, is for Stravinsky of a

Creative Typology and Craftsmanship 135

totally different nature than the principles governing Ravel's work. For Stravinsky, beauty is not an essential postulate of the quality of art, which in addition is not necessarily "pretty." The only thing Stravinsky considers important is that artifice should make a work musically truthful.

Stravinsky, as we well know, does not think that the aim of art should be to transpose into sounds the emotions of man or the beauties of nature, or to interpret them through his own vision. For him, the problem is to compose music with tones and rhythms, in accordance with established rules.

Human emotion, impressions of nature, as well as any theme of a ballet or opera, can be used by the composer as concrete points of departure, conscious or subconscious, but that is where their function ends: they are a springboard of the musical phenomenon, but never contaminate the creative process or the realization.

Despite the profound admiration Stravinsky has for the art of Ravel, for his technical perfection and for the fact that he knew exactly how to achieve what he proposed for himself, the sensual element of that art remains completely foreign to Stravinsky.

This proves, once more, how much certain superficial judgments upon the influences undergone by a composer remain on the surface of the true problem of his personality. Debussy certainly influenced Ravel in his language, and his harmonic and orchestral methods: Ravel influenced Debussy, and both of them influenced Stravinsky, who influenced them in turn. Yet could anything be more clearly different than these three types of artist, holding hands and turning their backs on one another?

When we deal with a personality having features as strong as those of Igor Stravinsky, the influence received, taken in the sense of a melodic reminiscence or a harmonic borrowing, is absolutely negligible. Every deliberately solicited influence is useful, for art is but an affiliation and the renewing of a link. Nothing "new" is ever invented in art: one discovers, thanks to one's gifts and intelligence, that which exists potentially, and one avails oneself of it.

A healthy influence, then, enriches a truly creative nature capable of assimilating it. But it absorbs or destroys an imitative personality.

During the entire course of his musical evolution, Stravinsky has undergone many influences, as did Bach, Mozart, Beethoven, Brahms, Wagner, Debussy, and Ravel. Is *Pelléas et Mélisande* a less beautiful work, or less original in itself, because Debussy could not have conceived it in quite the same manner had he not been already acquainted with Moussorgsky's *Boris Godounoff* or *Les Enfantines?* But in the *Deux Arabesques* the future Debussy is already foreshadowed. The *Firework* of Stravinsky, while assimilating or rejecting by evolution certain influences of a stylistic nature, already contains the germs of an originality, whose development was always to be logical.

A real understanding of Stravinsky's technique requires a perspective view of his work as a whole, the appreciation of each element in relation to the other, in function of the constructive moment. Each one of these problems has its assigned aim, its own law, and its particular mode of realization.

This technique, in its variety, is itself subordinated to a general principle of application which manifests itself through a constant evolution; it obeys a common denominator which constitutes the composer's artistic and spiritual discipline.

XXII

Thus, we believe that the greatness of Stravinsky's work is not to be found exclusively in the inexhaustible novelty of his technique and of his means of expression. The meaning of this work—in addition to its admirable beauty and its musical profundity, and beyond the fact that it possesses all the characteristics of an enduring and definitive art, in addition to the composer's immense personality, his unfailing professional mastery and his astonishing gift for unity in variety—is, above all, of a spiritual nature, by its æsthetic action, its example, and its teaching. This spiritual significance resides, for us, in:

1. The introduction of a "reactionary revolution" (and I am thinking here of the violent outbursts of the *Rite* as well as of the peaceful serenity of *Apollon-Musagète*), which freed the artistic tradition from academic routine by substituting "liberty at home" for "anarchy everywhere."

2. The substitution of the sense of lucid and intelligent creative individuality for egotistic expression.

3. The purification of false æsthetic concepts tending to make the musical art serve ends foreign to it: to "express" or to "signify" phenomena that cannot be expressed or signified by means of that art.

4. The fact also of placing realization in a perspective of abstract discipline freely accepted, instead of the free will of an unbridled imagination, or of the fabrication at any price of novelties with a pretense to originality.

5. The effort made to restore to the component factors of the musical art the universal notion of style, by substituting for the multiplicity of languages following a false convention the exclusive criterion of the artistic person-

ality and its determining importance. The effort made to reduce the autonomy of each one of these factors for the benefit of the music as a whole.

6. Finally, the utilization of the concrete or contingent for abstract and constructive purposes.

XXIII

At the moment of undertaking the biography of Igor Stravinsky, and the detailed analysis of his works, we are faced with the choice between two methods: either to tell the story of his life as it has developed until today, and then to discuss each work in particular, or else to place his works in the framework of the events of his life while following the chronological order.

The latter method seems to me more lively, communicative, and effective, since certain works have already been discussed in several of their aspects.

Moreover, as we well know, the concrete plays such an important role in the Stravinskyan morphology that the constraints themselves remain connected, in some cases, with the circumstances imposed by reality—circumstances that the composer makes his own, as though he had imposed them upon himself.

I also prefer not to divide the body of Stravinsky's works into periods limited by certain works. I know that this method is generally used in analytical works, and in particular those devoted to our composer, and I do not deny its convenience for outlining and discussion. And yet, for a body of works like that of Stravinsky, this very convenience is a drawback, in my opinion, for without insisting upon the fact that one more or less artificially established period necessarily trespasses upon another, a narrowly

Creative Typology and Craftsmanship 139

applied chronological system does not absolutely coincide with the real artistic evolution of Stravinsky.

Of course, this system of sharp divisions would be useful if we chose to admit that Stravinsky's creative evolution was made of leaps in opposite directions, following the apparent zigzags of his consecutive works, or that certain works put an end to an æsthetic or stylistic tendency in order to undertake an opposite one—in short, if we chose generally to admit that this evolution has not followed a logically determined path.

Now one of the essential aims of this work is precisely to affirm, contrary to that all too common impression, the unity of Stravinsky's work. We shall do it by assigning to each work its place as a step in a progressive renewal and as a manifestation of a constant tension toward one single goal.

The system of periods assimilated to the "genres" has already created so many misunderstandings about Stravinsky's work that by availing myself of it, were it only for the facility of expression, I would fall short of the goal that I have assigned myself.

As I said at the outset of this essay, we are not concerned with creating about Stravinsky another analytical system, but only with shedding light on the superficial character of certain overhasty affirmations, and to present his work in the frame of his æsthetic personality and in relation to his aspirations, apart from the critic's preferences.

PART II

CHAPTER V

Life and Works (1882–1920)

I

IGOR FEODOROVITCH STRAVINSKY was born June eighteenth (June fifth, according to the old Greek calendar), 1882, at Oranienbaum, near St. Petersburg, the summer resort of the old Russian capital, where his family ordinarily lived.

If one is to believe the astrologers, this is a fateful date. Born under the sign of the Gemini, Igor Stravinsky was particulary favored by the stars for an artistic vocation.

His father, of Polish descent, had acquired a reputation as bass singer at the Imperial Opera, where he filled the most important roles of the lyric repertory. He owed his celebrity not only to a perfect mastery of the vocal art, but to his remarkable gifts as an actor as well. Feodor Stravinsky, himself born of a family of well-to-do landowners, was a man of broad general and musical culture. He possessed a fine library of literary and musical works, of which the young Igor was later to avail himself freely, and from which he was to extract the popular texts of *Renard, Pribaoutki, Berceuses du Chat,* and *Chants Russes,* and in which he was to find inspiration as well for his text of *Les Noces*.

It is not without interest that the first musical impression that Stravinsky retained of his childhood, and that he recalls to us as a sort of motto in his *Chroniques,* should be of a physical and concrete nature.

Indeed, it is not an abstract impression, but rather an observation connected with his daily life.

Stravinsky tells us how he was impressed by a mute peasant, whose song consisted of only two meaningless syllables, which he alternated with incredible dexterity and in a very lively tempo.

He accompanied this inarticulate jabbering with a gesture, "placing the palm of his right hand under the left armpit, he moved the left arm by pressing the right hand against it." This manipulation had the effect of "producing dubious, but very rhythmic sounds."

Without going so far as to give a Freudian interpretation of a childhood recollection, as has been done with the "Dream of the Bird" of Leonardo da Vinci, and without seeking there for specific complexes, the fact that Stravinsky associates his first musical recollection with a concrete impression is not without significance, and gives a valid insight into the future æsthetic of the young boy.

To this strange gesticulation, which impressed him so much, Stravinsky adds the recollection of the village women singing in unison—and at home, the young boy made great efforts to reproduce the technique of these two manifestations of the music around him.

It is by these two phenomena, so the composer tells us, that he "became aware of himself as a musician."

A strange confession, yet how significant!

Until the age of nine, he knew music as an art only from a distance, through the walls of his nursery, for if much music was played at home, the young children were not allowed to be present.

At the age of nine, Stravinsky began his piano studies, and his progress in this domain was extremely rapid.

Having once acquired a certain dexterity of the fingers in handling the instrument, Stravinsky instinctively began to give himself over to improvisation, which from the beginning he took very seriously, to such an extent that he did not allow himself to be impressed by the little encouragement he received from his immediate family. At the same time, he began to apply himself to reading the operatic scores of his father's library, with as much pleasure as facility.

His first real contact with music as an organized art was at a performance of *A Life for the Czar,* of Glinka, for whom Stravinsky was always to retain an unreserved warmth and admiration.

It was also upon this occasion that, for the first time in his life, he heard an orchestra, and one organized in a way that always remained dear to him: clear, transparent, well balanced, and without padding or pretentiousness.

At about the same time, he heard another work of Glinka, his fairy opera, *Russlan and Ludmilla.* Igor's father took part in the performance, but Stravinsky retains another stirring memory of that eventful evening: that of a glance he had backstage at Tchaikowsky, who was to be carried away by cholera a few days later. These, then, are the first musical phenomena that were to occupy a place in his musical subconscious.

At the same time, Stravinsky entered the *Lycée* for his general education. By his own avowal and that of his professors, he did not particularly distinguish himself, and remained, for the most part, below average.

II

Apart from his life at school, which left Stravinsky with some dull memories, for he was not particularly attached to any one of his schoolmates, the young boy became more and more absorbed in the intense musical life of the capital. He began to frequent the opera and ballet performances, and to hear many symphonic concerts: he studied scores, and gave himself over more and more to the personal work of writing music.

The young self-taught musician did not seek as yet for a stylistic direction or for a personal æsthetic; what was most important to him was to learn technique thoroughly in all its complexity and in every detail and, apart from any preference, to become a "professional musician" in the most complete sense of the term.

He became more and more enthusiastic about counterpoint. He gave himself polyphonic problems as exercises, and applied them to his work as a budding composer.

Having completed his work at the *Lycée*, he enrolled at the law school of the university at St. Petersburg. But music dominated his thoughts more and more. At the university, Stravinsky became attached to one of his schoolmates, Vladimir Rimsky-Korsakoff, the son of the composer, who at that time had reached the peak of his fame. He then was the revered master of the younger Russian musical generation.

In 1901, Stravinsky's family spent their vacation in Germany, in the neighborhood of the locality where the Rimsky-Korsakoffs spent theirs. Young Igor took advantage of the opportunity by asking his friend to introduce him to the master, to whom he wished to submit a sample of his work. As he tells us in his *Chroniques*, Stravinsky had decided in any case not to allow himself to be discouraged, even if the judgment of the respected master should prove negative or indifferent. His faith in his vocation was already well rooted. He was to be a composer of music.

Rimsky-Korsakoff received the young man with kindness, showed an interest for some of his works, but in keeping with his severely pedagogical nature, he considered it enough to offer him some technical advice without passing any final judgment, encouraging or otherwise.

It was only later that the relationship between the old master and the beginner became closer and even intimate; when Stravinsky married his own cousin in 1906, Rimsky-Korsakoff was the witness for the young couple.

Until 1906, Stravinsky worked alone, but with much enthusiasm, and his knowledge of theory progressed with remarkable rapidity.

In 1906, Rimsky-Korsakoff accepted the young Stravinsky as a private pupil in orchestration, advising him against taking the usual courses at the conservatory of which he was the director. Stravinsky was to work with him for two years. These lessons were on a purely pedagogical plane, and Rimsky-Korsakoff never tried to force a particular stylistic tendency or an æsthetic direction upon his young pupil. He concerned himself only with teaching the musical aspirant the art of orchestration and nothing more. Stravinsky orchestrated classical works, like the Schubert Quartets, as well as fragments of the works of Rimsky-Korsakoff himself. He began to apply his newly acquired knowledge to his own music, as in his *Symphony in E Flat Major*, a purely academic work in which the young musician tried to mold his ideas, still eclectic, and composite in style, into the constructive frame of the large sonata form. However, the forceful personality of the future composer of the *Symphony of Psalms* did not as yet reveal itself there in any way.

In June, 1908, the sudden death of Rimsky-Korsakoff interrupted Stravinsky's studies, but already a significant work full of promise and implications had come into being as a result of this relationship: the *Feu d'Artifice* (*Firework*), composed upon the occasion of the marriage of Rimsky-Korsakoff's daughter to his other pupil, Maximilian Steinberg.

This work was preceded by a *Scherzo Fantastique* and, in addition to the symphony already mentioned, by a suite for voice and orchestra, *Le Faune et la Bergère*.

If the *Symphony in E Flat Major* can be placed under the academic sponsorship of some of the symphonies of Alexander Glazounoff (who at that time was for a certain part of the young musical generation a constructive counterinfluence to the popular and subjective tendencies of the Russian Five), it might still, as we have already observed, show certain indications of a feeling for pure form in the young Stravinsky. Nevertheless, the value of this work can only be historical, since it gives no indication of the composer's future direction and is in itself merely the exercise of a student, however gifted in the abstract symphonic form and in a correct, but hardly daring type of orchestration.

III

The future mystery of Stravinsky's personality is not revealed either in the suite, *Le Faune et la Bergère*, of the same year. It is one of those works that we are accustomed to qualifying as "full of promise"; nevertheless, certain coloristic tendencies show that something new had been introduced to the way in which Stravinsky had been read-

Life and Works (1882-1920) 149

ing scores, and integrating them into his own work. To his knowledge of the classics and the Russian and German masters of the nineteenth century, was now added that of Claude Debussy, Maurice Ravel, and Paul Dukas, as a first contact with the new French school.

This influence, hardly discernible in the suite, takes on a more pronounced importance in the *Scherzo Fantastique*, and, as we shall see later, in the *Feu d'Artifice* and *L'Oiseau de Feu*.

Here, a real orchestral virtuosity can already be observed, a seeking after coloristic timbres and atmospheric sonorities in a chromatically sensuous language that is sometimes rather violent.

But it is in the *Feu d'Artifice*, still strongly influenced by French impressionism in its stylistic and orchestral treatment, that Igor Stravinsky's future direction, made of will and clarity, first reveals itself.

Beyond the obvious influences of the Russian national school and the French contemporaries, and the apparent borrowings from *L'Apprenti Sorcier*, there arises a new personality, which, viewed in perspective, already seems clearly Stravinskyan.

Above all, the constructive character of the work, despite its descriptive point of departure, reveals a music that is formal and sufficient unto itself, apart from the poetic text. The *Feu d'Artifice* is a symphonic scherzo, whose title and subject are in no way indispensable to an understanding of its architectonic development and the determination of its value.

The melody, the harmony, and the rhythm, as well as the symphonic treatment, already indicate the characteristics of the future author of the *Rite of Spring* in their embryonic stage.

The themes are incisive, direct, abrupt, and the triumphal fanfare of the trumpet with its spiral, almost "pulcinellian" design, no longer has a Wagnerian ring.

A new harmony manifests itself, as well as a conception tending toward a tonal and diatonic polarization. The rhythm brings about pauses, abrupt foreshortenings, and a certain explosiveness such as had seldom been heard until then. Everything moves, everything stirs with lively motion, with dauntless dynamism in an arrangement of irregular meters with frequent off-beat accents—and this in an orchestra already somewhat characterized by the "extractive" significance of the timbres, by their clear contrasts, and by the crudeness of their colors made sharper and more violent by their isolation.

The *Feu d'Artifice* already leads directly to the meteoric *Petrouchka*, through the "Danse Infernale de Kashtchei" of the *Firebird*.

A *Chant Funèbre*, dedicated to the memory of Rimsky-Korsakoff, followed the *Feu d'Artifice:* it is impossible to analyze the work, since it remained in manuscript form in Russia, and Stravinsky himself does not possess a copy.

At the same period, from 1907 to 1908, Stravinsky wrote two songs to the poetry of Gorodetsky: "Novice" and "Sainte Rosée," *Four Études* for piano, and a vocal exercise, *Pastorale,* which he ultimately orchestrated for small woodwind ensemble.

Except for the fourth *Étude*, none of these works is as interesting as the *Feu d'Artifice*, for they still suffer from the absence of a well-defined direction.

The songs are pleasant, in a style popular at the time when they were composed. The *Pastorale*, especially in its ultimate instrumental presentation, has a bucolic charm and a perfect facility in writing. The *Études*, brilliantly chromatic and of a virtuoso style, are still part of the line of études born of Chopinesque pianism (Liadoff,

Life and Works (1882–1920)

Scriabin), but the fourth already shows a curious seeking after asymmetric rhythms in its metric oppositions and in its superpositions of binary and ternary meters.

IV

At this time a new personality appeared in the life of Igor Stravinsky—a strange character, full of contradictions, at once despotic and generous, a combined impresario of genius, a Barnum, a far-sighted and prodigal Macaenas—Serge Diaghileff. A type imaginable only in the setting of old Russia, a grand nonchalant lord and a dilletantish æsthetic of unfailing acumen, Diaghileff had for some time been introducing the national Russian art abroad and more especially in Paris, the artistic and intellectual center of the civilized world, with an exhibition of modern Russian painting, a series of operatic performances with Chaliapin in *Boris Godounoff*, a cycle of symphonic concerts of Russian music, and finally, what was to lead to that ensemble of artistic magic, the Ballets Russes.

For more than twenty years, the indefatigable activity of Serge Diaghileff was to exert a pronounced influence upon the entire artistic approach of the West. Nothing could impede this itinerant Russian. He "discovered" dancers of genius, choreographers, painters and stage designers; he inaugurated styles, always discovering whatever was new, with everything that implied in the way of chance and mistakes. Although some of his discoveries are now outmoded, others are permanent contributions, and that of Stravinsky should amply suffice to classify Diaghileff as a significant force in the renewal of contemporary music. He had instinctively divined potential genius upon a first hearing of the *Feu d'Artifice*—whose success at the first performance should have been quite insufficient to arouse such interest.

Serge Diaghileff, always alert, was very much interested in the young musician whose talent impressed him as above the ordinary.

As a test, he commissioned him to orchestrate two pieces of Chopin, which were included in the ballet, *Les Sylphides,* and shortly afterward he entrusted him with the composition of a new and important ballet, the text of which was to be the *Firebird,* taken from an old Russian folk tale. The work was to be given its first performance in the 1910 season of the Ballets Russes at the Paris Opera.

He was really showing a great deal of confidence in a young beginner who had not written very much and whose name was hardly known, even among the musical circles of the French capital.

Thus began an artistic collaboration that was to endure for twenty years, a collaboration to which we owe a whole series of musical masterpieces, and that little by little became a close friendship, in spite of often stormy discussions and frequent misunderstandings, caused by a difference in conception or opinion in certain instances—a collaboration that has now gone down in the history of music.

Diaghileff had become Stravinsky's standard bearer the world over, inspiring and performing his works. Stravinsky was now the star, the genius, of that admirable instrument for art in action that the Ballets Russes of Serge Diaghileff was to be during its twenty years of vibrant activity and constant search for renewal—sometimes artificial, but always sincere.

Life and Works (1882–1920)

V

In view of the importance that his personal relationship with Serge Diaghileff was to assume in Stravinsky's life and creative activity, it seems interesting to us to refer the reader to the composer's opinion as it is expressed in the *Chroniques*, several years after the death of the great impresario in Venice, in 1929. Stravinsky was particularly impressed by a quality in Diaghileff's personality that he himself possessed: "the degree of endurance and tenacity that he attained in the pursuit of his aim." For Stravinsky, Diaghileff's personality had another charm: "the quality of his intelligence and his mentality. He had an exceptional acumen, an extraordinary facility for seizing the immediate freshness and the novelty of an idea and for being instantly and unreasoningly carried away by it.

"That which he detested most in the world was platitude, incapacity, the lack of 'know how,' in a word, he hated and despised anything wishy-washy."

This very fruitful relationship was often interrupted by stormy discussions, but the struggle was always "terrifying and reassuring"; that is to say, Stravinsky judged these quarrels to be compatible with his own temperament, and found them not displeasing to him.

Before receiving Diaghileff's unexpected commission of the *Firebird*, which from that moment on classified Stravinsky as a young Russian composer to be reckoned with, and which gave him the first opportunity to be heard abroad in a setting as illustrious and important as that of the Ballets Russes at the Paris Opera, the composer devoted himself to the composition of a new lyric work, the *Nightingale*, an opera in three acts. The text, taken from Andersen's well-known Chinese tale, was written by his friend, Mitusoff, in close collaboration with Stravinsky himself.

At the end of the summer of 1909, Stravinsky finished the first act of the *Nightingale,* but the commission of the *Firebird* interrupted this work, and the two following acts were not composed until several years later. Of course the homogeneity of the entire work suffered as a result of such a long interruption, for since Stravinsky's personality renewed itself rapidly, his æsthetic as well as his lyrical and technical ideas were no longer the same, at least with regard to their maturity, when he was finishing the opera, as when the first act was composed.

It is preferable, then, if we consider Stravinsky's artistic evolution as it really took place, to look upon this first act as a distinct work, a link between *Feu d'Artifice* and the *Firebird,* by detaching it stylistically from the opera as a whole.

Later on, Stravinsky was to draw from extracts of the entire work a symphonic poem, *Le Chant du Rossignol,* but in this musical concentration of the opera, he made more particular use of the material of the last two acts.

VI

The first act of the *Nightingale* still shows in its language the marked influence of Debussy, but despite this persistent stylistic element, the work abounds in details that, when ultimately matured, were to become characteristic of Stravinsky's style. Despite the layers of complex harmonies often arising from the superposition of fourths and fifths, the writing already manifests a tendency toward diatonic expression in its melodic outlines.

Thus, the beautiful theme of the "Chant du Pêcheur," occurring several times in the first act, is the only one Stra-

Life and Works (1882–1920)

vinsky was to use in the symphonic version of *Le Chant du Rossignol*. It is simple in its design and has a clear, well-delineated plastic form.

It is interesting to discern in this first act the first appearance of the simultaneous superposition of the tonic harmony with its own dominant, a device that, after a considerable interruption, Stravinsky was to rediscover, and which he was to use very effectively in another context. In its crystallized harmony, in the transparence of its cold sharpened lines, in the expressive unfolding of a petrified dynamism, the prelude to the first act of the *Nightingale* already foreshadows the admirable second prelude to the *Rite of Spring*.

The lyric conception of the first act does not as yet reveal the well-defined attitude to be found in the composer's other theatrical works, but even in this first attempt at writing for the theater, Stravinsky proved himself a convinced opponent of synchronized realism and of an illustrative parallelism of action and music, as well as the use of the leitmotiv system to provide protagonists and psychological situations with "identity cards."

The "sonorous plane" already remains partially independent, and the drama of the *Nightingale* takes little account of the simultaneity of the music with the detail of the lyric action.

Stravinsky already begins to be concerned with a correspondence of two components, rather than with their fusion into a musical drama. The tale is told in one way on the stage and in another by the orchestra.

VII

Stravinsky, then, was temporarily obliged to abandon his work on the *Nightingale*. He devoted himself to the composition of the *Firebird* with full confidence in his creative forces and in his knowledge.

The work was completed in the summer of 1910 and performed almost immediately afterward at the Paris Opera. The young composer was present at the rehearsals and actively collaborated in the presentation of his first ballet, in which Michel Fokine, the young choreographer who had already proven himself with *Les Danses du Prince Igor* and with *Carnaval*, did the choreography. Thamar Karsavina was to interpret the principal role of the *Firebird*. The musical direction was given to Gabriel Pierné.

It was Stravinsky's first personal contact with Paris and with the European musical movement in its most dynamic form.

From the very outset, the *Firebird* was an immense success, with the public as well as with the press and the artists. Its sonorous and visual magic immediately filled the auditors and spectators with enthusiasm. Claude Debussy, Maurice Ravel, and Florent Schmitt warmly accepted the young Russian newcomer as one of their own, and from that moment on, Stravinsky asserted himself as one of the future masters of modern music and as a newly revealed force.

The success in Paris marked a step of the greatest importance in Igor Stravinsky's personal life and artistic career. From one day to the next he became almost famous. He entered squarely into Western musical life, of which he was soon to become the most important factor, the driving and directing force and the most powerful personality.

At the same time, Stravinsky's success radically changed Serge Diaghileff's entire conception of the Ballets Russes, thus opening a new and fruitful era in its

Life and Works (1882–1920) 157

activity. The Ballets Russes was no longer to export and exhibit Russian art in its narrow national aspect: in the future, it would create, bring new works into being, and this on an international scale. Diaghileff became a "producer," and by the same stroke Stravinsky became his great star and his genius for many years.

Despite the presence of remarkable innovations in the technical realization of the *Firebird*, of admirable finds in the harmonic, rhythmic, and orchestral realm, despite the indisputable musical value of the work itself, the music, except for the "Danse Infernale de Kashtchei," still bears within it a certain ambiguity in its æsthetic conception and in its technique.

The stage conception of the composer is still here, of necessity, that of a *ballet d'action*. It is the stage action that determines the form and its musical unfolding. Stravinsky still clearly aims at being descriptive. He tends to establish a parallelism between the poetic and the sonorous action, the former playing the role of initiator in the establishment of the musical planes.

Stravinsky consciously "subordinates" his contribution; he has not as yet æsthetically achieved the independence of the musical creation that he sensed only intuitively in the first act of the *Nightingale*. He strives to achieve the fusion of the various elements of the ballet: music, action, *décors*, costumes, and choreography.

It really is a paradox that the only music Stravinsky has written with deliberate descriptive and even illustrative intent should be able to dominate without question the entire spirit of the performance, carry it on its own wings, and finally leave it altogether and live its own life.

In 1919, Stravinsky extracted a symphonic suite from the *Firebird* (in 1945, he extracted still another), with an orchestration of the woodwinds somewhat simplified by the elimination of certain fragments whose musical value is inferior and which follow the stage action too closely. The work that had been conceived as applied music became one of the war horses of the symphonic repertory, one of the contemporary works most often played and most appreciated by varied publics throughout the entire world.

We must admit that, for once when he wanted to, Stravinsky did not completely succeed in subordinating his music to an extraneous aim: his inner nature was stronger than his conscious intent to oppose it. For this music, solely by its substance and its writing, avenged itself on the passive role that the composer thought he should give it.

As a ballet, except for scattered performances in Central Europe, the *Firebird* was not taken up again until 1944, in the United States, with a new choreography by Adolph Bolm and costumes and *décors* by Marc Chagall. As symphonic music, it has had a dizzy career, and the fact that it is appreciated by a young generation that never knew the original stage version demonstrates its intrinsic value and its quality as pure music.

In the *Firebird*, Stravinsky reveals the inventive genius of an achiever working on established terrain rather than that of an originator of principles and language, substituting his own treatment of the musical material for contemporary tendencies.

But in each aspect of the composition, the work abounds in wonderful inventions: a mastery of the melodic treatment, astonishing harmonic progressions, an unprecedented ease in the rhythm and movement, an irresistible dynamism, an organization of sounds such as had never been heard before. Magic colors and shimmering timbres of an unreal transparency appear on every page of the score.

But as we have already emphasized, we are dealing here

with personal contributions to a current conception rather than with the introduction of a different principle of expression.

Stravinsky is already present in the *Firebird*, particularly in the "Danse Infernale de Kashtchei," which could only be his own and which serves as a point of contact between the *Firebird* and *Petrouchka*, but he is only present in spots; he is not there completely, or alone.

The melody of the *Firebird* is built upon the tonal and modal plane of Russian folksong and on its Oriental inflections. It does not as yet have the direct, lapidary, squared-off line or the diatonic design of Stravinsky's typical melody. It continues the melodic line of the popular operas of Rimsky-Korsakoff or Borodin, without trying to innovate, except, of course, in the already mentioned "Danse Infernale" and somewhat also in certain parts of the lovely "Berceuse."

The harmonic language is full of ingenious discoveries as well: for example, the series of thirds in the woodwinds, in the "Introduction," rare and fresh modulations, and new and curious harmonic aggregates. But on the whole, the harmonic language shows clear traces of an ornamental chromaticism rather current at the time of Dukas, Debussy, and Ravel. However, the composer uses it with unquestionable mastery, and brings to it a real renewal.

Despite everything, a basic, concentrating diatonism shows itself in the presence, real or implied, of the tonal framework. However, the *Firebird* is dominated by the harmonic principle of the French school with its strange friction of seconds, its refined and piquant agglomeration of complex harmonies conceived vertically and sensually, its inversions of altered ninth and eleventh chords resulting in superpositions of fifths and fourths.

To this fertile and delicate soil, Stravinsky brings, as we have said, a rare inventive genius, and the riches of the master, but not yet of the leader.

The rhythmic vitality of the *Firebird* is remarkable in its intensity, and it is here that Stravinsky anticipates most clearly the essential aspect of his personality.

There is not one moment of rest in this music where everything moves, where even a tender and soft "Berceuse" (unfolding on a moving pedal point, an *ostinato* that leaves one transfixed) gives no respite. Similarly, the episodic character of the action, while rigorously respected by the composer, does not succeed in impeding the gushing flow of the music, whose rhythmic pulsation dominates the action even while it tries to subordinate itself to it.

But once again, with the exception of the "Danse de Kashtchei," Stravinsky works and innovates here on an already established rhythmic basis without modifying the current metric conception, despite the fact that he extracts from it dynamic effects that are remarkable in their novelty.

In the same way, Stravinsky uses the orchestra like a gigantic palette containing an unlimited number of potential nuances and colors, blending them into a homogeneous whole. We are still somewhat removed from that direct opposition of instrumental groups contrasted by their sonority, by their individual extraction, and by their self-sufficiency within the ensemble that envelops them.

Here we still have the "synthetic" orchestra of the period, instead of the analytical one that Stravinsky was to use later on.

But what effects, what an organization of novel, disembodied sonorities he obtains with this kaleidoscopic palette! A magic of sounds presides over his manipulations, an unprecedented intuition for dosing, mixing, and blend-

Life and Works (1882–1920) 161

ing the timbres into a multicolored and caressing shimmer, an icy sheen that creates a sonorous mystery.

As early as the "Introduction," a peculiar mood is created, to which we have not been accustomed, despite its somewhat Debussylike atmosphere. After the curious play of alternating major and minor thirds in the woodwinds with their capricious runs, the presentation of the *Firebird*, in the shimmering murmur of the strings in the high register, produces a silvery, unreal sonority whose effect has never been dulled, despite profuse borrowings, especially for the benefit of Hollywood-concocted film music.

The shimmer of the "Danse" of the *Firebird*, with its brief tremolos, the pastel shades contributed by the woodwinds and the syncopated intervention of the pizzicati in the basses, despite an apparent relationship with Scriabin's *Poème de l'Extase*, imparts a fresh, airy atmosphere through its sonorous effect.

The bassoon, exposing in its medium register the serene theme of the "Berceuse" on a double *ostinato* of harps and divided strings, is a find despite the Ravel-like orchestral basis dominating its conception (harmonically as well as orchestrally, in the ascending run accompanied by a harp glissando toward a major chord of the ninth). Likewise, the use of the brass, especially for the bold run of the trumpet in the "Danse de Kashtchei," the intervention of the percussion, and the use for melodic and coloristic purposes of the xylophone and the celesta, which trickle through the sonorous mass of the entire orchestra.

For quite a few years and to this very day, the orchestra of the *Firebird* has been used as a catalogue for magic sonorities. The technique of the cinema has made it its own somewhat arrogantly and exploits its elements in order to create "atmosphere" and a parallelism of mystery.

The evocative wealth of this technique has entered into the public domain, and it would be difficult to cite, even approximately, the number of times that the orchestral discoveries of the *Firebird* have been borrowed. Only one musician has consciously and definitely renounced this upon entering the distinctive path that was to become his own from that moment on, and that is Igor Stravinsky himself. On a fertile ground, Stravinsky has sown magnificent flowers and fruits of which he was never again to avail himself, since that ground was still not the one he really needed.

It is in the episode of Kashtchei that the composer already shows his true musical nature, or at least the direction it was to take in its later evolution. It is not as yet entirely Stravinsky. But it could not possibly be any other composer of his own generation. Through a rather detailed chromatic ornamentation whose atmosphere owes much to the style of the contemporary French school, a personal conception bursts forth frankly in a direct, steadfast, forward, and even bold spurt.

The melodic, harmonic, rhythmic, and orchestral components are already manifestly conceived as naturally interdependent. The laconic, brutal theme turning upon itself takes its full significance from the syncope of the ternary measure, implacably driven through the whole episode. The bass harmony is clearly directed toward a determined tonality despite the chromaticism of the derivative and ornamental lines. The obsessive meter is interrupted in its action only by broken accents which, like snaps of a whip, sustain the breathless and vibrating movement without stopping its momentum, displacing its point of departure to renew its dynamism. Fragments of a thematic design impress themselves upon the mind by a sort of stubborn repetition. The orchestra, continuing on

Life and Works (1882-1920)

the suggestions of the *Feu d'Artifice*, already anticipates that of *Petrouchka*, with its direct timbres, extracted from the orchestral mass, which do not seek to blend themselves in a unifying mixture, but go their respective ways. It is no longer the orchestration of music but rather an instrumental conception in which the individuality of each instrument is utilized for its own value and not as an element of a homogeneous whole. The mystery of orchestral envelopment is replaced here by instrumental directness, and blends by contrasts.

And yet this episode, so striking in every aspect of its conception, does not mar the over-all structure, or detract from its unity and homogeneity. All of the music surrounding it is of such mastery, of such variety and originality, that the disparate side is forgotten before an inexhaustible invention that preserves for this music all the seductiveness and hold it has upon the listener.

VIII

While the *Firebird* was being performed, Stravinsky took his family to France, and they spent their vacation at La Baule.

At that time, he composed two songs to the poetry of Paul Verlaine—"La Lune Blanche" and "Un Grand Sommeil Noir," works without too much distinction or special significance as far as the ensemble of his work is concerned: they are of a superficial type of Debussyism.

However, while still at work on the *Firebird* in St. Petersburg, Stravinsky had a kind of musical vision of a pagan rite taken from Russian antiquity—the ritual dance, before a group of sage elders, of a young girl marked for death, the ceremony being intended to propitiate the gods for the spring festival (a story from ancient Slavic mythology). Stravinsky spoke of it immediately to his friend the painter, Nicolas Roerich, who had specialized in the rites of prehistoric pagan Russia.

At the same time he communicated his ideas to Serge Diaghileff in Paris. The latter welcomed the project with genuine enthusiasm. Thus the idea of the *Rite of Spring* preceded the birth of *Petrouchka* in the chronological order of Stravinsky's conception, and coincided with the technical work of the *Firebird,* therefore also preceding the completion of the latter.

But a work like the *Rite of Spring,* as Stravinsky conceived it from the beginning, requires a well-thought-out and detailed elaboration, and planning on a broad scope. Stravinsky set aside, for a while, the completion of this monumental project, and, after his vacation at La Baule, went to Switzerland with his family. While awaiting the opportunity to concentrate on this work, he decided to compose another work, opposing the piano and the orchestra in a form that would not be that of the conventional concerto, but a sort of concert piece (*Konzertstück*).

The point of departure of the creative process was for him a concrete vision: that "of a puppet suddenly gone mad who exasperates the patience of the orchestra by his diabolical cascades of arpeggios. The orchestra retaliates in turn, with menacing trumpet blasts. The outcome is a terrific noise which, after reaching its climax, ends in the sorrowful collapse of the poor, plaintive puppet." *

The piano and the orchestra, then, are living entities, the sole protagonists of a musical drama. This concrete element has nothing of the visual about it but its point of departure: it is "the problem to be solved," retained in its construction, that determines the realization of the work conceived.

* *Chroniques de ma Vie.*

Life and Works (1882–1920)   165

Thus the third tableau of the future *Petrouchka* was born in the form of a piece for piano and orchestra, and the title adopted because of the similarity between the puppet gone mad and the "eternal and unhappy hero of every fair in every country." The musical point of departure, of whose form it was to become the center, is a pianistic passage, a discovery of genius, consisting in the simultaneous superposition of two major arpeggios, separated by the interval of the tritone, C to F sharp.

This passage, with its strident and sharp friction of major and minor seconds and minor thirds, has a totally new ring, an aspect at once burlesque and pathetic. It is a simple fanfare of the tonic in C major with a "shadow" that pursues it simultaneously.

It is not the tritone that makes for novelty. There are many examples of the use of its enharmonic qualities: among others, the first movement of *Scheherezade,* where Rimsky-Korsakoff modulates directly from C major to F sharp major by sustaining the dominant, reduced to its tones of the third and the seventh, which he considers alternately as F the seventh of the dominant of C major, or as its enharmonic, E sharp, the third of the dominant of F sharp major. Maurice Ravel, in the *Rhapsodie Espagnole,* makes use of the same enharmonic device with rare skill, by substituting the sonorous quality of the diminished fifth for a harmonic aggregate of augmented fourths, and by establishing a rapport with the bass, which determines it.

Several theories have been advanced about the character and the harmonic origin of this striking passage in the writing of *Petrouchka,* this curious and completely new fanfare. Some see there anticipations of greater and smaller appoggiaturas. This results in a very complex theory and is somewhat farfetched.

The theory putting this passage at the origin of polytonality, and considering it deliberately bitonal, seems to be on the wrong path.

Despite the graphic bitonalism, the parallel design of the two voices excludes any possibility of polyphonically different tonalities being used deliberately (as in the example of the *Rite* already cited, where one voice is doubled in major sevenths). The tonal planes require a contrapuntal structure that is excluded in a parallel design.

In my opinion, it is the instrument, the piano itself, that gave birth to this idea, concerning which quite a bit has been written.

I think it concerns a remarkable renewal of a pianistic style of writing, an alternation of white and black keys, a style dear to the virtuosity of Franz Liszt (and used in their piano works by Debussy and Ravel as well).

Stravinsky's discovery was to substitute for alternation the *simultaneity of attack,* to concentrate a spread-out passage, to verticalize a horizontal conception.

Stravinsky builds his entire musical movement around this discovery. It is a kind of pianistic recitative, in which, however, improvisation is totally absent, and where the constructive form remains fresh and vigorous.

At Clarens, the composer had his *Konzertstück* performed for Diaghileff (who had rather expected to hear the sketches of the *Rite of Spring*). Diaghileff immediately saw the musical and spectacular potentialities of this isolated musical fragment. The idea of the ballet of *Petrouchka* was born, and little by little its general lines were laid out: action, locale, period, realization. And Stravinsky began to compose his second ballet, which he worked on in Switzerland, at Beaulieu-sur-Mer, and at St. Petersburg.

Life and Works (1882-1920) 167

The painter Alexandre Benois made the stage-settings and the costumes, and Michel Fokine was once more entrusted with the choreography.

At Beaulieu-sur-Mer, the work on *Petrouchka* was interrupted by a serious illness. Hardly before he was well again, Stravinsky took up his work once more to finish it at Rome where the Diaghileff troupe, there on tour, rehearsed the fragments piece by piece, as they were completed.

The troupe having returned to Paris, the orchestral rehearsals began under the direction of the great conductor Pierre Monteux, whose activity has been closely connected with so many of Stravinsky's creations and with all contemporary music.

Pierre Monteux has, since then, become a faithful friend of the composer, who appreciates, above all, Monteux's faculty of perceiving the composer's intentions and the absence of all desire to impose a subjective and arbitrary conception upon a work.

On June thirteenth, the performance of *Petrouchka* at the Chatelet Theater, with Waslaw Nijinsky in the principal role and Karsavina in the role of the ballerina, had, from the beginning, a marked and resounding success. One fine morning, Igor Stravinsky found his name, until then rather difficult to pronounce and to remember, at the head of all contemporary music, the course of which he had changed most significantly and with far-reaching consequences.

IX

We have tried to explain in the first part of our work why the return to tradition imperceptibly and spontaneously inaugurated by *Petrouchka* had been an act of "revolutionary reaction," in that it put an end to perpetual æsthetic and technical revolution. Music had been progressing, step by step, toward the loss of its character as an absolute art, and the multiplicity of idioms was an insurmountable obstacle to the creation of a style.

Now *Petrouchka,* despite its seemingly picturesque and local color, is music of and not for the ballet. The work renounces, to a large extent, every idea of narrow correspondence by synchronization, and develops parallel with the poetic action while having an existence of its own; it grows in accordance with its own development and remains on a purely musical plane.

Each scene is a movement with a structure of its own, and all four movements constitute a whole, making the work sufficient unto itself, apart from any visual suggestion.

For the interludes between the scenes, which would normally have summarized the atmosphere or the action of a completed scene and evoked the atmosphere of the following, a simple drum roll is substituted—a purely temporal means to cut and unify the action without illustrating or explaining it.

The composer's lyrical conception, then, clearly deals here with two parallel and simultaneous actions rather than with an interpenetration of the welded factors of the drama, even when an action of a realistic or musical order (as in the episode of the barrel organ, or the magician with the flute) makes a synchronization of sound and gesture almost inevitable. The music reserves to itself all rights and possibilities to develop apart from any evocative factors.

During the full flower of the exacerbated chromaticism of the neoromantic school of Central Europe, born of Wagner and Richard Strauss and leading to Schoenberg-

Life and Works (1882–1920) 169

ian atonality through the "infinite melody"; of the sinuous and refined melody of French impressionism; of the sonorous mysticism of Scriabin in Russia and the magic shimmer of his own *Firebird,* Stravinsky throws us a sheaf of tonal melodies, diatonic, abrupt, direct, apparently vulgar, in short, clearly limited in their outline; melodies in which the blatant character of Russian folksong, authentic or re-created, combines in a fantastic melee with the Viennese waltz of Lanner, with the French streetsong, "Elle Avait une Jambe en Bois" (for which, it seems, the Society of Authors still collects royalties as an "inserted theme"), with the hackneyed refrains of fairs and streetsongs, and with fanfares made dissonant by the contrasting tonalities that loosen or bind them.

Everything here is new, unexpected, everything is in reaction against the existing state of affairs, everything proclaims an order, a discipline, and a style to which we had become unaccustomed. Their importance was not immediately perceived, but their unexpected appearance shocked the audience and compelled it to realize their necessity.

Through the apparent disorder of so many unrelated elements, there shines forth in Stravinsky's conception and its application in *Petrouchka* the direct path of clarity in tonal harmony and color contrast, already foreshadowed in *Le Feu d'Artifice* and the "Danse de Kashtchei."

With a few exceptions, such as the beginning of the second scene, or the "Sleight of Hand Trick," chromaticism is almost totally absent in *Petrouchka;* tonality rules as master. Stravinsky does with tonality as he pleases, takes it, lets it go, superposes it on others, but always holds onto it as to a *sine qua non* law.

The opening of the work, with its display of the "big accordion," in D major, with its shrill and plastic theme, and inner swarming of subsidiary voices, immediately transports us into an unequivocal musical setting, which goes its way unimpeded, like an irresistible movement started and then left to its own impetus. It is not a realistic fair, it is an orchestral, a musical fair. The genius of Stravinsky is present in every note, but his person is completely absent.

An unprecedented rhythmic animation holds sway in *Petrouchka*. Stravinsky juggles with the bar like a virtuoso or an acrobat. Indeed, so inexhaustible does the composer's invention seem as he creates new meters, breaks rules to breathe new life into them, or introduces an irregular meter into a squared-off movement, that we seem to be faced with a truly new rhythmic language. Breaks in the rhythm change the whole order of things, upset and displace everything, and all this to reach the anticipated goal with quasi-mechanical precision; a stroke putting everything into question, displacing and upsetting everything in order to arrive at his anticipated point with an almost mechanical accuracy. Stravinsky superposes binary and ternary rhythms with as much ease as if the process were in common use.

Rhythmic, irregular pivots with a measure of seven, eleven, or thirteen sixteenths are introduced into the obsessive, hammering movement; they distend the measure by throwing back the remains of a strong rhythm on a weak one; the syncope itself, displacing the accents and opposing them, takes on an unaccustomed importance.

But there is no element of laxness in this appearance of savagery; the whole complex construction is developed according to a conscious order with a sense of rhythmic balance, and with a method rigorously determined in every one of its details.

If everything here is conditioned by the rhythm, nothing is subordinate to it. With Stravinsky, the component factors mutually interpenetrate, and the function of the one affects that of the other, each for all and all for each.

The fact is that, in *Petrouchka*, the composer's working method no longer evolves from chance discoveries, harmonic series, or ingenious rhythms: it is subordinated to a rule, to a determining principle that will govern Stravinsky's technique from that moment on; throughout its evolution the component elements will no longer be autonomous in their action, but really "components."

The orchestra is no longer an unlimited potential of blended sonorities. From now on, its role will be to extract the individual instruments or the homogeneous groups from the mass, to oppose them, and to make them the "carriers" of their respective music and not the agents of spellbinding or magic.

In the first part of our work, we have sufficiently emphasized the uncompromising renewal of Stravinsky in *Petrouchka*. To exhaust everything that this work implicitly contributed to our art, we would have to go beyond the limits of our task, for it was *Petrouchka*, in its seeming innocence, that forced music to retreat from the equivocal road it had set out upon; it was *Petrouchka* that accomplished a revolutionary act with the bold conception of the "Danse Russe" in a striking C major, with almost no chromatic alteration; this was the work that introduced law and order and substituted it for hyperexpressive and arbitrary individualism; in short, it was *Petrouchka* that restored to tonality and its determining cadence their function as traditional restraints, by opposing itself to the "infinite melody," to harmony for harmony's sake, and by questioning color for its own sake and loose construction.

Stravinsky had become himself consciously; he had clearly chosen his doctrine and his method of work.

X

At the end of the Ballets Russes season in Paris, Stravinsky returned to his estate of Oustiloug in Russia to devote himself completely to the composition and the technical completion of the *Rite of Spring*. But meanwhile, he composed two songs to texts of the Russian poet Balmont, "Myosotis" and "Le Pigeon," works of great importance in the composer's evolution, and a cantata dedicated to Claude Debussy, *Le Roi des Etoiles*.

The two songs, still wavering between the diatonism of *Petrouchka* and the chromaticism of the *Nightingale*, might still be considered, with the trills of their moving pedal points, as sketches for the *Rite* and the last two acts of the opera.

Le Roi des Etoiles, because of the immense difficulty involved in performing it, its important orchestral ensemble, and its extremely complex choral writing, was never performed, at least to my knowledge, apart from a single rendition at Brussels. Upon first reading, the work seems to belong, æsthetically and technically, somewhere between the *Nightingale* and the *Rite of Spring*, at the dividing point between two different, if not opposite, directions.

The harmonic innovations are extremely complex— tonal superpositions resting upon prolonged pedal points, a very bold use of the appoggiatura, which already made its appearance in *Petrouchka* and which assumes a real importance in the *Rite* and *Les Noces*.

It may well be that *Le Roi des Etoiles* marks a negative point in his future direction, an exhaustive expression of a general conception to be eliminated, and it is toward that of the *Rite*, anticipated by *Petrouchka*, that the composer was definitely to direct himself.

Life and Works (1882–1920) 173

Certain technical devices in the harmonic superposition, in the use of the ambiguous third and that of modal opposition, were to become a part of the composer's stylistic tools, but it is evident that the judgment passed upon a work that has not been completely realized by its contact with the perceiving agent, the actual performance, can only be approximate and has no determining or even subjective value.

It was, then, to the *Rite of Spring* that Stravinsky devoted himself upon his return to Russia. This work was conceived without an illustrative plot, and was to develop itself simultaneously with the plastic acting out of the pagan rites of ancient Russia's spring festival.

These scenic actions were to be clearly subordinated in their succession and movement to the rigorously established musical composition.

Upon returning from Oustiloug, Stravinsky started to work at Clarens in Switzerland, during a stay interrupted by journeys to Central Europe (Berlin, Vienna, and Budapest), where he was present at the performance of *The Firebird*, and to Paris, where he became more and more intimately connected with Debussy (who was very much interested in the young Russian musician), with Maurice Ravel, who showed him at the piano his freshly composed *Daphnis et Chloé*. In his *Chroniques*, Stravinsky gives us his first impressions of the musical life in Central Europe: his meeting with Richard Strauss, who, after having heard the *Firebird*, advised him for the future never to begin a work pianissimo, because one must above all grip the audience at the outset, free after that to do as one pleases; the ironic reticence of the Viennese musicians; the enthusiastic reception at Budapest, etc.

The choice Diaghileff had made of Waslaw Nijinsky for the choreographic interpretation of the *Rite* seriously concerned the composer. Despite Stravinsky's great admiration for Nijinsky's talent as a dancer, he hardly believed him capable of grasping the musical significance and the plastic and constructive meaning of the *Rite.*

Little by little, the work, whose actual beginning, as we have said, was the last episode, "La Danse Sacrale de l'Élue," was finished, and on May twenty-ninth, 1913, Pierre Monteux conducted the first performance of the *Sacre du Printemps* at the Theatre des Champs Élysées.

So many things have been said and written about this first performance, this twentieth-century *Hernani,* about the scandal and the rumpus that it stirred up, so many snobs insist upon having been present (so that a theater with double capacity would have been necessary to hold them all), that we will not describe in detail once again "the greatest musical scandal of the century."

The fact remains that the performance took place in a stormy atmosphere where cries of indignation and protest were mixed with exclamations of approval and admiration: the noise in the audience drowned out the orchestra, which was quite loud, and the fist-fights between partisans and adversaries made the occasion a "memorable" one.

The *Rite of Spring,* by its "last-ditch" determination, by the frankness of its conviction, by the absence in it of any concession or compromise, and the unprecedented boldness of its technical conception, revolted all those who had remained attached to the previous stage of musical evolution. It stirred up the musical atmosphere like a brutal, virulent snap of a whip and pushed music at last out of the rut of an obsolete æsthetic.

Everything that *Petrouchka* anticipated in its apparently innocent and pleasant simplicity, in the attractiveness of its dizzy movement, primed by gay and easy themes, leads in the *Rite of Spring* to a bold complex

Life and Works (1882–1920) 175

principle, tried with the certainty of a method that seemed to have stood all the tests, and the application of which seemed to the composer to be the most natural thing in the world.

It is difficult to tell what is more admirable in the *Rite* —the boldness of the innovation or the total absence of hesitation in the realization, combined as it is with the absolute certainty of an uncompromising conviction that stops at nothing.

It is in the *Rite* that Stravinsky definitely manifests his creative objectivity; he organizes and unleashes its irresistible movement and molds its development, but allows it to flow out by the interplay of its own elements. He interferes only to warm, animate, and direct the work, but remains removed from the sonorous cataclysm whose temporal evolution he has created.

The relationship with *Petrouchka* always remains apparent in the technique as well as in the absence of a step-by-step parallelism between the poetic action and the musical background of the choreography. But the problem is different, and its resolution necessitates a treatment at a higher level of tension.

From the introduction of the first tableau, we feel ourselves immersed, so to speak, in a new world, from which every intention to evoke an atmosphere is banished. The unprecedented polyphony of the melodic and harmonic planes with the progressive entry of the tonal voices seems to take no account of their vertical resolution, and each plane is carried by a timbre which does not seek to blend itself with those that precede it, but retains its individuality; the effect of the simple parallel fourths in the clarinets, opposed to the trumpet, which, despite the *piano*, comes through the orchestra by its piercing register, all this in a harmonic halo of strings, a sort of breathless rhythmic respiration: this combination united for the creation of a mystery of pure music had something to surprise and disturb the Parisian ballet and music lovers of 1913.

And so it follows, one episode after another introducing unaccustomed elements, themes that turn on themselves, sonorous blocks that ram one another like clashing waves —each with its complex harmony, its instrumental armor, cutting, cruel, strident, implacable; everything carried by a rhythmic frenzy without precedent in the history of music. The meters, the various cuts are crossed and superposed. They clash without interpenetrating, in a hammering both obsessive and diversified, in which accents fall strictly, but always unexpectedly. In short, all the rules of the "good old program music" were upset and thrown into disorder by a primitive barbarian who seemed to know of no rules but those of his own wild fancy.

It took some time to realize how little the *Rite* tried to break laws, how small a place caprice occupied in a lucid and masterly realization, rigorously uncompromising in its application of a definite method.

In April of the following year, Pierre Monteux gave the first performance of the *Rite* in symphonic form. The work that in its stage version had been booed and whistled at in an atmosphere of scandal and indignation was feverishly acclaimed in its symphonic version by an informed and enthusiastic public.

What a wonderful vindication for Igor Stravinsky! A double vindication for the substance and the composition of the work as well as for its intrinsic value as absolute music!

XI

As we have already observed, the novelty of the *Rite* with regard to *Petrouchka* does not involve the already

Life and Works (1882–1920)

established general principle, but rather a difference in the particular problem solved and in the scale of the achievement. What *Petrouchka* presented in a seductive, stimulating, lively form, like a little pill one swallows down without noticing, the *Rite* imposed as a big dose, with a cruel and implacable intransigence, with the brutality of an overheated machine, each part of which was brought to a maximum degree of incandescence.

Petrouchka had shaken the musical art of the period. The *Rite of Spring* delivered a blow from which it was never again to recover, and which was to cause a definite break with acquired habits.

The composer, like an engineer or a magician, had created a universe of stone, which sang and moved of its own accord, but whose functioning he merely supervised and ordered with presence of mind and an infallible sense of logic.

A new or revived world, in which music was plastically conceived, arose at white heat from this orchestral music in which the sonorous planes, melodic and horizontal, clash without shattering, in which a violent outbreak alternates with the "unisons" of psalmodic themes to which mysterious appoggiaturas give a peculiar, equivocal aspect; in which a tonal or modal melody is treated in a contrapuntal manner as perspicacious as it is unexpected; in which the harmony is the resultant of a masterly polyphony, whose apparently pagan, barbarous primitivism was organized with an astonishing "Occidental" mastery of technique.

It is in the *Rite* that he definitely established this tonal harmonic polarization that we discussed at such length, this nucleus toward which the melodic planes converge and from which they radiate, with all the aggregates of their respective harmonies, and these short polytonal passages, given a provisional freedom, so to speak, by their main tonality. It is in the *Rite* that by manipulating, mangling, and manhandling tonality, Stravinsky triumphantly affirms its presence, its wealth, and its very necessity as the inexhaustible basis of the organic evolution of the musical art.

This uncompromising frankness in the conception of the definitive interdependence of all the component factors, the strident directness of their orchestration are what gave the *Rite* its apparently revolutionary character. Its inexhaustible rhythmic invention, its obsessive hammering, its disarticulated accents, upsetting one framework only to substitute for it another just as new and vibrant, and contrasting with the extraordinary strangeness and abstract mystery of the slow movements, with their simple themes, to which a unison at an interval of two octaves adds a sort of sonorous resonance, the constructive novelty of the conception based upon a principle of linking instead of a cellular development—everything was done that was sure to shock and horrify some hearers and upset others.

Even the melody is of a marvelous richness in this work, for side by side with authentic folk themes, Stravinsky creates others with an instinct so sure that one might say that he is participating in the re-creation of an anonymous folklore.

The *Rite* is the end of a direct evolution, started with the *Feu d'Artifice* and continued with the "Danse de Kashtchei" of the *Firebird*, and *Petrouchka*; it is the climax, the résumé, and at the same time, the "sum" from which a new logical evolution was to start, purifying itself as it passed through *Les Noces*, *L'Histoire du Soldat*, the *Octet*, the *Symphony of Psalms*, and *Apollon-Musagète*, up to the most recent works.

Life and Works (1882-1920) 179

In this regard, the *Rite of Spring* seems to me to be the most significant work of our time; the most pregnant with consequences is still, in my personal opinion, *Petrouchka*, which, in a more attractive form, had been the first work to pose the principle of the "revolutionary reaction" which Igor Stravinsky accomplished in the music of our time.

XII

While he was working on the *Rite*, Stravinsky composed a short cycle for voice and small ensemble of flutes, clarinets, strings, piano, and xylophone: *Trois Poésies de la Lyrique Japonaise*, as well as *Trois Petites Chansons* (*Souvenirs de mon Enfance*).

The first cycle, based upon old Japanese *haikai*, whose objective laconism corresponded perfectly with the composer's interests at the time, is, in my opinion, much closer to the *Rite* than to Schoenberg's *Pierrot Lunaire*, whose influence on this work has often been pointed out.

Stravinsky indeed had just heard that work in Berlin; but with the exception of certain passages where the tonality is not precise (but not atonal), and the use of certain instrumental devices, nothing is further removed from Stravinsky's spiritual æsthetic than the subjective and morbid expressionism of *Pierrot Lunaire*.

This is also true of the *Poèmes de Mallarmé*, composed by Maurice Ravel immediately afterward at Clarens, where he was orchestrating with Stravinsky some fragments of Moussorgsky's *Khovantchina*, upon Diaghileff's request. The *Poèmes* are often criticized for the same reason, although they represent Ravel at his purest and best, apart from certain superficial similarities.

The *Trois Petites Chansons* can be considered as a step

in the direction of the future vocal works, *Pribaoutki*, *Les Noces*, and *Renard*, in which the poetic text is treated, as we have already indicated, as a purely sonorous factor, for its syllabic action only, and with complete disregard for the poetic meaning.

XIII

A few days after the scandal of the *Sacre*, Stravinsky became seriously ill with typhoid fever, and spent several weeks hovering between life and death.

He was watched over with deep affection by his friends Maurice Ravel, Florent Schmitt, and Maurice Delage. Only recently, he evoked with tender emotion the memory of Ravel weeping by his bedside at the thought that he might succumb to the disease.

After recuperating, Stravinsky went back to Oustiloug for a short stay, and then returned to Switzerland where he installed himself and stayed for six years. He was to compose there a series of significant works. First, he finished his opera *Le Rossignol*, of which only the first act had been completed at the time.

We have already observed that with the marvelous faculty of self-renewal inherent in the composer's nature, the gap of several years between the completion of the first act and the following ones could not help but be perceptible, and detracted from the homogeneity and the stylistic and æsthetic unity of the work as a whole.

Indeed, although the same personality presides over the completion of *Le Rossignol*, it manifests itself there in various stages of its evolution and artistic maturity, all of which makes this work, perhaps the only one of Stravinsky's production, somewhat uneven in quality.

Life and Works (1882–1920)   181

When he later extracted from his opera the poem *Le Chant du Rossignol*, Stravinsky, as we have already said, made use almost exclusively of the materials of the second and third acts, and used only the beautiful "Chant du Pêcheur" of the first act.

In spite of many desirable elements that might have tempted any other musician with such a subject from the viewpoint of local color and superficial "Orientalism," it is thanks to a somewhat ceremonious coldness, a sort of lacquered iciness, that the music of *Le Rossignol* expresses a spiritual correspondence with the scene of Andersen's tale. Despite its harmonic refinement, the music has a rare lucidity and linear clarity.

From the interlacing of sinuous and inflected melodies, owing much to the *Lyrique Japonaise*, and the complex harmonies derived from the conception of the second prelude of the *Sacre du Printemps*, there arises a rhythmic pulsation almost metronomic in its regularity, which instead of creating agitation, crystallizes the musical action.

The Orientalism, despite the frequent use of Chinese modes and scales, the celestial and strange sonorities, arising directly from the magic of the *Firebird*, retains a quality of inwardness, thanks to its suspended ceremoniousness, which, in its artfulness, leads ultimately to the effect of ceremonious and icy Occidentalism of *Apollon-Musagète* (an altogether unexpected emotive effect of transparency, tenderness, and inner tranquillity).

By this device, the music moves in the heights of space, so to speak, avoiding every psychological or æsthetic equivocation. The contrast between the episodes according to the character of the protagonists—even if these be two nightingales—is achieved through the interpretation of an abstract rule of the game; Stravinsky would certainly not introduce the record of a real nightingale's song to recapture it authentically, for we are concerned here with musical, and not with realistic, truth.*

Le Rossignol, as much by its subject matter as by its technical treatment, proves once more how unwise it would be to try, at any price, to classify the work of Stravinsky as far as, let us say, *L'Histoire du Soldat,* in the "Russian period."

Many works on the composer neglect or simply disregard this annoying *Rossignol,* which proves very embarrassing any way you look at it; it comes at the height of the "Russian period," and yet bears absolutely no trace of it, either from the point of view of folklore or from that of workmanship. Since it belongs between the *Sacre, Renard,* and *Les Noces,* and was conceived in its outline before the *Firebird,* one really does not know what to do with this poor bird that sings so unseasonably, and detracts from a carefully elaborated theory an important element in its construction.

After attending the first performance of the *Rossignol* by the Diaghileff company, Stravinsky returned to Switzerland and there composed *Three Pieces for String Quartet,* and *Pribaoutki* ("Chansons Plaisantes"), the latter initiating the whole series of vocal phonetic works that were to culminate in *Les Noces* and particularly in *Renard.*

Apart from the vocal works, a series of piano pieces for two and four hands, ultimately orchestrated, show the same concern for direct and concrete action and intro-

---

* Mr. Tansman apparently refers here to *The Pines of Rome* (1924) of the Italian impressionist, Ottorino Respighi (1879–1936). In this work Respighi uses the recorded voice of a singing nightingale (translators' note).

duce the somewhat burlesque element of humor, inherent in the music and in the instruments producing it, without the composer manifesting his presence. At the same time this whole series of works for various combinations of instruments illustrates another one of the composer's interests, which fits with all the other postulates of his dynamic personality: his interest in an "individualized orchestra," an instrumental ensemble adapted to the needs of the particular work, in place of the ubiquitous symphonic orchestra.

If a man like Arnold Schoenberg shows the same preoccupations in the *Kammersymphonie*, and more especially in *Pierrot Lunaire,* they seem to be chiefly motivated in his case by an interest in timbres and the expressive effect of sonority. (The only work that might be cited in contemporary music as an example of the individualized chamber orchestra is Richard Strauss' suite, *Le Bourgeois Gentilhomme,* but here again, the technical realization is on an entirely different plane.)

The *Three Pieces for String Quartet* are perhaps still motivated by the same aspirations, since a seeking after combinations of timbre is quite apparent in them. But what follows is entirely different, as much from the æsthetic as from the technical point of view. It is the economy of means, the desire to eliminate everything that is not indispensable, and in short, to solve very diverse problems with adequate musical means, that was to lead the author to use different instrumental ensembles for different compositions. In addition, his concern with making the pure timbre stand out, which can be more effectively done in a small ensemble, is certainly one of his reasons for adopting this means.

Hence a whole series of works, short but pregnant with

implications, that were to lead to miraculous achievements: *Les Noces, Le Renard, L'Histoire du Soldat, Mavra,* and *Apollon-Musagète.*

We have seen that sometimes the reduced ensemble really originated with the necessity, not only for a musical, but for a financial economy, as was the case with *L'Histoire du Soldat;* this created a problem of choice and therefore an obstacle to be circumvented.

During this entire period the works were composed in a very mixed order. The composer abandoned one unfinished work to start another, then returned to the first, and so on. It is not possible for us to dwell too long upon this whole series of compositions, at once interesting in themselves and significant as sketches of music of wider scope and greater artistic value. In all these pieces Stravinsky causes things and beings to act as though apart from himself.

Pribaoutki for voice and small ensemble, *Three Stories for Children* for voice and piano ("Tilim-Boum," "The Song of the Bear," and "Lullaby"), *Berceuses du Chat* for voice and three clarinets, all based on the syllabic role of vocal emission; or *Three Easy Pieces* for four hands piano ("Marche," "Valse," "Polka"), and *Five Easy Pieces* for four hands piano ("Andante," "Napolitana," "Española," "Balalaika" and "Galop") conceived with easy first and second parts and conversely, and of which Stravinsky was later to make two suites for small orchestra of an altogether abstract burlesque character; or the later *Five Fingers* for children—all these pieces bear the mark of a technique at once artless and masterly in its simplicity, and were conceived as though they had developed of their own accord. The composer sometimes uses merely an ostinato with moving accents, a single accompanying voice, or a lucidly primitive scansion. However, as we have

Life and Works (1882–1920) 185

already noticed, the end result of all this creative activity, which so to speak tries out the terrain and measures its forces, consists for us in the important works: *Les Noces, Le Renard, L'Histoire du Soldat,* and later, *Mavra,* the *Octet,* and *Apollon-Musagète.*

In our general synthesis we have described the principles of this evolution: enrichment by renunciation, elimination of the superfluous, the refinement of what is indispensable, a sort of spiritual discretion, aiming at the ordered organization of the concrete essential and the abstract law of pure art, defined in its æsthetic and technical significance, and owing its emotive effect only to the interplay of its own elements, consciously chosen and adapted to the particular problem.

XIV

Owing to circumstances, works like *Les Noces* and *Le Renard* were thus composed alternatively, but even though it required several years for *Les Noces* to be completed in its final instrumental form, so that it was not performed until 1923, the conception of this work came before that of *Le Renard,* despite the fact that it is closer in style to the entire line of vocal works enumerated above.

Les Noces, in its conception and technique, touches upon the two poles that surround it, the *Rite of Spring* and *Le Renard.* It comes close to the *Rite* in its ritual, pagan, and primitive aspect, in its ideological point of departure, as well as in the stylistic evolution of its technical style. It resembles *Le Renard* in its vocal conception, the utilization of pan-Russian texts chosen for their syllabic expression and for the sonorous effect of the direct emission, without regard for their poetic meaning or even for their ritual origin.

With few exceptions, the choruses of *Les Noces* obey the same principle as the singers in the *Pribaoutki*, the *Berceuses du Chat*, and the four soloists who act as vocal instruments in the orchestra of *Le Renard*.

Les Noces, a new stage in Stravinsky's evolution, was considered from its first appearance as a perfect work, final and indisputable, not only with regard to the composer's production but to the musical art as well.

After laying out the plans for the *Noces Villageoises* as a ballet cantata based on the ancestral rites of a mock-marriage supplementing the spring ritual of the *Sacre*, Stravinsky had several collections of folk poetry sent to him from his father's library in Russia.

He was guided, in his choice of texts, neither by their literary significance nor by considerations of a definite epoch nor by the subject matter. He made his choice with regard only to the syllabic necessities as manifested on the melodic and rhythmic plane.

In 1917, the composition of *Les Noces* was completed. Its instrumental realization became the composer's new preoccupation. He had a clear vision of what he wanted, but he hesitated among several devices.

The problem was to oppose two blocks: one blown, the other percussive. The solution of this problem immediately proved very difficult to achieve practically.

After experimenting with several possibilities, one of which was even rather at an advanced stage, Stravinsky struck upon a solution of homogeneous sonority, in which the winds and the percussion were united in a manner as simple as it was new. Four pianos and a percussion battery were opposed to the mass of the "instrumental choirs," thus creating a metallic "harmonium" whose wealth of color one would never have imagined. By proportioning, polishing, and eliminating, Stravinsky had in-

Life and Works (1882–1920)   187

fallibly found, once again, the instrumental frame that the music of *Les Noces* necessitated by its essence.

The fact that, like *Petrouchka* and unlike the *Rite*, *Les Noces* was immediately understood and enthusiastically accepted despite its indisputable novelty is not in the least surprising. On the one hand, the public was beginning to adapt itself to the boldness of Stravinsky's language and order. But above all, the unity of the entire work in each of its technical elements had been made more apparent, more present, because of the simplicity of the technical realization.

We have justified the form of the *Rite* by a principle of style as far as each one of its episodes and the unity of the whole are concerned. For the system of melodic linking used so effectively in the *Sacre*, Stravinsky now substitutes in the constructive form the method of definite themes, which, by their return as a modern variant of the rondo, fix themselves by their presence upon the immediate perception.

In addition, the work contains a sort of theme that unifies it. It is framed by an analogous opening and close. All this makes the architectonic form more perceptible from the outset.

Even the character of the themes, despite their variety, has something that unifies rather than separates them: an often modal conception, a frequent use of the appoggiatura, a straightforward diatonism, and the use of a less complex polyphony, often treated somewhat like a descant in fifths, fourths, or octaves, making everything seem related to the rest.

The harmony, opposing itself to the choral masses, emphasizes a definite tonality. The tonal polarization, as rich as that in the *Rite*, is softened by the unification of the timbre. In *Les Noces*, the instrumental groups no longer contrast by their sharp and strident colors. They are leveled off by the neutralizing sonority of the pianos and a quasi-polyphonic battery of percussion.

The rhythm of *Les Noces* is a thing altogether unique. It dominates the entire melodic and harmonic structure of the work, even while constantly allowing melody and harmony to penetrate it in its development. Unity is achieved by the subservience of all the elements to the ensemble. Sometimes the pianos are only instruments of chordal percussion; the percussion battery seems to sing; the choruses act the part of wind instruments. Unique sonorities are born of the simplest instrumental combinations, such as the piano, the xylophone, and the triangle, whose unforgettable rhythmic stroke acts only as a function of its metric placement, its harmonic disposition, and its register.

What a stroke of genius to have produced with these three instruments that crystalline caesura, so striking in its high register! It comes after silences that are, so to speak, respiratory, so that it is awaited with expectation. It is based on a disposition of four tones, one of them repeated three times, which are distributed in such a way as to radiate an unprecedented harmonic resonance (fifth, sixth at the octave, fifth, fifth without tonic).

Only in the Dutch East Indies, particularly at Bali, have I heard a sound of like purity, arising from the qualities of a keyed instrument at once percussive and resonant (wood xylophone) and the pedal element of the bell (gongs and steel bars).

I do not know whether Stravinsky was familiar with Javanese and Balinese music at the time, and whether it could serve as a concrete point of departure for this sonorous murmuring that permeates and envelops *Les Noces*. Its effectiveness is striking in its novelty. The emotion produced by the struck and prolonged sound that the disposition of the registers surrounds with a halo of harmonic overtones, masterfully and intuitively arranged by the notes composing the harmony, always retains the same unforgettable intensity.

The melody of *Les Noces* partially reproduces the folk themes, chosen, like the text, for their adequate musical value, and not for reasons pertaining either to folklore or to synchronization with the action. It is also largely the product of the composer's imagination. As in the *Sacre*, Stravinsky in *Les Noces* seems, thanks to the authenticity and the impersonal character of the thematic curve, to have participated in the collective creation of organic, almost rocklike themes. But this melody always moves in such a manner that one does not know where the mechanical element stops and the human element begins.

There is no unbridled violence in *Les Noces*—here the music always goes forward, overcomes the obstacles with apparent ease. Oxygen penetrates through every pore into a cycle made of compartments, but in which air constantly circulates. Each component factor contributes to the unity, to the lucid order of materials constantly renewed and rich in their linear conciseness.

The choreography of Bronislava Nijinska, unlike that of her brother for the *Rite of Spring*, corresponded exactly to the composer's wishes. It was a construction of plastic, abstract movements, which never aimed at description or "historic reconstitution," and which grafted themselves as a visual action upon the musical action. Poetic similarity and Dalcrozian counterpoint were completely absent here: the choreography is based solely upon the relief of the initial musical idea—the ritual basis—and its musical embodiment.

Thus, *Les Noces* continues the line of *Petrouchka* and

the *Rite of Spring*, not merely as a new piece in a triptych inspired by Russian folklore, still less, with regard to the *Rite*, as another evocation of an ancient pagan rite, but above all, as a new result of an æsthetic and stylistic evolution directed toward an essential method of work and the co-ordination of all the component factors toward a single goal.

Even the most complex harmonic aggregates resulting from the crossing of the melodic lines seem softened and deprived of their strident aggressiveness, as a result of the unity of timbre and the inner plasticity of the melody, whose rhythmic character is more sustaining than it is polyrhythmic. In no other place is the superposition of diverse rhythms more frequent than in *Les Noces*, but the predominance of the choral melodic element absorbs and contradicts the whole mechanism of crossing, overlapping movements, neutralizes its apparent autonomy, and reduces it, even while contrasting with it, to the function of a moving support, of a framework, whose solidity is a function of its elasticity and even of its mobility.

XV

As we have already said, the composition of *Renard*, as well as that of the vocal and instrumental works already mentioned, were interspersed in the work of *Les Noces*. Stravinsky found for this work an admirable collaborator in the person of the great Swiss writer, the late C. F. Ramuz, whom we have already mentioned. During his stay in Switzerland, the composer became his warm and close friend. Ramuz is responsible for the French translation of *Pribaoutki*, the *Berceuses du Chat*, and *Renard*, which was not an easy task, considering the specific problem

Life and Works (1882–1920) 191

Stravinsky had set for himself in these works, the test of which was to be above all sonorous and syllabic, rather than poetic or literary.

Ramuz, therefore, had to find French words, corresponding by their sound to the Russian phonetics that had served as a concrete basis for the complete elaboration of the sound in the musical work.

In his penetrating book devoted to the Swiss period of Stravinsky's life, Ramuz describes this collaboration with the earthly humaneness so characteristic of his literary work, and gives us a striking picture of Stravinsky, the man, at work.

He describes the living side of his creative activity: his work table, with its many little gadgets for tracing, sharpening, and erasing, inks of every color, reminding one of a surgeon's table rather than that of a musician; the rare graphic precision of his manuscripts, with their markings in various kinds of inks, which took on little by little the aspect of a geographical map; the care with which he measured every note, every syllable, and every rest in view of the given problem.

Ramuz, whose humane personality was so close to that of Igor Stravinsky, succeeded with remarkable skill in his work as a translator. He restored to the French version of the texts their primitive, naïve side, their inarticulate sound, whose expressiveness remains a function of their syllabic emission, by making this oral emission something like an additional instrumental quality that supplements the timbre and the register of the tempered instruments.

The composition of *Renard* was resumed at the instigation of the Princesse de Polignac after several interruptions. During a stay of the composer in Paris, she requested him to write a stage work with chamber orchestra: Stravinsky suggested to her *Renard*, which he had already started, and set to work as soon as the text, or rather the *prétexte*, of the music was established.

Renard, according to Stravinsky's definition, is a "sung and played burlesque story, written for the stage." In the composer's intention, the stage and the orchestra pit were to represent two clearly defined places: "The piece is played by the buffoons, dancers, and acrobats, preferably on the stage; the orchestra is placed behind the stage. . . . The characters are silent and the voices are in the orchestra."

This stage conception, new as it might seem, corresponds perfectly to the static conceptions of Stravinsky's theater, to his principle of musical independence, and finally, to the demands of the particular problem. The text, borrowed from a collection of popular Russian folk tales, puts into play the characters of a fox, a cat, a ram, and a rooster in an intrigue whose dramatic inconsistency gives them full freedom of mimic action. It is sung by two tenors and two basses placed in the orchestra, where their voices blend as soloists, and, somehow, as "vocal instruments," into an instrumental ensemble composed of notes and syllables, whose dramatic significance is almost negligible.

The delivery of the sung text is in no way subordinated to the stage action. The latter consists in a mimic drama parallel to the development of the musical buffoonery in its plastic and acrobatic evolution, but without logical synchronization.

The musical ensemble, in addition to four "vocal soloists," consists of a flute, an English horn, an E flat clarinet, a bassoon, two horns, a trumpet, string quintet, a cymbalum, and percussion.

It is a sort of sung ballet, where the mute mimics act

Life and Works (1882–1920) 193

as buffoons simultaneously with the musical action. The melodic material of *Renard* consists of short motivs, whose grotesque character is due more to the onomatopoeic effects of the vocal and instrumental timbres than to intrinsically humorous elements, just as in the *Chansons Plaisantes*. The harmonic writing is considerably lightened, ventilated, so to speak, and perforated. The panting nervousness of the rhythm avoids a concentration of the caesuras, and keeps the sonorous material in a state of continuous dynamic impulsion, of tension created by successively linked thrusts.

Thus, by its style and its technical realization, *Renard* appears as one of the most objective of the composer's works. The music is more than ever independent of the simultaneity of the respective actions, as well as of the active participation of the person who began it.

It is a music for instruments: they are left to their own devices, like a record set in motion. The movement involved is not mechanical, however: on the contrary, it is an organic movement from which every subjective element is absent æsthetically, dramatically, and technically.

In the instrumental ensemble, the essential role is given to the famous cymbalum that Stravinsky had meticulously studied and for which he found many uses. In addition to its solo part as the rooster, it provides the fundamental element, acting as a foil for the burlesque and comical timbres of the winds, the trumpet, the percussive pizzicati of the strings, and the precipitous and breathless delivery of the "human vocal instruments."

XVI

This stay in Switzerland, far from the war in Russia, was interrupted by frequent journeys, which, apart from the one to Paris, brought Stravinsky for the first time to Spain, and several times to Rome, where he conducted several of his works and worked on *Les Noces* and *Renard.* The first Russian revolution took him there by surprise in the company of Diaghileff, Picasso, Massine, Cocteau, and Ansermet, who had, meanwhile, become conductor of the Ballets Russes, Pierre Monteux having accepted the leadership of the Boston Symphony Orchestra. Ansermet had then become the composer's personal friend and one of the most faithful interpreters of his works.

At a Russian-Italian benefit performance that took place shortly after the fall of Czarism, Diaghileff, embarrassed and not knowing how to replace the Russian national anthem, "God Protect the Czar," decided to substitute for it the famous folksong, "The Volga Boatmen."

He asked Stravinsky to write an orchestral version as quickly as possible. Stravinsky orchestrated the melody, and during the night dictated the score to Ansermet chord by chord. The following morning the orchestration was completed and played in the evening after the Italian anthem, in place of the Russian anthem.

Upon his return to Switzerland, Stravinsky suddenly found himself in very difficult financial circumstances. All of the personal income that he drew from his native country had been cut off, and, in addition, the political situation in that country filled him with concern.

With the small group of his Swiss friends—Ramuz, Ansermet, and the painter Auberjonois—the composer developed the idea of a work that could be played by a sort of traveling theater that would journey throughout Switzerland on tour. Thus came into being the first idea of *L'Histoire du Soldat.*

But Stravinsky first wanted to pay personal and traditional homage to Spain, which he had just visited, follow-

Life and Works (1882–1920) 195

ing the example of his dear Glinka's *Jota Aragonese* and *Nuit à Madrid*. He wrote a piece for player piano entitled *Madrid*, which he was ultimately to incorporate in the *Four Études* for orchestra (the three others being the reorchestrated pieces of the *Three Pieces for String Quartet* of 1914).

Very much concerned with assuring his family's subsistence and hoping to find a material solution to this problem in the collective exploitation of the future traveling theater, Stravinsky, together with Ramuz, began to seek for a subject that he might use as a basis for the music. Once again, it was in Afansieff's collection of Russian folk tales that they found a source whose national origin was sufficiently neutralized for the action to be located in any country.

This story of an imaginary soldier, a deserter, who after many adventures sells his violin (which symbolizes his soul) to the devil in exchange for worldly riches, might be Swiss as well as Russian. It is a part of that indeterminate folklore current in many countries, by a coincidence that is the result of similarity of circumstances and customs.

Ramuz was to provide the text, Auberjonois the *décors* and the costumes, Ansermet the orchestral direction, and Stravinsky, finally, was to compose the music.

There remained, then, but to complete the work and to find patrons to get the project under way. This last problem was not the easiest to solve. Finally, the well-known Swiss Maecenas, Mr. Werner Reinhardt of Winterthur, assumed the financial risks of the undertaking.

Stravinsky was later to thank him with a dedication of his *Three Pieces for Solo Clarinet*, for Mr. Reinhardt was an amateur performer of that instrument.

Encouraged by this patronage, everybody went actively to work. Stravinsky, out of a concern for an economy of means, as well as a preference for specific instrumental ensembles, decided upon seven instruments representing the extreme high and low registers in each group: violin and double bass, clarinet and bassoon, cornet and trombone and a one-man percussion battery, a type of acrobatic juggler originating with new-born jazz, who was given the percussion instruments. From this double limitation was born *L'Histoire du Soldat*, a true miracle of instrumental realization, of intuition and careful weighing, and of construction, in which the economy and the balance of the materials resulted in an unprecedented sonority.

It is certain that Stravinsky was very much interested at that time in the first attempts of jazz, with their primitive polyphony, their dislocated and vibrating rhythm, and their combinations of small instrumental ensembles in which the extractive treatment of the liberated timbres was related to the composer's personal instrumental predilections. Ansermet, upon his return from a tour of the United States with Diaghileff's Ballets Russes, brought him several collections of these little arrangements, the conception of which was so new. This concrete example may have inspired Stravinsky in the instrumental conception, and even in the rhythmic fabric of his work, as was to be the case for the *Ragtime*.

To this he added what looked like most disparate elements: Argentine tangos, a Spanish *passo-doble*, a waltz, a Bachlike choral and prelude, a Swiss fanfare, etc.

Out of this unimaginable conglomeration was born the most unified and homogeneous of Stravinsky's works, one of the most personal and engaging works of our time: *L'Histoire du Soldat*.

XVII

It is in *L'Histoire du Soldat* that the greater part of the critics see Stravinsky's break with his so-called "Russian period," and his choice of the new apparel of a cosmopolitan and vagabond musician, turning his back upon his past. This evolution, in their opinion, was to result inevitably in a drying up of his imagination and of his inventive genius, and in a certain cerebral coldness. According to others, the responsibility for having waylaid the composer is laid at the door step of *Pulcinella*. A strange way, indeed, of changing one's path, this new beginning with an accepted masterpiece!

Now the "Russian" quality of a man like Stravinsky goes far beyond the mere use of folklore as a working basis. Rather it is based upon psychological complexes that lie far too deep for them to be denied by an act of the will, which is, moreover, very improbable.

In our opinion, Stravinsky has never ceased to be basically Russian, just as he has never ceased to be a universal, Western musician. If, for some people, "Russia" is confused with perpetually unbridled barbarism, the proverbial "Slavic soul," or an artificial and factitious picturesqueness in the style of penny post cards, then, obviously, Stravinsky has gone beyond that stage.

L'Histoire du Soldat, while abandoning nothing, was enriched by a logical and natural renewal. It contributed something truly new in Stravinsky's art, something very different for which Stravinsky was most often to be denied recognition—I mean sensitivity.

A very curious phenomenon, indeed, that the extreme objectivity of the realization should result in a sensitive renewal. An apparently gay, captivating, rhythmic, and lively type of music, it carries within itself an element of infinite sadness, a pathetic solitude in its inexpressiveness: the solitude of Petrouchka's room, and of the palace of the Emperor of China of the *Rossignol*.

It is not that Stravinsky had forsaken any part of his subjective detachment, but rather that one perceives here the sensitive presence of the man. *L'Histoire du Soldat* is a humane work, and it is from this point of view, rather than upon the entirely superficial basis of the substitution of one source for another, that we must appreciate its immense significance: the humanization, always on a nonpersonal plane, of Stravinsky's sensitivity.

I know that it is not easy to explain this psychological phenomenon or to analyze it in words. But I think that every sensitive listener to *L'Histoire du Soldat* should feel the nostalgic and pathetic effect of this irresistible music, this impersonal but perceptible breath of tenderness, that was to animate—at least for those who do not seek after sensitivity in sentimental effusions, pathos in grandiloquence, and intensity in loud noise—all of the composer's future production, throughout the slow movement of the *Octet*, certain airs of *Mavra*, *Oedipus*, *Apollon-Musagète*, *The Symphony of Psalms*, to reach a climax in the breathtaking end of the *Symphony in C* or the trio of its Andante, in certain pages of the *Danses Concertantes* and of the *Symphony in Three Movements*.

Tenderness here is the result of a nobility of sentiment, tranquillity, serenity, and solitude which remain humane, and a seeming coldness vibrates with a sensitivity that is more precious for remaining hidden.

The purely musical structure and the interdependence of the elements in *L'Histoire du Soldat* have a surprisingly effective result. It is really impossible to tell whether the mobility of the rhythms and the individualization of the timbres, whose miraculous effect is a function of the economy of means, gave birth to the melodic lines and the harmonic results, or whether the melodies arising from the union of the most heterogeneous elements were born in their full-fledged setting and elaboration.

All seven instruments are treated as virtuosi, never as acrobats. Each instrument plays virtuoso passages, but never uses tricks that might alter its individuality.

They are treated as solo instruments, in combinations of two and three, thus creating, not composite sonorities, but autonomous timbres (in the sense of the unique sonorous effect and not of the musical function). Their combinations seem to create the timbres of a new instrument: I am now thinking of the dialogues between the violin and the double bass, the clarinet or the cornet and the violin, which "carry" their melodic material as though in the registers of a specific instrument. They remain a part of the dramatic action, while at the same time retaining their personality.

The work is conceived in separate parts, like stage music: it is a suite that develops simultaneously with the action, the latter being recited by a narrator and performed by the protagonists.

We are more or less concerned, then, with a mimic drama, performed, recited, and put to music: hence the title *Histoire*.

The numbers "Air de Marche," "Intermède du Violin," "Pastorale," "Petit Concert," "Danses," and "Choral" are characterized by miniature thematic developments.

The work is unified, in addition, by an emphasis upon certain instrumental passages, and by the use of the quality of a timbre as a theme or as a nucleus.

Thus, as we have already observed, the melodic line often seems to have been conceived in function of the performing instruments and even of their virtuosity. A certain incidental chromaticism is introduced here, not that of the *Firebird* or of certain pages of the *Rossignol*, but that which is related to jazz in its primitive and equivocal form, or to the *Sonatas for Unaccompanied Violin* of J. S. Bach.

Even the curve of the melody in *L'Histoire du Soldat* often reminds us of these sonatas, with the dislocated shifting of their intervals, often arising from an inversion at the octave of an adjacent tone, their discursive character, and their chromatic movement.

Stravinsky's melody unfolds itself here at full length; the polyphony is a result of the melodies rather than of contrapuntally treated or superposed themes. The harmony becomes tighter, more condensed, to the point of anticipating the supporting of homophony by a progression of chords, as in *Oedipus-Rex*.

We have already emphasized the importance of rhythm as the fundamental element in *L'Histoire du Soldat*, the source of melodic and harmonic movement as well as of the timbre, the unifying element of the sonorous polyphony of which it is an integral part.

The function of the percussion is no longer limited to the stressing of the accent. It is a "multiple man," performing almost as a melodic group, while retaining its function as a metric regulator, because of the percussive quality of its timbre.

For the rhythm is everywhere, in the notes, in their intervals, in the pauses, in the curves and in the patterns, in the resultant harmonies and in the timbre. It embraces and nourishes the entire musical drama without dominating it, yet providing it at the same time with a *raison d'être*.

Thus, it seems to me, *L'Histoire du Soldat* is a work that

in no way breaks with the past. On the contrary, while renewing the sensitivity of Stravinsky's art, it renounces nothing of his past. By defining a given stage in Stravinsky's evolution, it manifests a new aspect of his indivisible personality. This sensitivity, which, though subsisting in a latent state, had been somewhat suppressed in his preceding works, now asserts itself with a vibrating humaneness and a tenderness that remains free from exhibitionism. The composer's personality, far from bringing the work back to the ego, reveals itself only in the objective development of the musical material.

Stravinsky's humaneness never seeks to express or to signify, but it intervenes, perhaps subconsciously, in the lucid arrangement of all the factors, by giving them a life in which the man, if not the person, was always to be present from that time on.

XVIII

After completing *L'Histoire du Soldat,* Stravinsky manifested in another way his interest in the newly discovered jazz, the potential wealth of its melodic rhythms, and its instrumental combinations with their individualized timbres, by composing a *Ragtime for Eleven Instruments,* of which he was later to make an arrangement for piano solo.

The *Ragtime* really was the first attempt—followed by how many others—at integrating the instrumental technique of jazz into a stylized composition.

In this work, the rhythm is dislocated to the point of disintegrating the bar line, and uses metric possibilities only to provoke a melodic and harmonic competition by its mobility. Even the syncope loses its conventional meaning here as an accent on the uneven weak beat, for the notion of the strong and weak beats disappears in the dislocation of the meter.

For Stravinsky, this work creates a type and illustrates the concrete possibilities of a style that can no longer be ignored, and that engenders a purely linear result in its objective organization. We are simply dealing here, then, with a new set of materials, and not with a new way of thinking.

The *Piano Rag Music,* in its later form, corresponds to the same stylistic preoccupations, but the problem of pianistic virtuosity is considered in addition. (The art of his friend, the great pianist Artur Rubinstein, to whom the work was dedicated, was the concrete point of departure for this work.)

Nearly thirty years later, Stravinsky was to write a new work inspired by jazz, in which he even employed the ensemble now in use in bands, his recent *Ebony Concerto,* composed for Woody Herman's jazz orchestra. But here the artistic conception and technique correspond to the composer's present preoccupations rather than to those of 1917. We shall discuss it at the proper time.

The first performance of *L'Histoire du Soldat,* at Lausanne, was not repeated, despite its considerable success. Influenza had dispersed almost all of the protagonists, including Ludmila and Georges Pitoëff. Thus, the adventurous idea of an ambulant theater, and of the financial possibilities that went with it, was nipped in the bud. It was only several years after the war that the work was performed again in Paris at the "Concerts de Jean Wiener," and took its place among the most important works of contemporary music. The *Ragtime* was likewise performed after the war, under the composer's direction at the "Koussevitsky Concerts" at the Paris Opera.

At about the same time, Stravinsky extracted from the

Life and Works (1882–1920)

Firebird an orchestral suite in a version more reduced than the original, adding some fragments and eliminating others.

That same winter, while still in Switzerland, Stravinsky composed his *Four Russian Songs,* translated by Ramuz: "Ronde de Canard," "Chanson à Compter," "Le Moineau Est Assis," and "Le Chant Dissident," suggesting the syllabic style of *Pribaoutki,* except for the last, in which, despite the predominance of the phonetic factor, the text retains a poetic meaning and the melodic line seems to have a direction apart from the vocal sound.

XIX

The separate peace concluded by Russia put Stravinsky in an increasingly precarious financial situation. He asked Diaghileff to perform *L'Histoire du Soldat,* but the work was not a "World's First Performance," and since the composer had had it performed without the Ballets Russes, Diaghileff remained indifferent to the idea.

But the success of Scarlatti's *Femmes de Bonne Humeur,* orchestrated by Tommasini, stimulated Diaghileff to ask him for a work inspired by Pergolesi, for whom he knew Stravinsky had a genuine fondness.

Stravinsky, at that time, tended more and more toward a universal style, a purely musical language based upon a dogma whose premises he had found in the works of Bach and the great classics, and whose filiation he had followed through the old Italian school, which eventually resulted in that of the beginning of this century: Bellini, Donizetti, and Rossini.

This music, with its melodic and diatonic essence, had always corresponded to his personal aspirations, whether or not the basis was Russian.

When he agreed to write ballet music on the sparse themes of Pergolesi that Diaghileff had collected in the libraries of Italy and London, he was also charmed by the idea of working with Picasso for the *décors* and the costumes, and with Leonide Massine for the choreographic realization. But he found himself before a new æsthetic problem. Was it in the form of an arrangement, of a pastiche, or of a personal work that he was to conceive this undertaking—with respect or with admiration, as a purist or as a creator?

Stravinsky is no arranger, and his hesitations did not last long. He considered that it is admiration, and not respect, that is creative. "Respect does not beget children." To create, love demands possession: he decided upon love. He treated the Pergolesian themes as the concrete materials for a personal work, which was to be neither an archaic imitation nor a harmonization applied to a reconstitution, but used Pergolesi as a living and impersonal *prétexte*, a constraint to be overcome, without adapting himself to it, but rather adapting it to himself.

The reproaches leveled at him for being irreverent or impersonal did not concern him at all. He had anticipated them, and a man like Stravinsky could never be influenced by them.

In my opinion, *Pulcinella*, without being a work of capital importance in Stravinsky's production, is nevertheless significant. It is through this work that his style emphasized its natural relationship with the masters of the eighteenth and those of the beginning of the nineteenth centuries, a relationship arising from his predilection for the pure and direct lines and the undisguised clarity of their stylistic organization.

With few exceptions, this logical attitude, which consists in adopting the means of expression of a depersonalized style, this melodic Italianism, whose Vivaldian traces remain present in J. S. Bach, were to manifest themselves throughout his future production. Italianism was to become integrated in the composer's personality as the filter of his own style, the counterpart of his Slavic feeling for melody, though not in opposition to it. The discipline of Bach and the new polyphony of jazz—in *L'Histoire du Soldat*—thus act as a bridge between the two stages in the evolution of a personality that nevertheless remains more unified than ever.

After the "forsaking of Russianism," as manifested in *L'Histoire du Soldat,* an act already somewhat suspect in the eyes of some critics, *Pulcinella* was to become the source of constant misunderstandings concerning the principle of Stravinsky's evolution. He gained the admiration of those who found in *Pulcinella* what is not there, and lost the devotion of those who no longer saw in it what it nevertheless contains. The latter, indeed, think they can perceive in *Pulcinella,* and in the new orientation that it announced, the confirmation of the definite abandoning of a "Russian style," a sign of impending exhaustion, a temptation to borrow from academic models, the famous neoclassicism, in short, an impertinent deformation of the past and a manifest denunciation of the composer's personality.

Instead of considering *Pulcinella* as a fruitful and logical step, a direct though not a final result of his aspirations and of his preceding works, instead of perceiving the stylistic indications it contains, they looked upon it as a sort of double-faced flag.

Some said, "This, definitely, is modern music. Therefore let us hasten to imitate it, for apparently it ought not to be too difficult." Whereas others exclaimed, "Is that all? Did the mountain give birth to a mouse? After the *Firebird,*

Petrouchka, and the *Rite*, this is indeed a cruel disappointment!"

The interminable series of astonishingly superficial judgments, of so-called "returns" to Bach, to Handel, to Lully or to Rossini, had begun.

Ought we then to spoil our pleasure by seeking in Stravinsky's music for perpetual thrills, instead of simply enjoying his masterpieces with our sensitivity and our intelligence?

Let us rather put *Pulcinella* in its true place, without minimizing or exaggerating its significance. Let us consider it as one of Igor Stravinsky's works among others, whose musical material derived from Pergolesi, and which was composed at a definite period in his evolution, in function of what preceded and what was to follow.

Pulcinella is a tour de force because, without adopting a falsely archaic process of stylistic reconstitution, the composer succeeds in never betraying or deforming the Italian *divertimento* by the contributions of his own personality. The music, now graceful, now truculent, retains its lively character, its Neapolitan atmosphere. The style adopted in *Pulcinella* was to remain almost peculiar to itself, but it was to lead the composer, through *Mavra*, the *Octet* and the *Jeu de Cartes*, toward an increasingly transparent and spacious melodic invention and harmonic style.

CHAPTER VI

Life and Works (1920–1948)

I

AT THE end of 1919, Stravinsky finally left his Swiss refuge of so many years, which he was always to remember with warm gratitude.

He decided to establish himself in France, that country and especially Paris having regained, after the war, its position as the world center of art.

It was again during a vacation in Brittany that he finished his *Concertino for String Quartet* and his *Symphonies for Wind Instruments*, dedicated to the memory of Claude Debussy and written at the instigation of the *Revue Musicale*, directed by the late Henri Prunières, who was to publish in the supplement the choral finale, the *Tomb of Debussy*.

The two works are clearly connected with Stravinsky's production in Switzerland: *L'Histoire du Soldat, Les Noces, Renard,* and *Ragtime*.

The plural title of the *Symphonies for Wind Instruments* indicates that it was not the composer's intention to use the sonata form, which would have implied the singular, but that he intended, rather, to use an instrumental polyphonic ensemble. The thematic treatment by isolated sections recalls that of *L'Histoire du Soldat,* whereas the complex wealth of harmony and the amplitude of the sonority link it to the realization of *Les Noces,* and sometimes even to that of the *Rite of Spring.*

The admirable chorale at the end (anticipated at the beginning of the work) is of an altogether fresh beauty, a sort of static sequence of heavy harmonies, whose instrumental disposition creates a timbre at once grave and serene. The metric organization (in which the significant silences are more important than ever) creates an altogether abstract tragic and epic atmosphere heightening the action and the emotional intensity.

It is only in the last movement of the *Symphony of Psalms* and in certain fragments of *Oedipus-Rex* that we again find a continuation of this atmosphere, born, it seems to me, of certain ostinati in the *Rite* and of the last pages of the *Nightingale.*

The *Concertino for String Quartet* corresponds rather to the harmonic and rhythmic filiation of *L'Histoire du Soldat* and of the works based on jazz. Its dislocated meter, carrying and creating the thematic and harmonic material by its own evolution, gives it the dynamism and the purity of line of *L'Histoire,* though it lacks the latter's breathtaking humaneness.

In form it resembles the one-movement sonata; it is the "concertant" role of the first violin that determined the title, *Concertino.*

After his installation in the suburbs of Paris at Garches, Stravinsky followed the numerous tours of the Ballets Russes abroad, conducting the *Firebird* and *Petrouchka.* In London, he was present at a performance by Serge Koussevitsky of the *Symphonies for Wind Instruments.*

Life and Works (1920–1948)

The work remained completely misunderstood, and was received somewhat ironically by the British public.

Without insisting upon the fact that the strong inner quality of this composition deprives it of the qualities that make for popular success, the fact that it was placed on a "best-seller" program certainly did not contribute toward its favorable acceptance. It is difficult to please with psalmodic cantilenas and a finale completely solidified in the somberly static quality of its rocklike harmonies, after the sonorous magnificence and the easy picturesqueness of *Le Coq d'Or*.

After the season in London and upon Diaghileff's request, Stravinsky arranged and orchestrated certain parts of Tchaikowsky's ballet *The Sleeping Beauty*, which the Ballets Russes wished to make the main attraction for the following season.

At the same time, the composer conceived the idea of a short lyric work taken from a subject of the great Russian classicist (a classicist according to the period in which he lived, but more so by his discipline), Alexander Pushkin. Pushkin's works had already inspired many Russian musicians: to mention only Tchaikowsky's *Eugene Onegin* and *Pique-Dame*, Moussorgsky's *Boris Godounoff*, Rimsky's *Le Coq d'Or* and Glinka's *Russlan and Ludmilla*.

Who could be closer to Stravinsky than Pushkin? This essentially Russian artist established a fruitful relationship with the Western spirit. He is Russian spiritually and not ethnographically, Russian and universal, but in no way cosmopolitan.

The composer fixed upon a short story in verse, the *Little House of Kolomna*, in which a soldier, disguised as a maidservant, manages to get himself into the house of his sweetheart, only to be discovered later in the act of shaving. Diaghileff's collaborator, Boris Kochno, arranged the vocal text that was to become an opera buffa in one act: *Mavra*.

The work is placed, in the mind of the composer, under the sponsorship of the Russian musical tradition, as it had developed in connection with Western art, and apart from the purely folkloristic or popular conceptions. It is, therefore, the tradition of Glinka, Tchaikowsky, and Dargomishky, and not that of the Five, which was to legitimatize the national character of *Mavra*. Here, Stravinsky falls in line musically with a period that had a predilection for partly gypsy, partly Italian ballad.

Occupied at the same time with the work on Tchaikowsky's ballet and the recording of his works for the Pleyel Player Piano, Stravinsky completed the composition of *Mavra* at Biarritz. Meanwhile, the performance of *Renard* had been prepared by Diaghileff with a very spirited interpretation by Bronislava Nijinska. The latter was also entrusted with the interpretation of *Mavra*.

The two works, then, were performed by Diaghileff at the Paris Opera in the beginning of June, 1922. *Mavra* was received as a kind of whim, a work without musical importance for the present or the future.

Yet the work is a rare achievement in itself, and it had extremely significant repercussions in the composer's musical thought.

It is a curious fact that following this opera buffa, a work intended for the stage, the author undertook a series of works conceived in a purely musical form, with no poetic or lyric source whatever, starting with the *Octet for Woodwinds*, the *Concerto for Piano and Wind Orchestra*, and the *Sonata for Piano*.

We have already spoken about the construction of *Mavra* when we discussed Stravinsky's lyric conception in general. It is in *Mavra* that the composer was to inaugurate the formal delimitation of vocal melody by a return to separate "airs." He thus realigns himself with the formal tradition of the French and Italian opera, also taken up again by the Russian opera: in this conception the music holds back and freezes the action by the device of the sung air (as it had already partially frozen it in the *Rossignol*, and completely so in the *L'Histoire du Soldat* and *Renard*, solely as a result of its own inner development).

This convention is clearly opposed to that of the "infinite melody," of the musical drama that, by its deliberate synchronization, by its willful fusion of the music with the dramatic action, excludes the conventionality of the traditional rule of the game.

Mavra is a lyrical work, a classic opera buffa whose sections are unified by an instrumental linking and by the clearly organized stylistic conception, as well as by the objectivity of its inner musical motion.

The melody in *Mavra* has the round vulgarity of the streetsong, whose line is anticipated, familiar, and unfiltered by "good taste." This melody in no way denies the hackneyed element so dear to Stravinsky, as we were able to observe in *Petrouchka, Les Noces,* and *L'Histoire du Soldat*.

The harmonies often modulate by thirds on the common tone, tending toward a progressive simplification.

The rhythm, despite the vivaciousness of its flow and the asymmetric accentuation of the weak and strong beats, leans more and more upon a set meter very clearly marking the strong beats in the deep movements of the low-registered instruments, particularly the cellos and the contrabasses, which are more numerous than the violins.

It is in the play of the basses, often moving in the false

relation of a semitone, as in the *Prague Symphony* of Mozart, that the composer achieves his most astonishing modulations in an over-all harmony that is spacious, but hardly bold.

The polarization of the tone that was to result in the deliberate restraint of the *Serenade for Piano* insidiously substitutes itself here for that of a converging core and even for that of the tonality, though sometimes remaining merely implicit.

The tendency toward purely constructive form, ranging from the linking of episodes, as in the sectionalized suite, through the unification of themes, to the sonata form, already previously indicated, manifests itself more and more in Stravinsky's works.

We know that the composer does not assimilate himself with the things and circumstances that surround him. Rather, he assimilates them with himself, takes possession of them, and integrates them within his own nature.

It is for this reason that we have often observed how a Russian folksong, American jazz, a theme of Pergolesi, a Swiss fanfare, a hackneyed gypsy song, or a Rossinian theme will always be Stravinskyan, just as Beethoven's work, when viewed from a distance and through its evolution, retains the Beethovenian character: The *First Symphony,* the *Razumovsky Quartets,* the last quartets, and the sonatas for piano. By some unfathomable mystery, this genius is at home everywhere, because he remains himself everywhere; because, according to the perceiving definition of Ramuz: "You have never been a stranger anywhere on earth, you could never be one anywhere, having never lacked a connection with things, with life, having never been separated anywhere from *being,* which is the greatest of gifts." *

* C. F. Ramuz, *Souvenirs sur Igor Stravinsky.*

II

During his sojourn at Biarritz, where he was to remain until the end of 1924, Stravinsky composed, in addition to *Mavra*, the *Octet for Woodwinds*, the *Concerto for Piano and Wind Orchestra*, and the *Sonata for Piano*. The stay in Nice that followed it gave birth to *Oedipus-Rex*, *Apollon-Musagète*, and the *Symphony of Psalms*. All these sojourns were frequently interrupted by numerous visits to Paris and by tours abroad, among them his first journey to the United States. It was also at Biarritz that he finally completed the orchestration of *Les Noces*.

The *Octet for Woodwinds* (1923) and the *Piano Concerto* continue the composer's predilection for wind harmonies as well as his interest in individualized ensembles.

The *Octet*, despite its relative brevity, contains a limpid synthesis of the æsthetic elements and of the technical factors adopted by Stravinsky in the course of his evolution from *Petrouchka* to *Mavra*. The admirable clarity of its melodic lines, their discursive, constantly moving polyphony, inspired by Bach and colored by Rossini, the moving profundity of its slow movement where everything is music and nothing is for effect, the irresistible dynamism of the fugue finale combine with the often droll earthiness of *Renard* and do not exclude the inner mystery of the *Symphonies*. The chamber-music-like form, clear and limpid in its thematic conception, the rhythm where the syncopes lose their aggressiveness, all these combined qualities make the *Octet* a gem of constructive intelligence and humaneness.

We find the atmosphere of the *Octet* again in the delightful *Jeu de Cartes*, where, thanks to a manner broader in length and in instrumental variety, it blooms forth with a vivaciousness that is never forced and an always conscious abandon.

The *Concerto* marks the composer's beginnings, not only as a conductor, but also as a pianist in the interpretation of his own works.

Before he undertook this work, Stravinsky set about studying the piano conscientiously. The arrangement for piano of the three movements of *Petrouchka* amply demonstrates that it no longer held any secrets from him.

The *Concerto* was followed by the *Sonata* (1924) and the *Serenade for Piano* (1925), followed in turn by the *Capriccio for Piano and Orchestra* and the *Concerto for Two Pianos*.

The conception of the wind orchestra is probably due to the fact that the "scraped" strings do not constitute too good a foil for the plasticity and relief of the timbre of the piano: an old conflict, which Stravinsky solves simply by eliminating it. The *Concerto for Piano* stands out distinctly from among the works that surround it. It is masterly in its construction, in its instrumental framework, in its substance, and in the technique of its realization. It continues *Les Noces* and *L'Histoire du Soldat* by the ever renewed vitality of its movement. In the middle section, it anticipates the gravity and the serenity of the *Symphony of Psalms*, and also announces, by a certain hieratic quality, the moving sculptures of *Oedipus-Rex*.

From a purely instrumental point of view, there is no question here of "blending" the concerto instrument with the orchestra, or of making it an instrument apart. The climate is one of constant opposition, a discourse between two timbres, a dialogue animated by perpetual vitality.

After the beautiful introduction, of an intense gravity and profundity, the fast movement makes use of the percussive piano style dear to Bach and his contemporaries

Life and Works (1920–1948)

as well as to the clavichordists who preceded them, a *portamento* on the borderline between legato and staccato, in a discourse of a single uninterrupted organic flow.

The third movement manifests the same virulence and active dynamism. It is brutal in its impetuosity, except for the reminder of the grave slow introduction that is to serve it as a cadential link. A perfect architecture characterizes these two movements in which the form is closely tied to the musical discourse in a perfectly natural way, and gives them an infallible aspect of inner solidity.

The slow movement of the *Concerto* contains some of the most beautiful and moving pages that Stravinsky has written. Between the two cataclysmic movements that flank it, the reflective gravity of its atmosphere, the linear and emotional generosity of its continuous design, achieved with a remarkable economy of means, relates the *Concerto* to the future development of the *Symphony of Psalms,* the serene tenderness of *Apollon-Musagète,* and the monumental stability of *Oedipus-Rex.*

It was as soloist in his *Concerto* and as conductor directing his own works that Igor Stravinsky seriously began his career as a professional performer, a career that was to carry him through most of Europe as well as to the United States, and later to South America.

III

The *Sonata for Piano* of 1924 was also written under the patronage of the style of piano writing dear to J. S. Bach (particularly in the two- and three-part inventions). The first movement, in strict two-voice counterpoint, with thirds intervening from time to time in the right hand, opposes the legato triplets of the right hand to the moving staccati of the left hand. Stravinsky frequently uses this method of doubling a legato with a staccato of the same timbre or of dividing the strings into *arco* and pizzicato.

The second movement, nocturnal and meditative in character, moves in the midst of curious embellishments whose outer sections frame a short rhythmic intermezzo. It is followed by a toccatalike finale in the impulsive and percussive style of a dynamic polyphony.

The work is relatively short and resembles in form the rondo, varied, and the lied, rejuvenated by a fresh treatment.

The *Serenade for Piano*, composed by Stravinsky after his return from the United States, where he was received with immense enthusiasm, consists of four short movements: Hymn, Romanza, Rondoletto, and Cadenza Finale. In form and intent, the *Serenade* resembles the Mozartian serenades, night music, and cassations, or certain Italian *divertimenti*, transposed to a pianistic plane. The music is light and happy, and resembles the *Concerto* and the *Sonata*, though less strained in effect. The two outer movements remind one of certain phases of later modulations, and also anticipate *Oedipus-Rex* somewhat.

An A, around which the entire movement of the *Serenade* revolves, serves as a converging point. The latter is stabilized by a curious resonance, whose harmonic progression resembles in its strangeness *Les Noces* as well as the later *Symphony in C*.

IV

After this series of piano works, Stravinsky felt the need to compose a work of grander scope. He selected a myth of ancient Greece, whose static, immanent character corresponded at the time with his deeper aspirations. As

Life and Works (1920–1948)   217

he tells us in his *Chroniques,* he was inspired by the example of St. Francis who, when he spoke of the sublime, used French (his mother was French) to mark a difference from the native tongue that he used in everyday life: he thus chose Latin for his text, Latin being "a medium not dead, but turned to stone and so monumentalized as to have become immune from all risk of vulgarization."

Jean Cocteau, upon the composer's request, agreed to adapt the Sophoclean tragedy, the text of which was to be translated into Latin by Jean Danielou. It is impossible to explain Stravinsky's conception of this opera-oratorio better than by quoting the fragment of his *Chroniques* which discusses it: "How wonderful it is to compose music to a language of convention, almost of ritual, whose very nature imposes a lofty dignity. One is no longer dominated by the phrase, by the literal meaning of the words. Cast in an immutable mold, which adequately expresses their value, they require no further commentary. The text thus becomes purely phonetic material for the composer. He can dissect it at will and concentrate all his attention on its primary constituent element—that is to say, on the syllable."

Is this not, on another level, the same attitude with relation to the concrete that presided over the musical realization of the *Pribaoutki,* the *Berceuses du Chat, Le Renard,* and a large part of *Les Noces?*

With Stravinsky, the nature of intent and realization are closely related, so that his treatment of the text in *Oedipus-Rex* corresponds exactly to his theoretical conception.

We shall allow ourselves to quote once more the composer's *Chroniques,* which, while stating the problem of the æsthetic bearing of the work actually in progress, clarifies his general attitude, discussed at length at the beginning of this work: "I imposed upon myself this voluntary restraint by choosing a form of language sanctioned by time, and, so to speak, confirmed. The necessity of restraint, of a deliberately accepted 'bearing,' has its origin in the depth of our very nature, and is related not only to matters of art, but to all the conscious manifestations of human activity. It is the need for an order without which nothing is done, and with the disappearance of which everything disintegrates. Now all order requires restraint, but it is wrong to interpret this as an encroachment upon liberty. On the contrary, bearing and restraint contribute to its development, and only prevent it from becoming complete licentiousness. In the same way, the creative artist, when he borrows a form already established and recognized, finds himself in no way restrained in the expression of his personality. On the contrary, the latter stands out all the more, and gains still more relief, when it moves within a conventional and fixed frame."

Oedipus-Rex was completed at the beginning of 1927. It had its first performance on May thirtieth in Paris at the Sarah Bernhardt Theatre, with the Ballets Russes, but in concert form, as an oratorio. It was only later that the work was performed in its stage version at the Berlin Opera, under the direction of Otto Klemperer.

Like all of Stravinsky's lyric works, the opera-oratorio *Oedipus-Rex* is static in its action. The music freezes the dramatic action more than ever, for in this case, to the purely, æsthetic postulates personal to the composer, certain other factors are added: the monumental, even sculptural character of the subject itself and of the personages, the tragic hieratism of the sentiment, and finally, the very objectivity of Sophocles' epic conception.

"Greek" art, a term very much abused in the sense of "Attic" art, is not exclusively the linear purity of the Par-

Life and Works (1920–1948)   219

thenon, or the facial symmetry of Venus. It is also the stony tension of the Laocoön, the movement and élan of the Victory of Samothrace, the tragic fatality of the dramas of Æschylus and Sophocles, and the Eleusinian Mysteries. It is the objective attitude of the epic narration and of the presentation of the subject that make these manifestations Greek. The subject lives of its own accord, without the lyrical intervention of the narrator or of the artist to mark it with any element foreign to its own aim. Such is the classic attitude adapted by Stravinsky to his own *Oedipus-Rex*. The dramatic action develops only in the combined sonorities of the music and of the text. The role of the narrative in this dramatic action is conceived plastically. The actors do not perform, but sing the airs as "Spokesmen of the narrative." As a result, the action remains clearly static, crystallized in its monumental immobility emphasizing the abstract tragedy.

Here, after a long interruption, Stravinsky employs the usual symphonic orchestra, but the scoring is suggestive of the preoccupations that had resulted in the individualized instrumental ensembles of the "Swiss" period. The combinations of timbres of *L'Histoire du Soldat* and of *Renard* intervene in a significant and striking fashion, giving it the character of a mobile bas-relief.

Oedipus-Rex, by its cosmic, pagan character, is related to the *Rite* and to *Les Noces*.

The harmony is extremely simple. The subtle movements of the basses, which began with the writing of *Mavra*, are more especially responsible for carrying the often homophonic melody to modulatory points. These serve as supporting columns for a construction of emotive grandeur in which the conception of the Handelian oratorio results in a work most authentically Stravinskyan in conception.

V

It is surprising that no music critic ever tried to slip a "Greek" period into the evolution of Stravinsky's art. Indeed, after *Oedipus-Rex*, we were to have *Apollon-Musagète*, *Persephone*, a later work, entitled *Ode* (subdivided into Eulogy, Eclogue, and Epitaph), and finally, the composer has very recently completed a new ballet, *Orpheus*.

Commissioned by the Library of Congress at Washington, at the instigation of the well-known American music patron, Mrs. Elizabeth Sprague Coolidge, to compose for a contemporary music festival a ballet no more than about twenty-five minutes in length, for small orchestra, Stravinsky's choice fell upon Apollo inspiring the muses with their particular arts: *Apollon-Musagète*.

Having always had a clearly marked preference for the formula of the classic ballet, with its plastic feeling, and its absence of psychological or expressive aspirations, except those governed by a restrained mimic convention, Stravinsky conceived his work in the style of the ballets of Lully, that is to say, in the style of a period in which every stage device was regulated by a static rule of the game, despite the complexity of the stage performance.

Thus, the ballet, performed in Washington by Adolph Bolm and in Paris by Georges Balanchine, was performed in *tutus* on the traditional plan: *pas d'action, pas de deux,* variations, and coda. The entire choreographic action was based upon the allegory of plastic movements of the classic ballet. Wishing also to create his work upon the plane of a "white" music in which no intervention of contrast in the timbre might modulate the color, the composer made use of a string orchestra, whose volume he was

Life and Works (1920–1948) 221

further to reduce: he divided it into six parts, but in a peculiar manner, by emphasizing the "higher basses" and by treating the middle section lightly: first and second violins, violas, first and second violoncellos, and contrabasses. The work, freed from any concern for timbre, revolves only around a linear and melodic principle.

Stravinsky anticipated, without fearing it, however, a certain monotony in the dull atmosphere of the general sonority, further accentuated by the fact that he made no appeal to virtuosity to relieve this monochromatic flow of the musical material. He was concerned only with the purity of the essential melodic lines, going their way in an undeviated polyphony and without any concession to effect.

The work, for those who succeed in penetrating the sonorous web and grasping the inner substance, has much beauty and is one of those in which the tenderness and the humaneness of Stravinsky's genius are evidenced with rare success in a veritable sublimation of self-denial.

Despite its esoteric appearance, *Apollon* received a warm welcome at its first Parisian performance, although part of the public remained somewhat puzzled.

Numerous tours throughout Europe, as conductor and pianist, interrupted the composer's creative activity for some time. Acting on a request of Madame Ida Rubinstein, which went back to 1927, Stravinsky began a new ballet upon his return. His sincere admiration for Tchaikowsky, coinciding with the thirty-fifth anniversary of that composer's death, placed the contemplated work under this patronage.

According to Stravinsky's idea, the subject was to correspond with the very nature of the Tchaikowskyan muse, with her preference for fantastic elements.

Once more he started to read Andersen, who had already furnished the text for *Le Rossignol*. The tale of the snow maiden caught his attention, and he finally extracted from it the subject of his ballet *Le Baiser de la Fée*. The surface romanticism of this subject lends itself admirably to the plastic discipline of a classic ballet in *tutus*, with, in addition, rustic scenes, "which take place in the Swiss countryside with the characters dressed in the style of the first tourists, mixing with the friendly villagers in the good theatrical tradition."

In Stravinsky's æsthetic and technical evolution, *Le Baiser de la Fée* clearly reveals traces of the *Apollon*, which precedes it and anticipates the *Capriccio for Piano and Orchestra*, which was to follow it.

While using the thematic material borrowed from Tchaikowsky and taking possession of it in his habitual manner, Stravinsky builds his work upon a pattern of melodic planes, in which there is much to please the ear. The same tender serenity presides over the choice of themes and their instrumental and harmonic realization. There is a certain prettiness of design in the elegiac character of the adagios as well as in the jerky volubility of a rhythmic life that is always present, though without violent manifestations.

VI

After *Le Baiser de la Fée,* Stravinsky made a whole series of recordings of his works. To him, the chief significance of this work was that of a document fixing a definite interpretation, as opposed to the arbitrariness of so-called personal interpretations. In an important chapter of his *Poétique Musicale* devoted to the question of interpretation—one already touched upon in his *Chroniques*—Stravinsky also emphasizes the inevitable distortion of the

Life and Works (1920–1948)

timbre and the negative side of the "commodity of aural pleasure without disturbing oneself." He protests against everything that an exaggerated individualization can take away from, and even more, "contribute" to the authenticity of the composer's creative thought. He considers all his recordings useful above all for the creation of a tradition, and as an indication of what ought, and especially of what ought not, to be done, if his intentions as a composer are to be followed.

The year 1929 brought a great blow to the personal affections of Igor Stravinsky: the death in Venice of Serge Diaghileff. This loss of a friend and collaborator of twenty years, so closely connected with the composer's life and art, was profoundly felt by him.

More and more in demand as interpreter at the piano of his own works, Stravinsky started, in the summer of 1929, a new work for piano and orchestra, the *Capriccio,* which of all his piano works until then, was perhaps the most perfect and fluent. He found his inspiration in the style of Weber, particularly of the sonatas and the *Konzertstück,* as well as in Chopin for the purely instrumental brilliance of his pianistic quality, its sparkle rather than its expressiveness, and achieved a remarkable performance in these dazzling three movements.

He sought to develop his music by juxtaposing episodes "of varied genre which follow each other, and, by their nature, impart to the piece the capricious character from which it derives its name."

Even while claiming the example of Weber and availing himself of a pattern and a language whose charm and accessibility do not give way for one single instant, Stravinsky achieved a work striking in the originality of its content and craftsmanship, rich in constructive and instrumental imagination, and of a quasi-Mozartian flow.

Everything here is gay and cheerful, with the playful element later to be found in the *Jeu de Cartes.*

Once more, the work is related to those preceding it, and points to certain peculiarities which were to bear fruit in future works. The use of the arpeggio, with the ambiguous play of the major and minor third and omitted fifth, so characteristic of Stravinsky's style, here asserts its clearly thematic significance by anticipating the importance it was to assume in the *Danses Concertantes,* the *Scènes de Ballet,* and the *Symphony in Three Movements.*

The simultaneous linking of different degrees of the same tonality, particularly the tonic and the dominant, already observed in the *Rossignol,* make their reappearance here and are used with a definite method.

This is a work in which the virtuosity of the piano is manifested through a dazzling orchestration and in no way detracts by its factor of exhibition from the essence of the music itself. Stravinsky happily solved here the complex problem, which consists for him in charming without losing one thread of his personality.

Placed between two fast movements, more so by their liveliness than by the speed of their tempo, the middle movement, with its rhapsodic character of a seemingly improvised fantasy, takes on its full significance as a caprice of genius.

VII

Since we have already spoken at length of the *Symphony of Psalms* in its relationship to Stravinsky's conception of religious music, we shall no longer dwell upon this work, which, in our opinion, represents one of the summits of the musical art. It is difficult to analyze, so much do all of its component factors tend toward, by their equilibrium, and result in, granduer, emotion, and nobility. One feels almost hesitant to analyze technically a work of similar proportions, in which everything is inward, intangible, and indispensable. Born of *Les Noces* and *Oedipus-Rex,* the *Symphony of Psalms* is the sum of his maturity, in which a constant tension is allied to the unforgettable serenity of the last movement, based upon an astonishing pedal point of timpani, harp, and pianos.

Unifying thematic patterns run through the entire work, including the majestic double fugue in the middle, whose subject, derived from the first movement, is found again in the finale.

The orchestra, in which the woodwinds and the brasses predominate, uses only the basses of the strings, thus lightening and perforating the instrumental web, and creating an obstacle to the undesirable blending of sonorities. The *Symphony of Psalms* is the work of a creative genius and of a man of profound faith. It is the offering of the creator to the object of his faith, an offering from which, as we have said, all sacrilegious externalization is absent.

Commissioned of the composer in 1930 by the Boston Symphony Orchestra for the anniversary of its foundation, the work was performed in Boston in the same year. Despite its inward and austere character, the *Symphony of Psalms* impressed informed musicians from the day of its first performance in Boston and in Paris (under the composer's direction) as a definite and undisputed masterpiece. But, as was the case with *Octet, Mavra, Le Baiser de la Fée,* and *Apollon,* it disconcerted a number of the devout Stravinskyans who, despite the fact that they always hope for "something else" from him, never expect what he offers them.

While more and more admired by the young, Stravinsky

created an ever widening gulf between himself and those who had followed him "up to a certain point," those who lost track of him because of his self-renewal, in which, in place of variety, they discern only a disparate sterility, those who seek in music "their" pleasure and not the value of the music in itself.

Without being discouraged, Stravinsky proceeds along the path of a musical æsthetic that he chose for himself. He believes in "his" truth, and although sensitive to the absence of communion between the creative artist and the public, he prefers this absence of communion to one based upon misunderstanding or upon a concession on his part.

VIII

During a chance stay in Wiesbaden, in the course of a tour in Germany, Stravinsky was asked by the violinist Sam Duskin (through the intermediary of Mr. Willi Strecker, director of the Schott Publishers in Mainz) to compose a concerto for violin and orchestra, for which Dushkin was to have exclusive rights of performance for a certain time under the composer's direction.

Stravinsky hesitated somewhat: first, he was afraid to find in the young violinist the "virtuoso" type, whose attitude he detested, though not the professional ability. Reassured by a closer contact with Dushkin, he was still not sufficiently sure of his own knowledge of the violin. Yet nobody knows better than Stravinsky the theoretical possibilities of the instruments, and *L'Histoire du Soldat* proves that he had made a particular study of the technique of the violin. But is theoretical knowledge enough to compose a clearly violinistic work, and for a soloist? Assured of the technical collaboration of Dushkin, whose

Life and Works (1920–1948)

enthusiasm evoked a sympathetic response in him, Stravinsky began the *Concerto for Violin,* soon to be followed by the *Duo Concertant for Violin and Piano.*

Dushkin settled himself near the composer, first at Nice, and later in the Isère (where Stravinsky was to spend three years after the six years at Nice), and helped him with advice as to the specific instrumental possibilities of the violin. The work was finished and learned in time for a first performance over the Berlin radio, and later in most of the European and American centers.* This *Concerto* is somewhat related to the *Concerto for Piano,* the character of the style being transposed to the violinistic plane. It is firm and decisive in its lively movements, based upon the square structure of a variable and supple though solidly established rhythm, lyrical and melodic in its arias, which have a new contour. It shows a deliberate relationship with the style of the sonatas and the organ partitas of Bach. Indeed, unity is here obtained by the organic connection of the musical ideas rather than by the development of the thematic core.

The *Duo Concertant,* which follows it, is a rather developed work in which his preoccupation with a real polyphony and that of the realization of two heterogeneous timbres of struck and plucked strings is achieved with rare ingeniousness. Completed in July, 1932, the *Duo* was performed in Berlin in October of the same year, and the composer made a new tour of concerts throughout Europe, together with Dushkin.

* In 1941 Georges Balanchine used the score of the *Violin Concerto* for his ballet *Balustrade* (translators' note).

IX

In the beginning of 1933, at the request of Ida Rubinstein, Stravinsky began to write the music for André Gide's play: *Perséphone*.

Interrupted by several other trips abroad, the work was completed in March, 1934, and performed April thirtieth, 1934, at the Opera with Ida Rubinstein's ballet and a beautiful and sensitive choreographic realization by Kurt Jooss. The stage setting on the contrary was not at all in accordance with the composer's ideas. Moreover, it had been made without his or Gide's collaboration.

Perséphone, which is all too seldom performed in the concert hall, acts, in a way, as a bridge between the *Symphony of Psalms* and *Oedipus-Rex*, and some of the works that follow, such as the *Dumbarton Oaks Concerto* or the *Danses Concertantes*. We observe here the grave and severe element of certain pages of the *Symphony*, as well as the rather spasmodic rhythm of the works written between 1939 and 1942, with an accentuation of the modal ambiguities in a lightened harmonic dress in which the ingeniousness of the modulation makes up for the absence of complex superposed harmonies.

X

The work of great importance that was to follow *Perséphone* is the *Concerto for Two Pianos* (1935), whose first performances were reserved for the collaboration of the composer with his son, the pianist Soulima Stravinsky, who also accompanied him on his tour of South America.

The first movement, *con moto*, is all dynamism riddled with sixteenth notes. It brims over with unfailing vitality in the dialogues of the two instruments, the fusion of which results in the timbre of a single piano put into motion by a continuous contrapuntal play. The second movement is a nocturne with a long and beautiful melodic design, adorned with strange hues and resting upon a tranquil, respiratory, evenly pulsating accompaniment. The next movement is made of four variations, whose theme, instead of determining their evolution, crosses them as a function of a common core and unifies them in their variety: they are a careless barcarole, an impetuous second variation, a third in which the theme makes a way for itself through a chromaticism of the pianistic style, which is more than merely harmonic, and a fourth whose design is related in construction to the short intermezzo of the first movement. The work closes with a masterly fugue, preceded by a prelude of bold construction, and recalling more the great fugue of Beethoven, Opus 106, than those of Bach's conception.

The novelty of the conception of this fugue, monumental in its brevity, would in itself require a detailed analysis. But in a work like ours, where even analysis necessarily has to be of a synthetic nature, space is lacking to undertake this in a more exhaustive fashion.

The preamble enunciates with brilliant elocution the enlarged plan of the fugal theme that develops in the thick polyphony of four voices progressing in an atmosphere of resolute movement.

In this movement, the thematic development, opposing the subject and countersubject in bold clashes, is unified by the internal pulsation of a rhythm of repeated notes that continues its obsessive action to the limits of a coda, which sums up in a final concentrate all this polyphonic activity, and fixes it.

XI

The year 1935 gives us the charming *Jeu de Cartes*, a ballet in three "deals." The work, while displaying the characteristic traits of Stravinsky's technique, does not seem to propose any other problem apart from that of being exquisite music from beginning to end. A problem, as in the *Capriccio*, most difficult to solve, for despite the constant delight that this easy-going and carefree music gives us, it does not contain one single fragment that is not marked with the composer's personal stamp.

Even the loan from the overture of Rossini's *Barber*, so clearly evident, is integrated here with such appropriateness that its presence seems indispensable, and its absence would be felt as a gap. Each "deal" starts with an identical introduction: a pattern based on the interval of the seventh and the fifth, whose melodic and rhythmic simplicity determines the unity and serves as an opening. These unifying interludes, by their chronic function, are suggestive of the drum roll between the scenes in *Petrouchka*.

The melody, of an unlabored and cheerful gaiety, the spacious harmony, the voluble and infectious rhythm, the witty and dazzling orchestration, in which the timbre contributes more than ever its thematic material, makes this work a concert "suite" that it is high time to alternate with the *Firebird*, which, if one is to go by the usual orchestral repertory, is the only hit Stravinsky ever wrote— a personal hit for the conductor, obviously.

XII

We now arrive at the most recent decade of Stravinsky's artistic production: 1937–1947, which has given us nu-

Life and Works (1920–1948)   231

merous major works: the *Dumbarton Oaks Concerto*, the *Symphony in C*, the *Danses Concertantes*, *Ode*, the *Sonata for Two Pianos*, the *Babel Cantata*, the *Symphony in Three Movements*, as well as the *Concerto for Strings (Basel Concerto)* and the new ballet, *Orpheus* (the two last works are still unknown to me), and some minor works: *Tango for Piano or Orchestra*, *Circus Polka*, *Four Norwegian Moods*, *Scherzo à la Russe*, *Elegie for Unaccompanied Viola or Violin*, and *Ebony Concerto for Jazz Orchestra*.

We shall dwell especially upon the major works, despite the fact that each of the others has an indicative importance and a value in itself, as is the case with everything which comes from Stravinsky's pen.

All of this magnificent flowering of the last decade bears within it the mark of a maturity and an accomplished serenity whose character shows no trace of a stabilization that might exclude renewal and continuation.

More youthful than ever, Stravinsky's genius, guided by a unified, lucid discipline and method, continues to develop, constantly adapting new concrete phenomena and distributing them with the same effectiveness in the most varied directions.

No weakening hinders this advance, in which the power of artistic conviction takes precedence over external satisfactions.

The reaction to a body of works is temporary. Only the work itself remains a durable, ever present material to which each one can adjust his original reaction.

It might be that what I personally see in the body of Stravinsky's works is not there, for everything is possible. But, from now on, one thing is certain: what is there potentially still continues to escape many of our contemporaries, enmeshed as they are in a false purism or a false modernism.

It is very significant that the composer, while he applies himself to a different technical problem for each work, permits us to recognize in his production, sometimes at a great distance, embryonic riches momentarily put in reserve, so to speak, in earlier works. Thus, certain characteristics scarcely evident in *Renard* or *Pulcinella*, in which they fulfill episodic or secondary functions, suddenly take on a definite meaning in such recent works as the *Dumbarton Oaks Concerto*, or the *Danses Concertantes*. Others, barely perceptible, for example, in *Les Noces* or *L'Histoire du Soldat*, will only be found again in the *Ode* or in the *Symphony in Three Movements*, after having germinated during the entire period that separates these creations.

There is, in this use of earlier elements, no question of a retrogression or of a return to anything whatever. Likewise, their temporary or apparent abandonment never meant that the composer has turned his back upon his past or denies today that which he worshiped yesterday.

On the contrary, whether it is that the similarity of one detail calls for a similar treatment, or that a secondary element, present earlier, has reached its latent maturity after a long period of development, and has assumed major importance after having had only a secondary one, Stravinsky sees no reason for renouncing one iota of the vocabulary belonging to the public domain, and still less, the vocabulary that is his own.

XIII

The *Dumbarton Oaks Concerto* (1937–1938) was dedicated to Stravinsky's friends Mr. and Mrs. Bliss, and its

Life and Works (1920-1948)

title comes from the name of their estate, where an important international conference, which made Dumbarton Oaks famous, took place toward the end of the war. Judging by achievement alone, it would seem there is every reason to believe that Igor Stravinsky's work will prove more lasting than that of the diplomats.

Conceived for a small chamber-music ensemble, this *Concerto* achieves a wonderful quality of limpid balance and fertile invention, in a linear clarity where the harmony is always the result of melodic interweaving, and where the rhythm, whether pulsating or panting, clings closely to the flow of the thematic outline.

We observe in the *Concerto*, side by side with certain piquancies from *Pulcinella* and a broken rhythm recalling *Renard*, a clear prefiguration of the sonorous planes of the *Danses Concertantes*.

As was earlier the case of *Mavra*, the *Jeu de Cartes* and the *Dumbarton Oaks Concerto* after it accentuate Stravinsky's constructive aspirations more and more. It is followed by a whole family of formal works based upon traditional form to which the composer contributes an actual "presence." He retains only what is immutable, and eliminates everything that might hinder him by its connection with the formal conception of a definite period.

XIV

Thus, the *Symphony in C* (1938-1940) is more closely related to the symphonic form of Haydn than to that which was developed through the Beethovenian and post-Beethovenian evolution.

The development section is conceived more as a bridge between the exposition and the recapitulation than as a panel exploiting to the limit the thematic material in its detail.

The contrapuntal manipulation of the themes or of their parts, beginning, middle, and end, is here evident, but does not, as yet, assume the importance of a constructive principle.

The sprightly theme that introduces the first movement of the work imparts to the whole movement a direct and brisk tone by its unequivocally diatonic character. It moves, with its repeated notes and its descent of fourths, around an ensemble of strings in the tonic harmony. A harmony of Mozartian transparency, a rhythm made of quasi-metronomic pulsations, a limpid instrumentation in which no blurring interferes with the interplay of the groups, characterize this movement, whose apparent simplicity reveals, upon further hearing, an astonishing modulative inventiveness.

When he extracts a note from the harmonic basis and uses it enharmonically to avail himself of it as a common tone, Stravinsky steps past the tonal restraints and suddenly finds himself in another tonality, without seeming to have gone there. He is at home everywhere. He goes out by the door, comes in by the window, leaves again, one might think through the ceiling, takes advantage of every cranny, and all this with a naturalness, a gracefulness requiring as much harmonic intuition as it does lucidity.

From a slow movement where simple and serene melodies are interwoven, a fragment of pathetic, snarling violence is suddenly born; out of a scherzo of an almost pastoral character, despite its rhythmic complexity, there arises a finale whose impulsive beginning (as if it were based on a rhythmic fragment of the scale, to which an adjacent note is added at each repetition) results in an irresistibly active movement, to resolve itself at last into one of the most beautiful and astonishing pages Stravinsky has written.

The broadened theme of the first movement in its last part, B, C, G, is placed as though upon the transcendent summits of a harmonic resonance, in which the diatonism of the harmonies (containing, in a miraculous rearrangement, all the notes of the scale of C major, each one producing the entire series of harmonic tones) creates a halo of crystalline transparency.

The slow displacement of the theme, resulting either from the prolonging of a sustained tone or from a pause more palpable than a real sound, imparts to this page the character of appeased serenity of which we were aware on another plane in the second prelude of the *Rite,* in the finales of *Apollon* and of the *Symphony of Psalms.*

XV

In 1939, Stravinsky again went to the United States. He was invited there by Harvard University to give a course on musical poetics, which has since then been published in several languages, and which gives a clear and concise view of his æsthetic preoccupations of a dogmatic order.

The war surprised the composer in America, where as a result of circumstances he definitely established himself, and acquired a villa in Hollywood. It is from that center that he was to travel for his numerous concert engagements. After a sojourn of several years, he acquired American nationality.

I insist at this point upon discussing a question that has caused entirely too much ink to flow: Stravinsky's American citizenship—if only to avoid the suspicion of having left in the shade a certain element of questionable appearance. Certain fretful souls (and, it seems, more so in Switzerland than in France) have bitterly reproached him for having forsaken his French nationality, which he had acquired earlier, and become a citizen of the United States.

I wish above all to make understood, for those who may still have need, certain conditions peculiar to life in America. A foreigner, having established his permanent residence there, and exercising his activity there in a continuous manner, is not very favorably considered if he refuses to become a member of the American social community. An American finds it difficult to understand how someone who has the chance of becoming an American could hesitate to do so. It is, perhaps, surprising, but it is so, and it is impossible not to take it into account.

Stravinsky has definitely settled in the United States. He has found there a peaceful haven, the conditions of tranquillity and security essential to his work and to his age, and a neutral atmosphere that does not distract him from his artistic preoccupations by constant disturbances. If, by having changed his passport, he was able to avoid the continual annoyances of administrative red tape, as well as the reproach of wishing to distinguish himself in the famous American melting pot where he has found a hospitable and warm welcome, this does not at all influence his attachment for France, his spiritual affinity with that country, and his gratitude for what he owes it, which he emphasizes upon every occasion.

As for myself, I know quite a few authentic Frenchmen or bearers of French passports who certainly do not have the affection, tenderness, and love for France that Igor Stravinsky bears in his heart. In addition to this sentimental attitude toward the country that had been his

Life and Works (1920–1948) 237

most important field of action and from which his worldwide celebrity began, is he not more related to the French than to any other national type by his love for lucid and organized order, his concise intelligence, and even by his caustic wit?

Let me only recall our numerous conversations, such as the feverish one over the telephone that we picked up again every ten minutes during the night of the memorable Allied landing in Normandy: the days when we and our wives were glued to the radio, following with anxiety the changes of fortune of the Liberation of Paris, to affirm with certainty and conviction that the liberation of no city in the world could have moved Igor Stravinsky as much as that of Paris. Likewise, the misfortunes of no other country in the world could have affected Stravinsky as closely as those of France. And it certainly is not his American naturalization that could cause any change in an attitude so deeply rooted in an intimate sentiment and a constant affinity of intelligence and taste.

But let us now return to Igor Stravinsky's hospitable house in Hollywood, where the composer's love for order and method is effectively combined with the harmonious taste and the artistic sense of his charming wife, Vera Stravinsky, who was able to create for him an intimate and domestic hearth.

After crossing the living room, furnished in sober taste, and the little den, we arrive, through a corridor (where, on the shelves, scores are placed next to a rich assortment of French liqueurs and cognacs) at his workroom, isolated and soundproofed.

This room is an American transposition of the famous Swiss workroom that Ramuz describes for us in such lively fashion, and where *L'Histoire du Soldat* and so many other works were composed. Two pianos, one a grand, the other a half-muted upright, occupy a good half of it. The work desk is encumbered by a quantity of odd objects: multicolored pencils, inks, erasers, clef makers, chronometers, and a collection of gadgets of which I think only Stravinsky knows the exact usage.

The drawers contain manuscripts, business papers, documents, his correspondence, everything arranged in irreproachable order, in such a manner that everything is within hand's reach, as in a filing cabinet.

On the walls pictures and drawings by his son Theodore, by Picasso, Fernand Léger, and Eugène Berman, placed next to family photographs, together with a framed extract of a contemporary newspaper containing a very bad criticism of a new work of "Herr Ludwig van Beethoven," a telegram, also framed, on the subject of the first performance of the *Scènes de Ballet* (about which more later on), reproductions of Callot, etc.

Stravinsky methodically spends a good part of his day there: all morning, after his daily calisthenics, and a good part of the afternoon.

After lunch, which takes place at two o'clock (and Stravinsky cannot be dragged away from his work table one minute before), he likes to play a game of Chinese checkers, an indispensable form of relaxation for him. This game has a real importance in the distribution of Stravinsky's time. He is very fond of it, knows it well, and is not a very good loser. He is so accustomed to the discipline of a game after his meal that he thought it worth while to give us a set in order to have it at his disposal each time he came with Mrs. Stravinsky to our house to dine. He even takes one along with him on his train trips. I hope that he will forgive me this little indiscretion, since it is dictated only by a sentiment of tenderness and by a desire to show the familiar and human side of the man.

Life and Works (1920–1948)

The intimate circle of his friends, at least during the period we spent in Hollywood, from the end of 1941 to April, 1946, was very limited apart from his purely social and professional relations: it included the remarkable Russian actor, Vladimir Sokoloff, and his wife; the well-known dancer and choreographer, Adolph Bolm, and his wife; Nadia Boulanger, for whom he has a sincere and warm admiration; the painter, Eugène Berman; his lawyer and friend Aaron Sapiro, whom Stravinsky considers as his "business nurse," only to list the more intimate ones.

My wife and I often spent whole hours with Stravinsky playing the organ works of Bach, and we went through all of them several times.

It goes without saying that everyone who has any importance in the universal world of art, living in or passing through Hollywood, as well as anyone who is young and animated by sincere aspirations, finds the path to Stravinsky's house.

For every Frenchman who comes to California, this house is practically a consulate, where he is assured a warm welcome, simply because he is French.

But this house has nothing of the atmosphere of a shrine, in the manner of Bayreuth. Stravinsky always remains affable, putting at ease those for whom he has opened his door, without any show of superiority or condescension, and always retains his simplicity. But he cannot be complacent when it comes to judging music. He remains as objective as possible, but his integrity makes him organically incapable of complimenting or flattering what he does not sincerely respect. He skillfully sets the question aside or eludes it wittily rather than committing himself against his wishes. He says nothing if his opinion is not asked, but he gives *only* his opinion once it is asked.

I remember how, after the performance of a mediocre

contemporary work, the composer asked Stravinsky what he thought of it. His reply was as concise as it was caustic: "I think the title of the work is excellent."

In the expression of his opinions, Stravinsky can be extremely direct and outspoken, and his sense of repartee is developed to a rare, almost French degree. Questioned once as to what he thought of the works of a composer at the time very much in vogue in the United States, Stravinsky replied point blank: "I will tell you when he has composed *one*."

Repartees of this kind are innumerable. I might also quote his famous reply to a Parisian composer, as pretentious as he was mediocre, who, upon first meeting Stravinsky, asked him what day he might come to show him his works.

Stravinsky, taking out his appointment book and slowly turning over many pages, answered, "Never."

The free part of his working day, as well as his meals, is spent in the garden that Igor and Vera Stravinsky take care of with a particular fondness. Stravinsky knows each plant and flower in it, he is concerned with their life and growth, just as he takes interest in his canaries who, from their cage, fill the dining room with their voluble song. Everything is organized in the life of the artist, but nothing seems pedantic or conventional.

Is it necessary to say that Stravinsky's intellectual culture is enormous, that he is interested in everything alive, as in everything abstract and speculative? How many times have we discussed the most diverse problems until the early hours of the morning, beginning with the latest bit of political gossip, to end with a discussion on the intimate meaning of the Epistles of Saint Paul, passing through the æsthetics of Bach, the style of Gide, the

Life and Works (1920–1948)

relationship between Spinoza and Bergson, Spanish mysticism as it reveals itself in the country's art, etc.

Stravinsky's knowledge is always profound. It goes to the very roots. A superficial judgment never invalidates his views. If he discusses a subject, he speaks of it with complete knowledge and with a determined conviction that might be open to discussion, but that always represents a profound and legitimate view on the subject.

Here, then, is the intimate circle in which Igor Stravinsky has been working since 1940. It seemed important to me to describe it to some extent, in order to share with my readers the atmosphere that prevails there: one of order, neatness, and for myself, of affection and friendship.

XVI

As we have said, a whole series of works were composed there, not one of which leaves us indifferent, despite the circumstantial character of some of them.

First, the *Tango for Piano* (1940) and an arrangement for chorus and orchestra of the *Star Spangled Banner* (1941); much has been written concerning the latter, which even provoked the intervention of the Boston police, since Massachusetts state law forbids any arrangement of the national anthem. (Evidently, this law has never noticed, in all these years, Pinkerton's air in *Madam Butterfly*.) Then the year 1941–1942 gives us an important work, the *Danses Concertantes*, composed at the request of Mr. Werner Janssen, conductor of the Los Angeles Symphony Orchestra.*

Two years later this music was to serve as the basis for

---

* Mr. Janssen has retired from his position as conductor of the Los Angeles Symphony Orchestra since the writing of this book (translators' note).

a ballet of the same name. The abstract choreography of Georges Balachine and the admirable costumes and *décors* of Eugène Berman make it one of the gems of modern ballet.

The *Danses Concertantes* is composed for chamber orchestra, comprising one of each woodwind, two horns, a trumpet, a trombone, timpani, and strings; in its perceptive character, the work corresponds to the return to tradition of characteristic certain earlier works: it has the pleasing melodic quality of the *Jeu de Cartes,* the harmonic and rhythmic concentration of *L'Histoire du Soldat,* the pulsating complexity of the *Dumbarton Oaks Concerto,* the wealth of modulation of the *Symphony in C,* and yet retains the appearance of a new work in which no repetition is apparent.

As is often the case with Stravinsky, the theme of the first part, March-Introduction, is built upon conjunct notes of the scale, which turn upon themselves. The B flat major of the bass tonality finds itself "crossed" from the beginning by a play of the seventh, whose alteration from A to A flat causes the whole work to pivot between B flat major and the dominant of E flat major. Likewise, a fragment in G major, by the introduction of a counterpoint in the basses with an arpeggiated pattern (in which the D and altered D sharp serve either as the fifth of G or as the third of B), retains the atmosphere of equivocal tonality characteristic of the composer's tonal planes. The whole movement, which by the tranquillity of its conception also sometimes suggests *Pulcinella,* with its phrases suspended on a fourth sixteenth note, extended by a quarter note, has an immediately pleasing effect, so natural and easy does everything about it appear (example 10).

A *pas d'action* in song form opposes a rhythmic and

Ex. 10 Danses Concertantes, Movement III, Thème Varié
(Arranged for two Pianos)

resolute pattern, somewhat suggestive of the beginning of the finale of the *Symphony in C*, to a *meno mosso* of extreme tenderness, in which four divided violins overflow on a high pedal point of the flute and the clarinet, leading to a lovely modulation in G major, which itself is led into E major by the composer's favorite play on the third (example 9, see page 88).

A re-exposition of the first theme brings us to the third movement, Theme and Variations, exposed by the woodwinds. A suite of four variations: Allegretto, Scherzando, Andantino, and Tempo Giusto (in the style of a tarantella), with a never failing ingeniousness, and a resolute *pas d'action* bring about the restatement of the March-Conclusion.

The style of the *Danses Concertantes* is constantly interesting. We find here once more the composer's predilection for themes based on the use of the tonal arpeggio, already affirmed in the first measures of the *Capriccio*. The ambiguous play of the major and the minor third is here used with rare effectiveness, restricted as the composer is by the use of only three available notes.

This results not in the classic modulation of the third, which implies the passing from one tonality to another, but in a kind of balance between the two simultaneously maintained tonalities, a pivoting between the two that gives the developing melody its mobile and freely flexible character.

The faculty for modulation, properly speaking, manifests its richness to the full in the course of the work. We cited, earlier, the extract of the *pas d'action* as a small example of what Stravinsky can obtain in this direction, from a four-voice harmony, to find himself "elsewhere" very naturally.

The work is conceived as a suite of dance rhythms or dance movements, with no definite subject, and in which the music gives rise to the plastic movements of the human body. There is no action other than that proceeding from the formal planes of the music itself.

It is strange that the very character of certain themes in this work should, despite its instrumental conception, bring to mind the syllabic writing of the vocal works of the period of the *Pribaoutki*. The instruments seem to converse, to be inflected by virtue of a kind of phonetic of the melodic phrase.

The whole section following the exposition of the theme and variations gives this impression of a discursive language, with its departure on the weak eighth note, its short contrapuntal passages of conjunct sixteenths or repeated notes, its pizzicati, which, from time to time, accentuate a legato pattern of the basses (example 10, see page 243).

The orchestration of the *Danses Concertantes* is always based on a scoring opposing one group to another, as

Life and Works (1920–1948)

the beginning already illustrates. To the close melodic playing of the strings Stravinsky opposes the pattern of the bassoon limping on three notes, of which the B flat is ornamented, at the moment of coincidence, by the trombone and scanned by the timpani.

That same year, Stravinsky also composed two occasional works: *The Circus Polka for a Young Elephant,* commissioned by a circus for an elephant ballet—a burlesque, comical work, whose instrumentation accentuates Stravinsky's humorous side, instrumental and nonexpressive in origin, and which, in its peroration, superposes its development upon an unexpected intervention of Schubert's *Marche Militaire.* Then came the four charming *Norwegian Moods,* based upon popular themes: it is a witty, pleasing work, but has no importance in Stravinsky's production other than as an amusement, an occasional diversion.

XVII

The year 1942 gives us two new works, significant despite their relative brevity: *Ode* (Elegiac Song in Three Movements), and the short but striking *Sonata for Two Pianos,* so charming in the pure arrangement of its lines.

Ode was composed in the memory of Nathalie Koussevitsky, wife of the well-known conductor, Serge Koussevitsky (who, as founder of the Editions Musicales Russes, was, with his wife, Stravinsky's publisher for many years).

It is, therefore, the idea of an in memoriam that motivated the title *Ode* as well as the subtitles given to the movements comprising the work.

There is nothing in the elements of the *Ode* to remind one of the title dear to Pindar and Boileau. No rhetoric is mingled with its two outer movements, which are of a noble and serene quality. The first movement, Eulogy, presents a curious synthesis of chromatically melodic design with a clearly diatonic harmonic base.

The chords at the beginning suggest certain harmonic characteristics of the *Rite,* in the low register of the horns and the middle register of the trumpets. The chromatic melodic phrase of the strings develops in the atmosphere of a rich polyphony, sustained by a light pulsation of the horns, which maintain the tonal predominance.

This entire movement evolves without brilliance, in an atmosphere of evenness, whose seeming monotony contributes to an altogether inner and somewhat proud grandeur.

A second and livelier movement, rather in the atmosphere of a Weber "hunting song," with its horn calls, contains many curious harmonic details in which the composer's rich modulative imagination manifests itself.

But it is the last movement, Epitaph, that gives its particular emotive significance to the entire work by its element of calm, by the extreme economy of its means, and by the pure polyphony of two simple lines of the same timbre sharing different notes of the same phrase. The opening theme, exposed by the two flutes and the clarinet, constantly interrupted by the oboe and the bassoon, is striking in its serenity, and the whole movement, suggests by its atmosphere, a fragment of another in memoriam: the *Symphonies for Wind Instruments.*

Rarely has so much been said with so little. The transparency of the realization is the most impressive feature in this *Ode,* which will leave indifferent any auditor in need of startling brilliance to feel the power of its inwardness, and in which the "dull" factor of a deliberate monochromaticism contributes to its emotional weight.

XVIII

It is this same transparency carried to the extreme of fragility that we find again in the *Sonata for Two Pianos*. The very simplicity of its principle and of its structure gives it the appearance of an unimportant work. And yet, its substance is rich and its structure is extremely arresting.

But we have so taken the habit of confusing volume with content, and brilliancy with richness, that simplicity often impresses us as a lack of inventiveness or as a sign of poverty.

From this viewpoint, the *Sonata* strikes us as significant work, for, without having the importance of the symphonies or the *Danses Concertantes*, it presents a most revealing aspect of the artist's creativeness, in its fragile and carefully designed realization: the work displays but a single timbre, and in its polyphony the idea of contrasting timbres never interferes in a distracting manner.

Very concise—since its total duration corresponds more or less to that of one single movement of a contemporary sonata—it says in its three movements everything it has to say, and nothing more. It is a constructive laconism, and not the absence of inventiveness, which gives the *Sonata* its perfect balance, and a complete absence of prolixity.

The first movement of the *Sonata* is almost entirely based upon a contrapuntal superposition of melodic lines, evolving simultaneously upon the tonic and the dominant of F major and the dominants of F and C major (example 11).

By the ingenious device of alternating the B flat, the composer imperceptibly slips toward the tonic and the

Ex. 11 Sonata For Two Pianos, Movement I
Moderato (♩=63)

dominant of C major. This whole evolution is based upon a polyphony of four voices, with the intervention, from time to time, of a bass doubled in staccato. A modulation in E major brings us to a short transitional episode, within which fragments of the second theme, supported by a group of asymmetrically placed chords, leads to the second theme in F major, with a figuration of the dominant. The reappearance of the main theme, at first augmented and later in its original form, ends this movement in a harmonic combination of the horizontal planes of the tonic and the dominant.

The second movement is a theme and variations. The theme itself, of a Palestrinalike gravity, exposes a figuration in two voices around an inner *cantus firmus* in G major, to which is added the entrance of the low basses, thus displacing the *cantus* to a high register.

The first variation contrasts with the severity of the initial theme by a charming motif in D major, harmonized in G major. The seventh of D major, sometimes C sharp, sometimes altered to C natural, causes this entire variation to pivot in an ambiguity of tonic and dominant. In the following variation a pianistic style, born of the toccatas and the violin sonatas of Bach, frames a variant of the theme in staccato mordants displacing the tonal framework of D major.

The third variation is a fughetta in four voices in a fast and resolute tempo. The fourth variation, with its austere polyphony of two low voices, is unfolded over the resonance of the spacious harmonies of the first piano. These harmonies serve, so to speak, as converging poles toward an A, a fifth, as a pedal point. The disposition of augmented and diminished fourths and fifths sometimes reminds one of some patterns in the harmonic planes of *Le Rossignol.*

The finale is constructed in a combined rondo and song form. Its initial theme, as well as the middle trio, are of a Russian melodic character. This trio, with its singing theme in G major, develops with a curious inner figuration in D major, limping upon three conjunct notes, whose tonic sometimes leaps to the octave. A bridge of three measures, in a changing meter, with a sustained G pedal point, brings the recapitulation of the initial movement in its tonality of B flat, "squinting" toward F major, and, as in the first movement, the four voices are resolved in a harmonic aggregate of tonic-dominant, thus giving the key to the technical problem of the entire work.

XIX

Stravinsky has of late been requested more and more frequently to conduct his works in most of the musical centers of the United States and Canada. It seems interesting to me to consider his career as a conductor somewhat more closely.

The world of music remembers the debut of Stravinsky in that role in Paris (*Ragtime,* the *Symphony of Psalms,* the *Dumbarton Oaks Concerto,* etc.). These beginnings were rhythmically precise and sure, but technically awkward, for the composer's intentions never were fully realized, due to a lack of experience in the organizing of the sonorous planes and the dynamic elaboration, in short, of a sufficient knowledge of the rules of the game, which serve as a point of contact between the conductor and his ensemble.

In this regard, we are surprised by the metamorphosis accomplished by Stravinsky by virtue of experience and especially of arduous work, as well as of an undoubted gift as a leader. I had the opportunity to hear in the United States several of his renditions of former works, and all of his first performances of recent works, and I have the impression that no one knows better than the composer how to obtain that fidelity, that security of the ensemble joined to a solicitude for details, and that undefinable atmosphere of authenticity that comes of inner conviction.

I made this little digression because this victory, due to a voluntary discipline—this acqusition of the conductor's craft, with all its indispensable little tricks—is very characteristic of Stravinsky's genius, in that it implies application, a desire to do things thoroughly, and a loathing for amateurish approximation.

Stravinsky conducts with the same constant lucidity as he composes. He is concerned with realizing exactly what he has put into his music, for he considers, as we have already said, that what he has put into a work corresponds exactly to his intentions, and that every interpretive element, seeking to bring to it a subjective conception, goes beyond the composer's indications, and necessarily falsifies the authenticity of the work.

Consequently, for Stravinsky, the truly great interpreter is one who, after having penetrated a work with regard to the composer's intentions, knows how to limit his personal role to that of the precise intermediary between the creative message and the perceiving agent—the auditor. Stravinsky's views on this question, so thorny and delicate, have, as we know, been clearly exposed in his theoretical writings. But I have had many occasions to observe to what extent he remains faithful to them on the practical plane, and with what professional conscientiousness he applies them to his own performances.

XX

The year 1944 gives us, first, three works of small dimensions: *Scherzo à la Russe*, *Babel*, and *Elegie for Viola or Violin Solo*, and, later, the *Scènes de Ballet*.

But the future *Symphony in Three Movements* was already in gestation, Stravinsky having worked on sketches of the first movement several years earlier. In 1942, he already was able to play for me (with instrumental annotations) fragments from it, not only sectioned off, but also considerably developed, and later to be entirely integrated into the first movement.

At that time, Stravinsky thought of including this material in a symphonic work with a piano concertant. But later on he became aware of other problems, from the constructive as well as from the instrumental point of view: the problem of the unified timbre of legato and staccato produced by the opposition of the piano and the harp, that of the elements of the "concertini" etc.

XXI

The *Scherzo à la Russe* was composed at the request of Paul Whiteman, the famous promoter of symphonic jazz, which had given birth to the *Rhapsody in Blue* of the late George Gershwin. If it is true that Paul Whiteman is partially responsible for the discovery of George Gershwin, he seems to have been a little late in his discovery of Igor Stravinsky.

The Russian quality of this short *Scherzo*, like that of certain parts of the *Sonata for Two Pianos,* has nothing of the brilliant and dynamic character of the *Rite* or *Les Noces,* or of the Orientalism of the *Firebird.* The Russian quality here is amiable and placid, and recalls by its infectiousness certain turns of the airs in *Mavra.*

Here, on a plane freed of any harmonic surcharge, the smooth and unconstrained material is developed, ornamented by delightful modulations, in an orchestral frame that does not try to be picturesque, but is replete with well-imagined piquancies. The work is related by the directness of its conception to the *Norwegian Moods.*

The *Babel Cantata* represents a fragment of a collective work, based upon extracts from Genesis. Each chapter was written by a different composer, upon the request of Nathaniel Shilkret, who commissioned the work. The work as a whole, for orchestra, chorus, and narrator, is subdivided in the following manner: *Prologue,* by Arnold Schoenberg; *The Creation,* by Nathaniel Shilkret; *The Fall of Man,* by Alexandre Tansman; *Cain and Abel,* by Darius Milhaud; *The Deluge,* by Mario Castelnuovo-Te-

Life and Works (1920–1948) 253

desco; *The Message,* by Ernest Toch; and *Babel,* by Igor Stravinsky. Other movements by Béla Bartók, Paul Hindemith, and Serge Prokofieff were expected, and were later to be integrated in this suite.

The ensemble of the work was given its first performance at Los Angeles in October, 1946, under the direction of Werner Janssen.

As we have already indicated, *Babel* has no evocative or illustrative aim whatever, and is developed upon a purely abstract plane.

The work opens with a slow pattern in eighth notes of the violoncellos and the contrabasses, somewhat suggestive of the opening measures of the *Firebird.* Little by little, a quasi-static progression begins to develop around harmonies based upon a diminished fifth, two minor thirds, and a minor second, over the somber background of the pizzicati basses, which gradually brighten.

The construction of the tower corresponds chronologically to a fugal fragment, whose mobile, architectonic character, as each voice makes a way for itself as it enters, produces a parallelism of constructive thought without expressive imagery.

The core around which this polyphonic progression radiates is the tower, the chaos bringing on the apparition of the voice of the Eternal as a "quotation." This quotation, as we have said, is exposed by the chorus.

A lively fragment, though devoid of cinematographic violence—a device that would have tempted many other musicians at the point when the tower is destroyed—brings us back to the status quo of the beginning. The entire work, whose duration is about seven minutes, is in a very strict form. The part leading to the fugue impresses me particularly as having great beauty. It is related in its "static" motion, though upon another plane, to the end of the *Symphony in C,* with a sort of greater tension, and a more ascending direction, which gives the fragment more intensity and less serenity.

The *Elegie for Solo Viola or Violin,* was composed in the memory of Alphonse Onnou, member and founder of the famous Pro-Arte Quartet of Brussels, an ensemble to which our whole generation of musicians owes a debt of gratitude.

The instrumental problem Stravinsky had to solve in this short work is the same as the one Bach proposed himself in the *Unaccompanied Violin and Cello Sonatas:* that of a balance of polyphonic lines developing within the limited register of four strings, with regard to the position of the fingers upon the strings as well as to the unity of the timbre, the realization of the ensemble taking place in the setting of a simultaneous, legato attack.

In view of the elegiac character of the piece, Stravinsky considered it important to avoid any brusque attack of the arpeggio made necessary by the harmonies. He reduced his polyphony to two voices, but by displacing the registers, he succeeded in avoiding the monotony of a final stabilization of two adjacent strings, and thus created the illusion of a multiple counterpoint.

The *Elegie* is constructed in song form. The two outer movements in F major, with constant alterations of the third and the sixth, develop upon an equivocal tonal framework, leaning strongly, however, toward the principal tonality. A generous melodic line, moving in its tranquillity, is placed contrapuntally against an arpeggiated pattern that leads it through several harmonic pitfalls. A monodic bridge leads to a very effectively written fugal fragment, and then returns to the identical recapitulation of the main theme.

Life and Works (1920–1948)

The whole piece, with its sober lines of "a slow two-part invention," is bathed in serenity and peacefulness.

XXII

The origin of the *Scènes de Ballet* is of a rather particular character. The work was composed as a part of a spectacle, commissioned by Broadway's greatest producer, Billy Rose. It dealt with an apotheosis of the five living arts. Stravinsky was asked to write the music for a classic ballet in the style of *Giselle*, though without any definite subject.

It was to be, then, a suite of connected musical numbers that could serve for plastic evolutions, with a plot to be determined later.

I have until now abstained as much as possible from telling anecdotes. But a rather humorous incident is related to the first performance of these *Scènes de Ballet* —an incident confirming a manner of thinking very characteristic of certain artistic circles, and of which, unfortunately, neither the United States nor even Broadway or Hollywood have a monopoly.

I do not think I would be lacking in discretion in relating this little anecdote.

It is the custom in the United States to precede the first performance of a work in New York by a preview in some less important center. This preview helps to refine the performance, to make certain practical changes, and, above all, to anticipate the reaction of the public. Assuming the existence of a standardized taste in the entire country, the producers consider that this test reflects the collective taste of the public, and therefore, the very worth of the work.

Thus, the entire spectacle was performed for the first time in Philadelphia, including the *Scènes de Ballet* in its choreographic form, which represented the type of "great music."

After this preview, Stravinsky received a telegram from the managers, which he immediately read to me over the telephone. The telegram was worded somewhat in this manner: "Great success. Could be sensational if you authorize the arranger, Mr. X, to add some details to the orchestration. Mr. X arranges even the works of Cole Porter. Wire if agreed."

This telegram is now among the framed souvenirs in Stravinsky's workroom. The composer's reply was as laconic as it was concrete: "I am satisfied with great success. Igor Stravinsky."

I do not think that the promoters of this sensational spectacle ever understood why Stravinsky lacked ambition to the extent of denying himself a sensational success, so easily obtainable with the help of a few little changes by such a famous arranger, who orchestrates *even* for Mr. Cole Porter!

The *Scènes de Ballet* (of which an excellent recording was recently made under the composer's direction) was conceived according to the same plastic plan as the *Danses Concertantes*. The work comprises the following movements: Introduction, Dances (*corps de ballet*), Variation of the Ballerina, Pantomime, *Pas de Deux*, Second Pantomime, Variation of the Dancer, Variation of the Ballerina, Dances (*corps de ballet*), and Apotheosis. Any indication of a relationship to a fixed text is eliminated from the musical conception of the work.

The short, slow Introduction exposes in five-eighths rhythm a melodic pattern of the violas, violoncellos, and contrabasses, with a third alternating in major and minor, against the harmonic background of two horns. This pattern, interrupted by brutal caesuras, leads to the second movement where the same manipulation governs a new tonal plan: an inversion of the position of the arpeggio having now displaced the third, it is the alteration of D to D sharp that is substituted for that of B to B flat.

After a horn solo in B major, progressing to the accompaniment of a string ensemble in alternating B major and B minor, a lovely, lyrical theme, seemingly suspended, in mid-air, appears in the strings. It is supported by an arpeggiated play of the woodwinds and a rhythmic framework of the horns and the timpani.

A short reprise introduces a new and discursive episode, exposed by the two oboes against a pulsating background of the strings. Thanks to its thematic unity, this movement resembles a miniature of the great variation form, treated with rare skill. The pulsating element serves as a bridge introducing the Dance of the Ballerina in a six-eighths meter frequently combining the ternary and binary measures.

The first Pantomime begins with sustained harmonies of the woodwinds, further accented by the unfolded arpeggios of the strings, and leads to an andantino, of a typically "tiptoe dance" character, with the leaps accentuated by the oboes and the flute stepping over a light pulsation of the strings.

The *Pas de Deux* marks the appearance of a deliberately pompous theme, exposed by the trumpet against a counterpoint of the horn. A short allegretto is used as an intermezzo, and the theme reappears, accompanied this time in the manner best suited to its pseudopathetic character: tremolos of the low strings and broad chords in triplets at the piano.

The second Pantomime is resolute and alert. To a

rhythm of dotted eighths in the melodic design, it opposes one of two sixteenths on the strong beats and a syncope of the divided basses in *arco* and pizzicato (a rhythmic pattern somewhat related to certain Brahmsian conceptions).

A variation of the Dancer, direct and determined, is followed by that of the Ballerina, in which an enchanting melodic design of the second violins finds its way against a tonal harmonic background in D major in an ingenious and supple rhythm.

The new Pantomime (a variant of the theme formerly given out by the trumpet, but exposed this time by the violins) is linked to a new and lively evolution of the *corps de ballet*.

A masterly Apotheosis, in which a wonderful use of the resources of the old devices of the tremolo and the trill results in an impressively novel and forceful effect (with its "struck" harmonies supporting a syncopated pattern of the woodwinds in a strict counterpoint in the opposite direction), closes this magnificent suite, rich in substance, and of a realization as new as it is well balanced.

XXIII

Two works mark Stravinsky's production for the year 1945. The abyss separating their practical *prétextes* is rather significant. I can testify that the composer worked at each one of them with the same severity, the same gusto, and the same seeking after perfection in their realization.

They are the *Ebony Concerto,* composed at the request of Woody Herman for his jazz orchestra, and the *Symphony in Three Movements,* composed at the request of the New York Philharmonic Orchestra. The *Symphony* shortly precedes the *Concerto.*

Life and Works (1920–1948)

In many ways, the *Concerto* caused Stravinsky more concern than the *Symphony*. For to the composer's purely personal problems were added here his almost total ignorance of the functioning of a jazz band, as well as of the use of a whole set of instruments of which he had never availed himself until that time: the guitar, the entire saxophone family, a specific battery, and finally, a whole collection of instrumental devices that are part of the stylistic idiom of the jazz band.

It was with as much surprise as intense admiration that I saw the greatest composer of our time, as well as one of the greatest of all time, humbly applying himself to this new problem, like a student at the Conservatoire, seeking to extract from it all its latent possibilities, and working at it with the same conscientious application that he had given a few months before to his *Symphony*, a capital work in his recent production and one of the summits of his art.

That is when I clearly realized *de visu*, that Igor Stravinsky is not only the greatest musician of our time, but the greatest artist as well.

I went back to the period of the Florentine Renaissance, and thought of the hesitations, of the mystical and æsthetic revolts of Giovanni Beltraffio, while he watched Leonardo da Vinci working with the same earnestness and profundity at the painting of the head of Christ or of an Apostle of the "Last Supper," as at the solution of an acoustical problem, a botanical phenomenon, or the expression of a human grimace in its various manifestations.

For the Florentine painter, too, it was the attitude that counted above all, the human contribution to what nature has offered there as a potential gift, the concrete source as a basis for the artifice of the creator.

The composer's problem in the *Ebony Concerto* was, then, to take hold of and to adopt something without adapting himself, to integrate without assimilating. From that point of view, and without giving this work an exaggerated importance, the *Concerto* is a perfect achievement, a problem solved within the restraints imposed by circumstances upon the creator, with no surrender of the latter's personality.

The *Ebony Concerto* is undoubtedly a work in jazz style, just as *Pulcinella* was Pergolesian. Yet it is as authentically Stravinsky's as *Pulcinella*.

The jazz formula here has nothing in common with the rhythmic dislocation of the *Ragtime* or the *Piano Rag Music*, where it sometimes results in the annihilation or the disintegration of the bar line.

On the contrary, it is the melodic material here that defines the rhythmic movement. The latter, despite its diversity, its hiatus, or its syncopated re-entries, never loses its metric bearing, like a metronome beating only intermittently, but making one aware nevertheless of the organized regularity of its pulsation.

The work is also curious in that the composer, despite the novelty of his problem, obtains new sonorities, even in the jazz idiom, thanks to a rare intuition for the careful distribution and contrasting of timbres, so that he enriches a language that he was supposed to have assimilated as a ready-made form with discoveries in this reserved domain worthy of a Duke Ellington.

The *Ebony Concerto* is pleasing throughout. It abounds in those ingenious and original modulations of which we have already found many examples in the *Dumbarton Oaks Concerto* and in the *Danses Concertantes*, suggesting it sometimes by the thematic design or the rhythm, which seems interrupted but never becomes dislocated.

The clarinet is given a somewhat concertizing part, since Woody Herman is a virtuoso of that instrument, very popular in that musical milieu.

It is more than evident that, by comparison with the *Symphony in Three Movements,* about to be analyzed, the *Ebony Concerto* should be considered as a musical amusement. But, as we have observed, this seeming amusement is the result of careful work on the part of an artist who considers nothing easy or of minor importance, but who devotes himself to each problem with the same discipline, without distinction among the sources of the works undertaken. With Igor Stravinsky, nothing is ever taken for granted.

XXIV

The *Symphony in Three Movements* is the last work to be considered here, since our knowledge of Stravinsky's work stops with this composition.

I have already mentioned the beautiful "Gloria" worked at intermittently by Stravinsky in 1946, before my return to Europe. Since then, two new works that I have not as yet been able to hear or to read have been added to the composer's list.

The first is a *Concerto for String Orchestra,* composed at the end of 1946 at the request of Paul Sacher for the jubilee of his string ensemble of Basel. The work was performed at Basel, some time ago, under Paul Sacher's direction.

The second is a new ballet, *Orpheus,* whose first performance by the choreographer Georges Balanchine was expected in New York for that season. In September, 1947, Stravinsky wrote me that the work was almost finished. I presume, therefore, that it was finished at the moment of this writing.

It is, then, with the *Symphony in Three Movements* that we must close our work for the moment, even if we must later add analyses of works to come.

I consider this opus as a sum of Stravinsky's work. It touches upon all the phases of the composer's artistic evolution, without being in the least a repetition or a recapitulation. The *Symphony* preserves the aspect of an absolutely new composition, and contains a wealth of material that could be the source of numerous developments. It is an achievement, perfect in the maturity of the thought it expresses and the firmness of its construction; a work remarkable in its youthfulness and vitality, rich in substance and inexhaustible in its movement. In this work all the "apparent Stravinskys" meet each other through a new Stravinsky in a concentrated creative harmony. Like a pillar, it supports, with its perfection, an evolution that is logical but many sided: *Petrouchka*, the *Rite*, *Les Noces*, *L'Histoire du Soldat*, *Oedipus-Rex*, *Apollon*, the *Symphony of Psalms*, and the *Symphony in C*. It is the master column of that harmonious edifice that Igor Stravinsky built with his musical works.

One must have misunderstood the musical phenomenon of Stravinsky completely, and partly, as well, the musical phenomenon in general, to see, as is the case with certain critics, only repetition and a return to certain earlier techniques in what constitutes a definite confirmation of the creative unity of this rich personality, embraces his most salient characteristics, touches upon all the implied facets of his evolution, and culminates in a masterpiece of striking originality and independence.

Life and Works (1920–1948)   263

What an admirable answer the creative presence in this symphony offers to those who try with as much incompetence as bad faith to detect some weakening of the composer's creative faculty!

With what conviction and serenity this work affirms in each one of its notes, "I am still here, and now more than ever!" With what rare mastery it codifies Stravinsky's whole contribution to our art, over a period of forty years, only to start out again toward new discoveries—for this work is at once a summing up and a new departure.

The interdependence of all the component factors of the material and the craftsmanship results in this symphony in an unprecedented success. The sureness of the realization might cause one to believe that the composer posed himself only one problem: the avoidance of any deviation from his creative thought.

This impression, of course, is altogether false, for never was the composer's musical thought filtered with such lucidity, with such discrimination between the indispensable and the superfluous, a conciseness as eloquent and a more discerning distribution of his riches. As we have said, Stravinsky's presence is manifested here with incontestable identity, in a purely positive manner, and with nothing retrospective. The work, in its novelty, is thus related to diverse organic manifestations of Stravinsky's art. It ties together all the denominators common to the various stages of his path as an artist. It makes use of many factors, latent until now, and here manifesting themselves in full force.

By its points of contact, the *Symphony in Three Movements* has the eruptive explosiveness and the breathtaking pulsation of certain fragments of the *Rite of Spring*, the active rhythmic movement of *Petrouchka* and *Les Noces*, the constant charm of the melodic spontaneity of the *Jeu de Cartes*, the lightness and animation of the *Octet* or the *Capriccio*, the astonishing plasticity of the timbres for which the utilization in concertino of diverse groups originates in *L'Histoire du Soldat*, the moving tension of the *Symphony of Psalms*, the peaceful serenity of the *Apollon-Musagète*, the solid construction of the concerti and of the Symphony in C, and finally the discursive virulence of the *Concerto for Two Pianos*.

It possesses the stylistic unity necessary for all those elements which, while expressing themselves in a language characteristic of Stravinsky's method, combine for the realization of a definitive and fresh work.

Explosive as a cannon ball at the summit of an ascending scale, the unison of the first theme of the opening allegro asserts itself, from the outset, with direct violence. It seems difficult to classify the melodic morphology of this theme, to relate it to some known type of Stravinskyan melody. Upon first glance, its markedly graphic appearance brings to mind the *Capriccio* with its skipping intervals, and the *Octet*. And yet the intense and almost dramatic character of its lyricism reveals a note seldom perceived until then in Stravinsky's themes.

Exposed by the strings in unison, the horns, and the piano, the pattern is continued by the wind instruments, while the strings scan the weak accents, with strident harmonies of simultaneous major and minor thirds, creating a diversity of rhythm by virtue of an application of the "melodic syncope" (example 2, see page 72).

Leaning upon the notes of the second and fourth beats of the theme, this scansion is resolved in a subsidiary melodic pattern, determining by its composition the entire development that follows (example 12).

The inner activity of the ascending scales maintains, as in a certain variation of the *Octet*, a magnetic tension

Life and Works (1920–1948)

Ex. 12 Symphony in Three Movements, Movement I

toward the A flat, the sustained supporting note of the thematic design.

From the initial play of the thirds arises the theme unifying the whole movement in a deployed arpeggio, with omitted fifth, exposed at first by the horns and later taken up by the trumpet. The workmanship of this theme is familiar to us since the *Capriccio:* its conception of the tonic harmony, spread out by alternating thirds, runs through almost all of Stravinsky's recent production, while its purely harmonic character already illustrated the style of the *Rite* and the *Rossignol* (example 7, see page 83).

Passing through a sort of basso ostinato, it leads to a pulsating and dramatic rhythmic development that, with its pizzicato eighth notes and its ornamented triplets of the strings and the piano, recalls somewhat the atmosphere of the "Danse Sacrale," though on an altogether different plane.

To the moving pedal point of the basses, creating a second derivative mobility by the alternation of the binary and ternary measures, and to its purely mechanical action, is added an organic, respiratory rhythm, contributing an increasingly lively element to the re-entrance of the woodwinds and the horns.

Stravinsky imparts a new aspect to this thematic disposition found again, in various forms, in several of his earlier works. It is not an arbitrary invention, but a traditional method employed since J. S. Bach. Closer to us, Brahms uses it with telling effect in the first movement of his Third Symphony in F, by opposing to the F major of the theme, an apparent F minor of the basses (the A flat of the design being harmonized as a diminished seventh). Here, too, this process is based upon an arpeggiated theme with omitted fifth: F, A flat, F.

It is around this same problem of a spread-out theme and a constant play of major and minor—whether it is through an alternation of the thirds of the horizontal pattern, or a superposition of two tonics, or, finally, a clear, simultaneous opposition of a major theme to its minor, that the conception of the harmonic plane of this movement evolves, and even, to a certain extent, the entire symphony, though, of course, the plane of construction and realization is entirely different from that of Brahms.

We might cite numerous examples of this tendency, manifesting itself in the technical analysis of the work without ever being noticeable or obsessive upon hearing.

It is a "pillar" about which the harmonic architecture of the work radiates, but an internal pillar traversing the entire edifice, supporting and unifying it by the same constraint (example 2, see page 72).

Thus, in the first episode of the development, the pedal point of the basses could just as well be A minor as F major, but the superposition of the higher pedal point, exposing the dominants of A flat and F major, directs the entire tonality toward the latter, because of the simultaneity of tonic and dominant.

This arpeggiated movement is contracted, as is the fragment of the first superposed theme, to the interval of the third, and finally results in a repeated note. The

Life and Works (1920–1948)

theme is then taken up again with a scalar movement of the basses and the bassoons, in eighths, still ornamented by the syncope of the violins and the violas, and leads to a new variant, in three-fourths meter, of the arpeggiated tonal episode. This arrangement, directed in an atmosphere of progressive modulation toward a constant harmonic renewal, is reabsorbed into a progression of strident harmonies, then originating in a new phase of the development.

A rhythmic pattern of the horns (the G major chord), whose obsessive repetition is somewhat suggestive of certain planes of the *Danses Concertantes,* is the source of a series of concertini, in which the groups, as though brought up to a platform, oppose their respective timbres in a transparent but rigorous polyphony.

The piano introduces its metallic timbre in ingenious "two-part inventions," dividing or unifying the groups of the woodwinds and the strings, with watchful reminders of the rhythmic harmonies of the three horns.

In a development of broad scope there appears a new episode of the link, in which, upon an astonishing double ostinato of the violins and the piano, the woodwinds introduce a theme in three-eighths with a diverting intervention in three-sixteenths, displacing its point of departure, and leading to the return of the earlier ostinato episode in G major (example 13).

A concise re-exposition of the thematic material leads back, by a dynamic diminuendo (not one of volume) to the rhythm of the repeated note in the basses, finally to resolve itself into a clarinet solo over a sustained harmony.

The construction of this Allegro follows the sonata form rather strictly, but is more closely related, this time, to the Beethovenian conception, particularly of the first Allegro of the Fifth Symphony.

Ex. 13 Symphony in Three Movements, Movement I

The mastery and the originality with which Stravinsky treats this large form by integrating it completely with its own substance is very Beethovenian in a spiritual way as well, despite the absolute classicism of the composer's æsthetic attitude.

The second movement, Andante, opposes, from the first measure, its melodic D major to a D minor of the basses (example 8, see page 86).

The division of the contrabasses into *arco* and pizzicato emphasizes this modal doubling by a percussive scansion. It is not the main theme of this movement, constructed in song form, but a melodic and harmonic introduction, serving it as an introduction and a background. The theme, simple and lyrical as a theme of the *Jeu de Cartes*, is exposed by the flute, and travels in its evolution through all the registers of the instrument. It finally arrives at the fundamental D, where it is stabilized in opposition to the buzzing of the clarinets in the low register.

Passing from the binary to the ternary, through a garland of figurations characteristic of the Lento of the *Capriccio,* it encounters the element of the repeated notes of the first movement, which had already manifested their pulsating presence in the introduction. A suite of concertini, in which the harp intervenes with its resonant timbre, in combination with either the woodwinds or the strings, leads to a lyric episode of great beauty, with its four solo violins, two solo violas, and the harp, related by its sweet and peaceful tenderness to that of the *pas d'action* of the *Danses Concertantes.*

This episode serves as a transitional bridge to a Piu Mosso (Trio of the Song), of really pathetic character and a very chamber-music-like conception. The concertini of the particular groups are unified here by the timbre of the harp, used as a polyphonic and not as an arpeggiating or glissando instrument. An ingenious harmonic transition of three measures leads to the restatement of the main theme in its original bimodal aspect. An ascending scale, finishing upon its extended sixteenth, as on a suspended breath, gently closes this tender and moving piece.

An *attacca* interlude links the slow movement with the Finale. It consists in seven measures of chords, whose pattern in seconds and rhythmic design is related to the lyric episode of the Andante, and whose harmonic substance is reabsorbed in a dominant chord (with anticipation of the tonic) of D major, bursting forth with assurance in the *con moto* Finale.

Explosive and as if liberated, this Finale, in spite of its moments of quiet and peacefulness, is one of the most violent, rhythmically unfettered pages written by Stravinsky since the *Rite of Spring.*

Built upon the organic linking of the various episodes,

and carried away by the unity of the movement, which rules as master, the Finale adopts that form of fragmentary opposition always handled successfully by Stravinsky.

Exposed once more from a bimodal aspect, and accented by the downward motion of the basses with their alternating thirds, the movement, after a theme based upon entirely developed arpeggios, takes on an episode based upon three conjunct notes turning upon themselves, leading to a short new outburst that stops abruptly upon reaching its goal (example 5, see page 77).

The timbres of the piano and the harp, each of them making an individual contribution to preceding movements, intervene here in a compact block and create a group of struck and plucked chords, resulting in a metallic sonority of prolonged resonance. An episode in the form of a concertino of two bassoons—whose apparent unison is partially ornamented by a minor second that encroaches from above or below and produces a rhythmic rather than melodic polyphony—changes gradually into a new episode opposing the piano, the harp, the first violins, and the contrabasses in a play of a bimodal G unequivocal in its direct affirmation. This device is an identical repetition of the ostinato figure in the first movement.

A variant of the preceding episode in conjunct notes reappears in a concertino for solo string trio, against a background of the piano and clarinets. The strings playing tutti link this episode to the next one by means of a short bridge in B major–minor, whose pattern, taken up again by the harp, leads back, after a breathless, pulsating passage, to a new fragmentary aspect of the theme. A short fragment, serving as an interlude, introduces a fugal variant very curious in its construction and its instrumental disposition (exposition by the trombone and piano, then by the harp), resulting, by the birth of a new metric cut, in a coda extraordinarily violent in rhythm and timbre. Like the *Scènes de Ballet*, the work closes with striking sonorities, arrived at by an astonishing treatment of the old device of the tremolo of the clarinets and the horns, with the stress of the note upon the octave against a moving background of deployed basses, in the strikingly forceful atmosphere of a resonating block.

XXV

I had intended to avoid, as much as possible, the excessive use of overtechnical terms that might make the reading too arduous and thereby cause the reader's attention to dwell upon details at the expense of the whole.

I have often observed how an analysis overladen with details results in an effect opposite to that which it intends, and makes the assimilation of the ensemble more difficult even for a professional musician.

And yet it seemed indispensable to analyze technically a work where details play such an important part, and where the elaboration of the clearly self-imposed problem is sometimes predetermining. I have limited myself to details whose omission would render the very understanding of the work doubtful and of which a knowledge might be taken for granted in the case of readers somewhat advanced in the study of harmony.

We have insisted upon the particular interdependence of the component factors in Stravinsky's working methods, upon that interpenetration as a result of which each one of these factors determines the others, in particular or as a whole. We were thus led to speak of harmonic melodies, melodic rhythms, of harmonies spread out thematically, and of rhythmic melodies.

For the composer's craftsmanship omits nothing, indeed, all the latent possibilities of an idea, of a phrase, a chord, or a metric cut are examined, weighed, and utilized after having been filtered. The composer meticulously analyzes all the wealth that a melodic pattern might offer him in the shifting of the harmonic modulation.

Let us take a characteristic example with a simple thematic contour, frequent with Stravinsky: a deployed major arpeggio with fifth omitted: C-E-C.

The very inflection of the pattern is inherent in the composer's phrasing, not only by the nature of the tones, but by his predilection for the inversion of lower adjacent tone to the octave (as the second to the seventh, the third to the sixth, the unison to the octave, etc.).

Every one of the tones in this pattern, C-E-C, is considered as a possible pivot for a modulation. Even without the use of enharmonics, the theme, as a whole, can be a part of many tonal combinations: C major or A minor, the major eleventh of C minor, the altered eleventh of E flat, the altered seventh of the fifth of D flat, the thirteenth of C major, the dominant of B major or minor with altered fifth; the seventh of the first degree of F major, the thirteenth of A minor; the eleventh of G major or minor etc.

We see then what the simple melodic device of a major third, considered with regard to its harmonic possibilities, can offer in the way of variously directed modulations. A practically unlimited field is thus opened to the intuitive and perspicacious organization of Stravinsky, who knows how to extract from it every possible meaning and to use it in an intelligent synthesis.

The chief characteristic of the composer's method is the fact that his work in discovering the concrete element that he uses as musical material is never done according to intellectual pedantry or haphazard discoveries. It always remains upon the higher plane of the intelligence analyzing, extracting, filtering, measuring, polishing, and co-ordinating, in the joy of creating a balanced organism out of these discoveries.

One might say that each sound presents itself to Stravinsky's imagination with the whole series of its harmonics, each melodic design with its modulatory possibilities, each chord with its melodic deployment, each rhythm with the potentialities of dynamic and chronic movement that the author is called upon to direct.

We know well that this is only an image and that all these details find their place after much arduous work, but the result leads us to believe it, and that is what counts. The musical cuisine can be appreciated only after analysis, particularly in the case of Stravinsky, who considers it important to offer us the result and not the source.

Thus, for many, the evolution of Stravinsky's art might appear arid and thankless in its deliberate renunciation of every external appeal, of what tries above all to please. Stravinsky himself in his *Chroniques* answers his critics, in a manner as meaningful as it is moving:

"I shall never be seen sacrificing that which I love and to which I aspire to satisfy the claims of people who, in their blindness, are not even aware that they are inviting me to go backward.

"Let it be well understood! What they want is obsolete for me, and to follow them would be to do violence to myself. . . . I do not know what tomorrow will bring. I can only be aware of what is true for me today. That is the truth which I am called upon to serve, and I serve it with full consciousness."

Conclusion

HAVING arrived at the end of this work, I am perfectly aware of the extent to which it seems to have been conceived in the form of a eulogy.

As I observed at the beginning, there would be no valid reason to undertake this work if it were not inevitably to lead to such a conclusion. But what is of importance here is that this conclusion is based only upon the concrete elements constituting the real value of a body of works, judged in accordance with its own quality and in function of the artistic aspirations peculiar to the composer and to him alone.

This work, then, has nothing to do with an analysis based upon subjective admiration, or with a necessary affinity of tendency or affiliation of school. On the contrary! I have explained with all possible frankness where the lesson ends and the influence begins—that is to say, the extent to which Stravinsky's luminous example could and should be followed as a discipline and as an artistic attitude enriching every genuine personality and helping it to express itself. I have also remarked to what extent indiscreet prowling around this powerful and overwhelming personality or imitation of his style would be equivalent to unconditional surrender.

Intelligence and a creative gift are not acquired, and intelligence is part of the gift. What can be learned is the manner of applying intelligence to one's gift, the way of putting it to work and of causing it to order and organize the manifestation of the gift. It is from this point of view, as a law of a general order, that Stravinsky's lesson can prove particularly fruitful.

It is, above all, as we have said, the fact of having imparted a human quality to the source of musical creation, of having brought it back among men, far from the misty realm where the absence of control was bringing about the absence of order, of having returned human craft to art as one of its component factors, and of having organized his material by following the rules and laws established by tradition, that makes Stravinsky the greatest artist of our time. It is here that his luminous example can have the greatest influence.

It is the importance of the body of his own works that gives Stravinsky a place among the greatest musicians of all time. Here he must be left alone, for he belongs to history. For my part, I consider it a rare privilege to have lived for more than four years close to him, to his work, and to his method. I think that this intimacy has helped me to draw from Stravinsky's example only what was of use to me to remain myself.

It is, then, from the conscious viewpoint of intelligence that we must make contact with Stravinsky's art. Intelligence precludes imitation. Only ignorance is servile and passive.

The sensitive reaction to Stravinsky's art, as to all art, is certainly not the result of an act of the will. It exists or it

Conclusion 277

does not exist, and we are not responsible for it. But to react, we must be in possession of everything that perception demands of an æsthetic reaction, and, at the same time, we must be free of all the extra-artistic rubbish encumbering it.

Stravinsky helps us to arrive, with greater ease and conviction, at this unadorned æsthetic reaction, free from the artificial postulates of a facile subjectivism applying the criteria of personal taste to the definition of musical value.

The lesson of Stravinsky will thus make it possible for each one of us to express himself according to his own personality and nature, in the same way that each one avails himself of the universal conventions of tempo, the bar line, chromatic accidentals, instruments, and registers.

It is, then, with the expression of an objective admiration for his genius, as well as of a tender and faithful personal affection, that I close this humble work, dedicated to a universal artist and a complete man: Igor Stravinsky.

PARIS, LONDON, PORTO D'ISCHIA (NAPLES).
May–September 1947

Chronological Catalogue of Works

Title	Publisher	Date
Symphony in E Flat	Jurgenson-Schott	1906–1907
Le Faune et la Bergère, for Voice and Orchestra	Belaieff	1906–1907
Scherzo Fantastique, for Orchestra	Jurgenson-Schott	1907–1908
Feu d'Artifice, Fantasy for Orchestra	Schott	1907–1908
Three Songs, for Voice and Piano Novice, Sainte Rosée (text by S. Gorodetsky) Pastorale (without words)	Jurgenson	1908
Four Études, for Piano	Jurgenson	1908
The Firebird, Choreographic Tale	Jurgenson-Schott	1909–1910
Two Songs (text by Paul Verlaine)	Jurgenson	1910
Petrouchka, Burlesque Scenes in Four Parts	Edition Russe	1910–1911
Le Roi des Etoiles, Cantata for Chorus and	Jurgenson	1911

Title	Publisher	Date
Orchestra (text by C. Balmont)		
Two Songs (text by C. Balmont)	Jurgenson	1911
The Rite of Spring, Choreographic Scenes of Pagan Russia	Edition Russe	1912–1913
Three Japanese Lyrical Poems, for Voice and Small Instrumental Ensemble	Edition Russe	1913
Souvenirs of My Childhood, Three Little Songs for Voice and Piano	Edition Russe	1913
Le Rossignol, Lyric Tale in Three Scenes	Edition Russe	1908–1914
Three Pieces for String Quartet	Edition Russe	1914
Pribaoutki (Pleasant Songs), Four Songs for Voice and Small Ensemble	Edition Russe	1914
Three Easy Pieces for Piano Four Hands (Second Grade) (March, Waltz, Polka)	Chester	1915
Three Stories for Children, for Voice and Piano (Tilim-Boum, Song of the Bear, Lullaby)	Chester	1915
Berceuses du Chat, for Voice and Three Clarinets	Edition Russe	1915–1916
Four A Cappella Choruses, for Women's Voices	Chester-Schott	1914–1917
Le Renard, Burlesque Story, Sung and Played, for Four Men's	Chester	1916–1917

Title	Publisher	Date
Voices and Chamber Orchestra		
Five Easy Pieces for Piano Four Hands (First Grade) Andante, Neapolitana, Española, Balalaika, Galop)	Chester	1917
Le Chant du Rossignol, Symphonic Poem for Orchestra, after the Lyric Tale, *Le Rossignol*	Edition Russe	1917
Song of the Volga Boatmen, for Wind Orchestra	Chester	1917
Étude for Pianola	Duo-Art-Aeolian	1917
Histoire du Soldat, Recited, Played and Danced (text by C. F. Ramuz, after Russian Folk Tales)	Chester	1918
Three Pieces for Clarinet Solo	Chester	1918
Ragtime for Eleven Instruments	Chester	1918
Four Russian Songs, for Voice and Piano	Chester	1918–1919
Piano-Rag Music, for Piano	Chester	1919
Pulcinella, Ballet with Voice and Small Orchestra, on Themes, Fragments, and Pieces by Pergolesi	Chester	1919
Concertino for String Quartet	Hansen	1920
Symphonies for Wind Instruments, to the Memory of Debussy	Edition Russe	1920
The Five Fingers, Little Piano Pieces for Children	Chester	1921

282 Igor Stravinsky

Title	Publisher	Date
Suite for Small Orchestra, (Orchestral Version of the Easy Pieces: March, Waltz, Galop, Polka)	Chester	1921
Three Movements from Petrouchka, Transcription for Piano	Edition Russe	1921
Mavra, Opera Buffa in One Act	Edition Russe	1921
Octet for Wind Instruments	Edition Russe	1922–1923
Les Noces, Russian Choreographic Scenes in Four Parts	Chester	1917–1923
Concerto for Piano, Orchestra, Contrabasses, and Timpani	Edition Russe	1923–1924
Sonata for Piano	Edition Russe	1924
Serenade in A, for Piano	Edition Russe	1925
Suite Number Two, for Small Orchestra (Orchestral Version of the Easy Pieces, Andante, Napolitana, Española, Balalaika)	Chester	1925
Oedipus-Rex, Opera-Oratorio in Two Parts, Sung in Latin, Libretto by Jean Cocteau, after Sophocles	Edition Russe	1926–1927
Apollon-Musagète, Ballet in Two Scenes	Edition Russe	1927–1928
Le Baiser de la Fée, Ballet in Four Scenes	Edition Russe	1928
Capriccio for Piano and Orchestra	Edition Russe	1929
Four Études for Orchestra (Symphonic Transcription of the Three Pieces for String Quartet and of the Étude for Pianola)	Edition Russe	1928–1930

Chronological Catalogue of Works

Title	Publisher	Date
Symphony of Psalms, for Orchestra and Chorus	Edition Russe	1930
Concerto for Violin and Orchestra	Schott	1931
Duo-Concertant for Violin and Piano	Edition Russe	1932
Berceuse from *The Firebird,* transcribed for Violin and Piano	Schott	1932
Scherzo from *The Firebird,* transcribed for Violin and Piano	Schott	1933
Souvenirs of My Childhood, Transcription for Voice and Small Ensemble	Edition Russe	1913–1933
Pastorale (From the *Three Songs*) Transcription for Violin and Piano; Transcription for Violin and Four Wind Instruments	Edition Russe	1932–1934
Perséphone, Melodrama in Three Movements (text by André Gide)	Edition Russe	1933–1934
Suite Italienne, from the Ballet *Pulcinella,* Transcription for Violoncello and Piano; Transcription for Violin and Piano	Edition Russe	1934
Divertimento for Orchestra (Transcription also for Violin and Piano)	Edition Russe	1934
Concerto for Two Pianos	Schott	1935
Jeu de Cartes, Ballet in Three Deals	Schott	1936
Airs from the *Rossignol* and *Chinese March,* Transcription for Violin and Piano	Edition Russe	1935–1937

Title	Publisher	Date
Song of Paracha, from *Mavra*, Transcription for Voice or Violin and Piano	Edition Russe	1935–1937
Danse Russe from *Petrouchka*, Transcription for Violin and Piano	Edition Russe	1935–1937
Dumbarton Oaks Concerto in E Flat for Chamber Orchestra	Schott	1937–1938
Symphony in C	Schott (London)	1938–1940
Tango, for One or Two Pianos	Mercury	1940
The Star-Spangled Banner, for Orchestra and Mixed Chorus or Piano and Mixed Chorus	Mercury	1941
Danses Concertantes, for Chamber Orchestra	Associated Music Pub., N. Y.	1941–1942
Circus-Polka, for Orchestra or Piano	Associated Music Pub., N. Y.	1942
Norwegian Moods, Four Episodes for Orchestra	Associated Music Pub., N. Y.	1942
Ode, Elegiac Song in Three Movements	Associated Music Pub., N. Y.	1943
Sonata for Two Pianos	Chappell and Co.	1943–1944
Scherzo à la Russe, for Orchestra	Chappell and Co.	1944
Babel, Cantata for Men's Chorus, Orchestra and Narrator	(Manuscript)	1944
Elegy for Viola or Violin Solo	Chappell and Co.	1944
Scènes de Ballet, for Orchestra	Associated Music Pub., N. Y.	1944

Chronological Catalogue of Works

Title	Publisher	Date
Symphony in Three Movements	Schott, London (AMP)	1945
Ebony Concerto, for Wind Orchestra	Charing Music Corp.	1945
The Firebird, New Version, Symphonic Suite	Leeds Music Corp.	1945
Concerto for String Orchestra	Boosey and Hawkes	1946
Petrouchka, New Version for Orchestra	Boosey and Hawkes	1947
Orpheus, Ballet	Boosey and Hawkes	1947
Mass in C	Boosey and Hawkes	1946–1948
The Rake's Progress, Opera (text by W. H. Auden)	(In Preparation)	1947

Index

Afansieff, 195
A Life for the Czar, 145
Analysis of Stravinsky's work (*see* Criticism *and* Meaning and Understanding)
Ansermet, 194, 195
Apollon-Musagète, 13, 35, 49, 51, 77, 85, 86, 110, 113, 117, 119, 126, 137, 178, 184, 198, 215, 220-221
Apollonian principle, 35, 38, 46, 126
Appreciation (*see* Criticism)
Art and music compared (*see* Musical philosophy)
Art of music (*see* Musical philosophy)
Artist, definition of, iv
Artistic conception (*see* Attitude toward work)
Artistic discipline (*see also* Attitude toward work), 9-11, 17, 37-38, 56, 71, 128
Artistic objectivity, 37-38
Atonality, 59
Attitude toward work, 9-11, 14, 15-16, 17, 18, 19, 21-22, 23, 24, 25, 36, 39, 41, 43, 48, 51, 66-67, 71, 78, 80, 89, 90-91, 103, 126, 127, 129, 130-131, 132, 135, 196, 204, 211, 226
Auberjonois, 194, 195

Babel Cantata, 231, 251, 252
Bach, J. S., 30, 40, 45, 46, 53-54, 73, 112, 121, 136, 200, 203, 215, 229, 266
Bach, Philip Emanuel, 119
Balanchine, Georges, 117, 119, 220, 227, 261
Ballet music, 24, 25, 114-115, 116-117
Ballets Russes, 151, 152, 153, 156-157, 172, 194, 208, 209
Balmont, 172
Balustrade, 227
Barber of Seville, 42, 230
Basel Concerto (*see Concerto for Strings*)
Beaulieu-sur-Mer, 166, 167
Beethoven, 40, 44, 45, 50, 73, 79, 82, 91, 107, 113, 119, 123, 136, 212, 229, 233

288 Index

Bellini, 76, 203
Benois, Alexandre, 167
Berceuses du Chat, 19, 109, 143, 184, 186, 217
Berg, Alban, 59
Berlin, 45, 173, 226, 227
Berman, Eugène, 239
Biarritz, 210, 213
Biographies, Stravinsky (*see also Chroniques de ma Vie* and *Poétique Musicale*), v, ix, 114-115
Bizet, 45
Bleefield, Charles, vi
Bleefield, Therese, vi
Bliss, Mr. and Mrs., 232
Bolm, Adolph, 158, 220, 239
Boris Godounoff, 136, 151, 209
Borodin, 159
"Borrowed" music (*see also* Attitude toward work and Method of writing)
Boston Symphony Orchestra, 194, 225
Boulanger, Nadia, 239
Brahms, 45, 66, 119, 136, 266
Brussels, 45
Budapest, 173

Cadence (*see* Tonality)
Caesura, 75, 78
Capriccio concerti, 51, 77, 85, 111
Capriccio for Piano and Orchestra, 214, 222
Carnaval, 156
Cavalleria Rusticana, 32
Chabrier, 45
Chagall, Marc, 158
Chaliapin, 151
Chamber music, 110
Chamber orchestra, 11
Chansons Plaisantes, 193

Chant Funèbre, 150
Chants Russes, 143
Chopin, 113, 152
Chromaticism, 78, 89, 101
Chroniques de ma Vie (*see also* Biographies, Stravinsky), v, 8, 12, 18, 25, 70, 127, 132, 133, 144, 146, 153, 164, 173, 217
Circus Polka for a Young Elephant, 231, 245
Clarens, 166, 173, 179
Classicism, 7-8, 35-36, 38, 101, 119
Cocteau, 194
Color, 102-103, 104, 109, 110, 158, 220-221
Commentaries (*see* Criticism)
Composition methods (*see* Method of writing)
Concerto for Piano and Wind Orchestra, 13, 85, 111, 210, 213, 214
Concerto for String Orchestra, 261
Concertino for String Quartet, 207, 208
Concerto for Strings, 231
Concerto for the Left Hand, 134
Concerto for Two Pianos, 85, 111, 214, 228-229
Concerto for Violin, 112, 227
Contemporary artists (*see also* Stravinsky and future geniuses), xi
"Conventions" in music (*see* Tradition)
Counterpoint, 59-60, 83
Creative approach (*see* Attitude toward work)
Creative effort (*see also* Trends in Stravinsky's work), vx, 11, 87
Creative movement in music, xi

Index

Criticism, xi, xii, 5-6, 15, 26-27, 47-50, 52-53, 62-65, 69, 113-114, 115, 118, 120-121, 122, 127, 128, 134-135, 137-138, 160-163, 168-171, 172, 177-180, 181, 187, 188-189, 196, 197-201, 205-206, 209, 210, 213, 225-226, 230, 231-232, 245-246, 247, 259, 261, 262-271, 273, 275-277
Cymbalum, 19

Dahl, Ingolf, 22
Danses Concertantes, 49, 52, 77, 80, 86, 88, 97, 112, 113, 117, 118, 119, 198, 228, 241-242
Daphnis et Chloé, 173
Dargomishky, 210
Da Vinci, Leonardo, iv, 30, 39, 66, 70, 144
Debussy, Claude, 30, 44, 45, 56, 107, 135, 136, 149, 156, 159, 163, 166, 172, 173, 207
Degas, 30
De Gourmont, Rémy, 10
De Schloezer, Boris, 25, 119
Deux Arabesques, 136
Devices, musical, 32
Diaghileff, Serge, 151-153, 156-157, 164, 166, 167, 173, 179, 182, 194, 203, 209, 210, 223
Dionysiac principle, 35, 38
Discipline (*see* Artistic discipline)
Dodecaphonic System (*see* Twelve-tone school)
Dogmatism (*see* Attitude toward work)
Donizetti, 76, 203
Dukas, Paul, 45, 81, 149, 159
Dumbarton Oaks Concerto, 52, 112, 118, 228, 231, 232-233

Duo Concertant, 14, 112, 227
Dushkin, Sam, 226, 227

Ebony Concerto for Jazz Orchestra, 14, 202, 258-261
Écossaises, 44
Education (*see* Personal data)
Elegie for Unaccompanied Viola or Violin, 231, 251
Ellington, Duke, 260
Eroica, 82, 123
Eugene Onegin, 209
Evaluation of Stravinsky's work (*see* Criticism)
Expressionism, 84, 103

Family life, 237-241
Femmes de Bonne Humeur, 203
Feu d'Artifice (*see Le Feu d'Artifice*)
Firebird, 26, 46, 51, 64, 78, 80, 84, 97, 100, 101, 112, 114, 150, 156, 157, 158, 159-163, 169, 173, 178, 181, 182, 200, 208
Firework (*see Le Feu d'Artifice*)
Five Easy Pieces, 184
Five Fingers, 184
Flight of the Bumblebee, 70
Fokine, Michel, 117, 156, 167
Form, 47, 60
Four Études, 150, 195
Four Norwegian Moods, 231
Four Russian Songs, 19, 109, 203
French school, 149, 159, 162

Galatea, 39
Genesis Suite, 129
Germany, 226
Gershwin, George, 252
Giselle, 115, 255
Glazounoff, Alexander, 148

Glinka, 45, 145, 195, 209, 210
Gluck, 66
Gorodetsky, 150
Gounod, 45

Harmonic language (*see* Harmony)
Harmony, 47, 60, 71, 72, 81, 82, 85, 87, 88, 89, 90, 101, 149, 150, 177, 200, 208, 234
Harvard University, 235
Haydn, 45, 86, 119, 233
Herman, Woody, 202, 258, 261
Hollywood, 235

Iberia, 44
Ibsen, 32
Impressionism, 34, 169
Influence of Stravinsky, 55-56, 57, 62
Influences on Stravinsky's work (*see also* Criticism), 135-136, 148, 149, 151, 204-205, 210
Instrumental ensembles, 12, 13, 100, 104
Instrumentation (*see* Instrumental ensembles *and* Orchestral conception)
Interpretation (*see* Criticism *and* Meaning and Understanding)
Innovations (*see* Novelty in music)
Inversion, 78

Janssen, Werner, 241
Jazz, 196, 201, 208, 252
Jeu de Cartes, 42, 52, 113, 119, 206, 213, 224, 230, 233
Jota Aragonese, 195

Kammersymphonie, 183
Karsavina, 167
Khovantchina, 179

Klemperer, Otto, 218
Kochno, Boris, 209
Koussevitsky, Nathalie, 245
Koussevitsky, Serge, 208, 245

Language of music, 7
"La Lune Blanche," 163
L'Apprenti Sorcier, 149
Le Baiser de la Fée, 52, 113, 119, 222
Le Bourgeois Gentilhomme, 183
Le Chant du Rossignol, 154, 155, 181
Le Coq d'Or, 209
Le Faune et la Bergère, 148
Le Feu d'Artifice, 15, 48, 100, 101, 136, 148, 149, 150, 151-152, 169, 178
Le Jeu des Deux Cités, 84
Leoncavallo, 32
"Le Pigeon," 172
Le Renard, 19, 51, 97, 104, 105, 109, 112, 113, 120, 143, 180, 182, 184, 190, 191-194, 207, 210, 211
Le Roi des Etoiles, 172
Le Rossignol, 180, 198, 211
Les Danses du Prince Igor, 156
Les Enfantes, 136
Les Noces, 13-14, 19, 20, 44, 46, 49, 51, 77, 97, 100, 104, 105, 109, 113, 114, 119, 120, 144, 172, 178, 180, 182, 184, 185, 186-190, 207, 208, 211
Les Sylphides, 152
L'Histoire du Soldat, 11, 13, 51, 77, 83, 94, 96, 104, 105, 108, 112, 113, 116, 120, 178, 182, 184, 185, 194, 196-201, 202, 204, 205, 207, 208, 211
Liadoff, 150
Library of Congress, 220
Lifar, Serge, 114-115
Liszt, Franz, 166

Index 291

Little House of Kolomna, 209
Logic in Stravinsky's work, 43, 51
L'Oiseau de Feu, 149
London, 208
Los Angeles Symphony Orchestra, 241
Lyrical composition, 21, 24, 25, 117, 120, 168

Madrid, 195
Maecenas, 130, 195
Malipero, Francesco, 48-49
Mascagni, 32
Massine, Leonide, 194, 204
Mavra, 46, 51, 97, 112, 113, 119, 184, 198, 206, 209-212, 213, 233
Meaning and understanding, 103-104, 120, 122, 127, 136, 137, 187, 209
Melodic theme (*see* Melody)
Melody, 47, 59, 71, 72, 75, 76, 78, 79, 82, 84, 85, 87, 90, 97, 101, 102, 110, 149, 200
Meter (*see also* Rhythm), 77, 79, 95, 97, 100, 208
Method of writing (*see also* Technique), 4, 9-10, 12, 13, 14, 18-19, 23, 24, 30, 41, 63, 64-65, 71, 72, 73-74, 77-100, 105-112, 118, 121-122, 124, 157, 184, 185, 186, 191, 192-193, 196, 199, 204, 212, 215-216, 218, 224, 227, 230, 232, 234-235, 242-245, 254, 260, 263
Michelangelo, 66
Missa Solemnis, 131
Mitusoff, 154
Modernism, 36
Modern music (*see also* Modernism), xii-xiii, 55, 205
Modulation, 87-89, 91-92, 101

Molière, 30
Monteux, Pierre, 167, 174, 176, 194
Monteverdi, 66
Mossolov, Alexander, 70
Moussorgsky, 136, 179, 209
Mozart, 30, 40, 82, 86, 119, 136
Musical devices (*see* Devices, musical)
Musical effects, 14-15
Musical Jest, 82
Musical philosophy, 26-29, 30-33, 40, 61, 66-67, 69-70, 111, 113, 115-116, 122-123, 133-134, 135-136, 205, 218-219
Musicotherapy, 33
"Myosotis," 172

Neoclassicism, 125
Neoromanticism, 124, 168
New York Philharmonic Orchestra, 258
Nightingale, 64, 78, 84, 95, 101, 113, 153, 154, 155, 172, 208
Nijinska, Bronislava, 189, 210
Nijinsky, Waslaw, 117, 167, 173
Noces Villageuises, 186
Novelty in music, 42, 63, 100, 107, 108, 187
Nuit à Madrid, 195

Objectivity (*see* Artistic objectivity)
Octet for Wind Instruments, 49, 110, 118, 178, 198, 206, 210
Octet for Woodwinds, 213
Ode, 52, 78, 85, 105, 118, 220, 245
Odet, 112
Oedipus-Rex, 21, 52, 85, 113, 119, 126, 198, 200, 208, 214, 215, 217, 218-219, 228
Onnou, Alphonse, 254

Orchestral conception, 100, 106, 107, 108, 109
Orchestration, 47, 101, 104, 160, 194
Order (*see also* Attitude toward work), 75
Organization (*see* Method of writing)
Orpheus, 40, 113, 220, 231, 261
Oustiloug, 173, 180

Pagliacci, 32
Paris, 19, 45, 173, 194, 207
Parsifal, 132
Passions, 131
Pastorale, 150
Pause, use of, 94
Pelléas et Mélisande, 136
Pergolesi, 41, 46, 125, 203, 204
Perséphone, 52, 113, 220, 228
Personal data (*see also* Stravinsky's personality), 143-147, 167, 180, 194, 203, 207, 235-236
Personal style (*see also* Stravinsky's personality), 78, 91
Petrouchka, 15, 25, 44, 47, 50, 51, 60, 71, 77, 80, 81, 82, 83, 84, 96, 97, 99, 100, 101, 102, 104, 106, 112, 118, 125, 150, 159, 163, 164, 165, 166, 167, 168-171, 174-176, 187, 208, 211, 213
Philosophy of art, general (*see* Musical philosophy)
Philosophy of music (*see* Musical philosophy)
Philosophy of Stravinsky (*see* Attitude toward work)
Phrase (*see also* Melody), 77
Piano Rag-Music, 96, 202
Picasso, 194, 204
Piccini, 66
Picturesqueness, 104

Pierrot Lunaire, 58, 179, 183
Pique-Dame, 209
Pitoëff, Georges, 202
Pitoëff, Ludmila, 202
Pleasant Songs, 19, 109
Pleyel's, 19, 210
Poèmes de Mallarmé, 179
Poétique Musicale, v, 8, 25, 35, 70, 222
Polyphony, 47, 60, 78, 79, 82, 83, 84, 99, 208
Pribaoutki, 19, 143, 180, 182, 184, 186, 217
Prince Igor, 45
Princesse de Polignac, 191
Pro-Arte Quartet, 254
Problem and restraint (*see* Method of writing)
"Problem music," 49
Prunières, Henri, 207
Psychological cause and effect, 23, 30, 37, 126, 198
Pulcinella, 113, 119, 125, 204-206
Purpose of music, 32, 34, 131
Pushkin, Alexander, 209
Pygmalion, 39

Racz, Aladar, 19
Ragtime for Eleven Instruments or for Piano, 94, 95, 96, 112, 196, 202, 207
Ramuz, C. F., 12, 18, 65, 190-191, 195, 212
Ravel, Maurice, 45, 56, 81, 86, 107, 134-135, 136, 149, 156, 159, 165, 166, 179, 180
Razoumovsky, 44
Razumovsky Quartets, 212
Reinhardt, Werner, 195
Religious music (*see also* Symphony of Psalms), 128-133
Rembrandt, 30
Renard (*see Le Renard*)

Index

Respighi, 182
Restraint (*see also* Method of writing), 110
Rhapsodie Espagnole, 165
Rhapsody in Blue, 252
Rhythm, 47, 72-73, 75, 79, 85, 87, 91, 93-100, 101, 109, 149, 150, 160, 234
Rimsky-Korsakoff, 45, 81, 146, 147, 148, 150, 159, 165, 209
Rite of Spring, 14, 35, 44, 46, 49, 51, 71, 73, 77, 78, 82, 83, 84, 97, 99, 104, 105, 106, 108, 109, 112, 114, 119, 126, 127, 137, 149, 155, 164, 166, 172, 173, 174-176, 177-179, 185, 208
Roerich, Nicolas, 164
Roland-Manuel, 41
Romanticism, 7-8, 16, 29, 35-36, 38
Romantic period (*see* Romanticism)
Rome, 167, 194
Rose, Billy, 255
Rossignol (*see Le Rossignol*)
Rossini, 41, 42, 46, 76, 203, 230
Rubinstein, Artur, 202
Rubinstein, Mme. Ida, 221, 228
"Rule of the game" (*see* Method of writing)
"Russian element," 44, 50
Russian music, 45
"Russian period," 182, 197
Russian Revolution, 12, 193, 194
Russlan and Ludmilla, 145, 209

Sacher, Paul, 261
Sacre (*see Sacre du Printemps*)
Sacre du Printemps, 49, 174, 182
St. Petersburg, 143, 163, 166
Sapiro, Aaron, 239

Scarlatti, 46, 203
Scènes de Ballet, 48, 52, 77, 86, 88, 108, 113, 114, 115-116, 119, 251, 255-258
Schaeffner, André, v
Scheherezade, 45
Schelling, 22
Scherzo à la Russe, 231, 251
Scherzo Fantastique, 148, 149
Schmitt, Florent, 180
Schoenberg, Arnold, 58-59, 168, 179, 183
Schubert, 88
Scriabin, 81, 150, 169
Serenade for Piano, 111, 212, 216
Shakespeare, 30
Significance (*see* Meaning and understanding)
Sincerity (*see* Attitude toward work)
Sukoloff, Vladimir, 239
Sonata for Two Pianos, 85, 87, 88, 111, 118, 231, 245
Sonata for Piano, 210, 213, 215
Sonatas for Unaccompanied Violin, 200
Souvenirs de mon Enfance (*see Trois Petites Chansons*)
Souvenirs sur Igor Stravinsky (*see also* Biographies, Stravinsky), 12, 18, 212
Spain, 194-195
Staff-stencil-ruler, 92
Star Spangled Banner arrangement, 241
Steel Foundry, The, 70
Steinberg, Maximilian, 148
Strauss, Richard, 168, 173, 183
Stravinsky and future geniuses, xi
Stravinsky as a "case," x, xii
Stravinsky as a conductor, 250-251

Stravinsky as a revolutionary, 34, 104, 167-168, 177
Stravinsky compared with others (*see* Criticism)
Stravinsky, Igor, Biographies of (*see* Biographies, Stravinsky)
Stravinsky's musical theory, xiv
Stravinsky phenomenon (*see* Stravinsky as a "case")
Stravinsky's lyrical works (*see* Lyrical composition)
Stravinsky's personality (*see also* Attitude toward work), ix, x, xiii, xiv, 8, 18, 19, 20, 22, 54-55, 64, 75-76, 92, 127-128, 134, 154, 201
Stravinsky's reaction (*see* Attitude toward work)
Stravinsky's technique (*see* Technique)
Stravinsky's work, general (*see* Criticism)
Stravinsky's working methods (*see* Method of writing)
Stravinsky, Vera, 238, 240
Strecker, Willi, 226
Style of music, 7, 13
Switzerland, 12, 19, 166, 190
Syllables in music (*see* Words)
Symphonies for Wind Instruments, 13, 51, 97, 110, 112, 207, 208
Symphony in C, 85, 88, 198, 216, 231, 233
Symphony in E Flat Major, 147, 148
Symphony in Three Movements, 42, 48, 72, 77, 80, 85, 86, 91, 97, 100, 108, 110, 112, 198, 231, 258, 261-271
Symphony of Psalms, 49, 50, 52, 108, 118, 129, 131, 148, 178, 198, 208, 224-225, 228
Syncopation, 96

Tango for Piano or Orchestra, 231
Tansman, v, vi
Tchaikowsky, 36, 41, 145, 209, 210, 221
Technique (*see also* Method of writing), 4, 5, 43, 44, 63, 80, 91, 100, 105, 108-109, 120, 128, 136-138, 160, 162-163, 165, 168-171, 173, 177, 187-188, 192-193, 208, 211-212, 221, 228-229, 234, 242, 247-249, 254, 256-258, 264-271, 272
Terence, 55
Theater music, 24
Thematic invention (*see* Thematic pattern)
Thematic pattern, 72, 78
Theories about Stravinsky's work, xiii-xiv, 23-24, 113, 120, 166-167, 197, 205
The Pines of Rome, 182
The Sleeping Beauty, 209
Three Easy Pieces, 184
Three Pieces for Solo Clarinet, 85
Three Pieces for String Quartet, 182, 183
Three Stories for Children, 184
Timbre (*see also* Modulation), 100, 101-102, 103, 104, 105, 107, 112, 158
Tomb of Debussy, 207
Tommasini, 203
Tonality, 57-58, 71, 78, 81, 82, 83, 84, 89, 90, 91, 95, 150, 177-178, 234
"Tower of Babel," 129-31
Tradition, 3, 6, 32, 62, 81, 104, 108, 118, 125, 164, 167
Trends in Stravinsky's work, xv, 26, 48-49, 52, 80, 81, 93,

Index

102, 104, 111, 162, 186, 197, 203
Tristan, 60
Trois Petites Chansons, 179
Trois Poésies de la Lyrique Japonaise, 179
Twelve-tone school, 58-62

"Un Grand Sommeil Noir," 163

Valéry, 30
Venice, 153
Verdi, 46
Verlaine, Paul, 163
Vienna, 45, 173
Virtuosity, 104, 111
Vivaldi, Antonio, 40, 54

Wagner, 56, 66, 78-79, 81, 107, 136, 168
Weber, 36, 41, 44, 223
Whiteman, Paul, 252
Wind Octet, 51
Words, 19-20, 180
Working techniques (*see* Attitude toward work *and* Method of writing)

Zola, 32

CPSIA information can be obtained at www.ICGtesting.com
Printed in the USA
LVOW031749200911

247097LV00002B/124/P

9 781163 186695